THE UNITED STATES of SPORTS

Sports Illustrated KIDS

Writer Bill Syken
Editor Mark Bechtel
Designer Beth Bugler
Photo Editor Linda Bonenfant
Reporter Jeremy Fuchs
Copy Editor Jill Jaroff
Production Manager Hillary Leary

Published by Liberty Street,
an imprint of Time Inc. Books
225 Liberty Street
New York, NY 10281

ISBN: 978-1-5478-0000-1
Library of Congress Control Number:
2018905915

First edition, 2018
1 QGV 18
2 4 6 8 10 9 7 5 3 1

We welcome your comments and suggestions
about Time Inc. Books.
Please write to us at:

Time Inc. Books
Attention: Book Editors
P.O. Box 62310
Tampa, FL 33662-2310
(800) 765-6400

timeincbooks.com

Time Inc. Books products
may be purchased for business or
promotional use. For information on
bulk purchases, please contact
Christi Crowley in the Special Sales
Department at (845) 895-9858.

THE
UNITED STATES
OF SPORTS

Bill Syken

Illustrations by Beth Bugler

CONTENTS

Elephants and tigers and trees, oh my! Who's got the coolest mascots? Look inside to see how they compare.

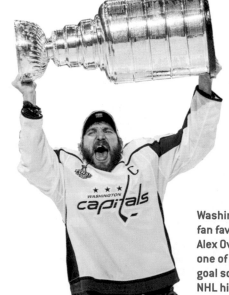

Pennsylvania has a pretty crowded trophy shelf, with hardware from each of the major pro championships.

Washington, D.C., fan favorite Alex Ovechkin is one of the top goal scorers in NHL history.

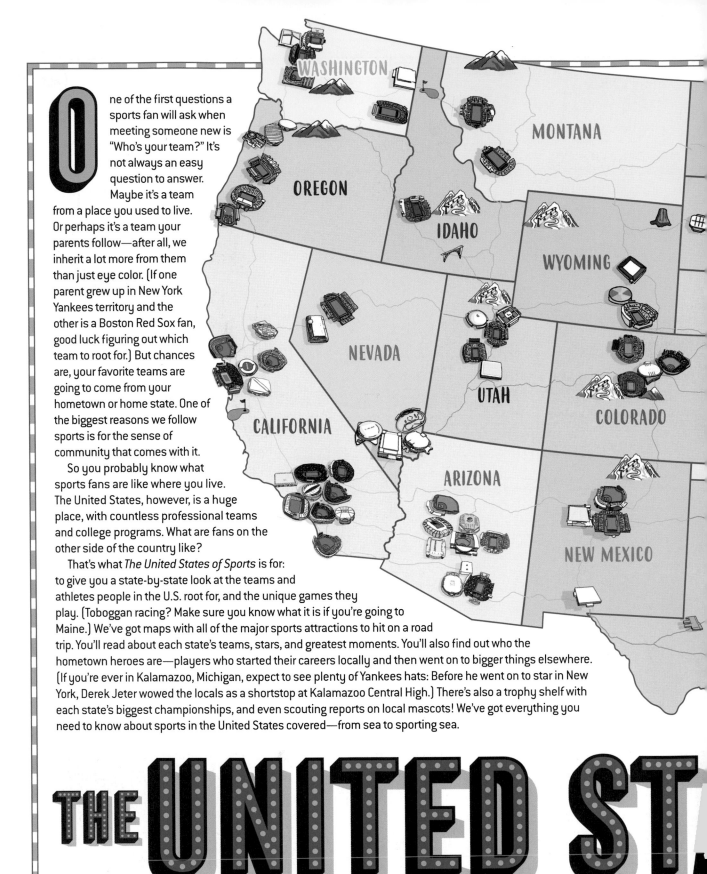

One of the first questions a sports fan will ask when meeting someone new is "Who's your team?" It's not always an easy question to answer. Maybe it's a team from a place you used to live. Or perhaps it's a team your parents follow—after all, we inherit a lot more from them than just eye color. (If one parent grew up in New York Yankees territory and the other is a Boston Red Sox fan, good luck figuring out which team to root for.) But chances are, your favorite teams are going to come from your hometown or home state. One of the biggest reasons we follow sports is for the sense of community that comes with it.

So you probably know what sports fans are like where you live. The United States, however, is a huge place, with countless professional teams and college programs. What are fans on the other side of the country like?

That's what *The United States of Sports* is for: to give you a state-by-state look at the teams and athletes people in the U.S. root for, and the unique games they play. (Toboggan racing? Make sure you know what it is if you're going to Maine.) We've got maps with all of the major sports attractions to hit on a road trip. You'll read about each state's teams, stars, and greatest moments. You'll also find out who the hometown heroes are—players who started their careers locally and then went on to bigger things elsewhere. (If you're ever in Kalamazoo, Michigan, expect to see plenty of Yankees hats: Before he went on to star in New York, Derek Jeter wowed the locals as a shortstop at Kalamazoo Central High.) There's also a trophy shelf with each state's biggest championships, and even scouting reports on local mascots! We've got everything you need to know about sports in the United States covered—from sea to sporting sea.

THE UNITED STA

NEW HAMPSHIRE
VERMONT
MASSACHUSETTS
CONNECTICUT
MAINE
NORTH DAKOTA
MINNESOTA
SOUTH DAKOTA
WISCONSIN
MICHIGAN
NEW YORK
NEBRASKA
IOWA
PENNSYLVANIA
RHODE ISLAND
NEW JERSEY
DELAWARE
MARYLAND
WASHINGTON, D.C.
INDIANA
OHIO
ILLINOIS
WEST VIRGINIA
VIRGINIA
KANSAS
MISSOURI
KENTUCKY
NORTH CAROLINA
OKLAHOMA
TENNESSEE
SOUTH CAROLINA
ALASKA
ARKANSAS
MISSISSIPPI
ALABAMA
GEORGIA
TEXAS
LOUISIANA
FLORIDA
HAWAII

TES OF SPORTS

ALABAMA

Double A **Birmingham Barons**
Mobile BayBears
Montgomery Biscuits

The **Barons** gained national attention in 1994 when Michael Jordan left the NBA to play outfield in Birmingham.

ⓘ INSIDER INFO

When NBA legend Michael Jordan played baseball for the Birmingham Barons, he wanted to travel in comfort. So he bought a 45-foot, $350,000 bus for the team. That season Jordan hit .202 with three home runs. He soon returned to the NBA.

★ALABAMA STAR★

Nick Saban

With Alabama's comeback win over Georgia in the 2017 championship game, Nick Saban won his fifth national title at Alabama. It was his sixth overall—he won one with LSU in 2003—which tied him with Alabama legend Bear Bryant. Saban's coaching method has been called the Process, because he encourages players to think about the small tasks that are immediately in front of them rather than worrying about end results that may be months off: Lift weights hard, execute plays correctly in practice, and come game time, beat the man in front of you. In the classroom, don't worry about graduation, just concentrate on writing your next paper. The Process is now widely imitated because, for Saban, focusing on little moments has brought such big results.

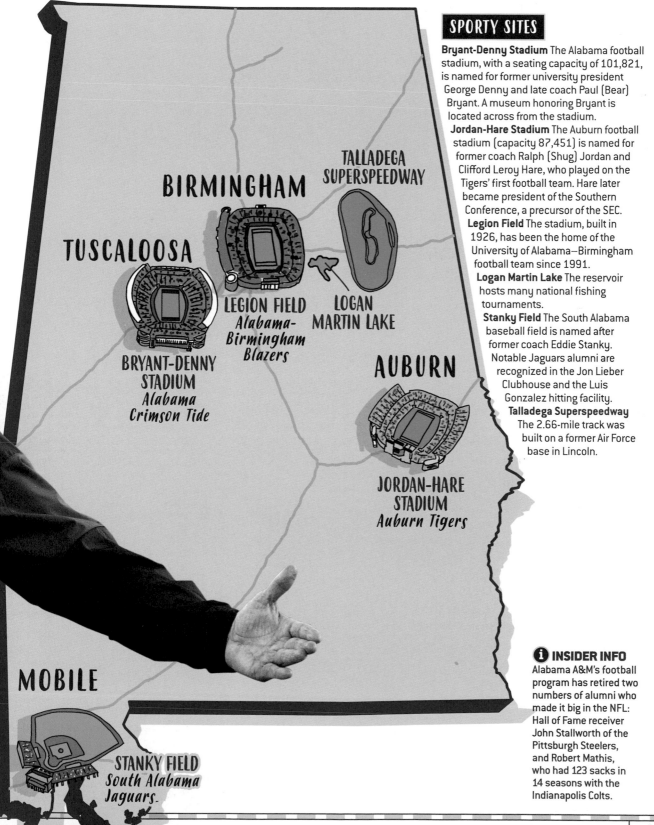

BIRMINGHAM

TALLADEGA SUPERSPEEDWAY

TUSCALOOSA

LEGION FIELD
Alabama-Birmingham Blazers

LOGAN MARTIN LAKE

BRYANT-DENNY STADIUM
Alabama Crimson Tide

AUBURN

JORDAN-HARE STADIUM
Auburn Tigers

MOBILE

STANKY FIELD
South Alabama Jaguars

SPORTY SITES

Bryant-Denny Stadium The Alabama football stadium, with a seating capacity of 101,821, is named for former university president George Denny and late coach Paul (Bear) Bryant. A museum honoring Bryant is located across from the stadium.

Jordan-Hare Stadium The Auburn football stadium (capacity 87,451) is named for former coach Ralph (Shug) Jordan and Clifford Leroy Hare, who played on the Tigers' first football team. Hare later became president of the Southern Conference, a precursor of the SEC.

Legion Field The stadium, built in 1926, has been the home of the University of Alabama–Birmingham football team since 1991.

Logan Martin Lake The reservoir hosts many national fishing tournaments.

Stanky Field The South Alabama baseball field is named after former coach Eddie Stanky. Notable Jaguars alumni are recognized in the Jon Lieber Clubhouse and the Luis Gonzalez hitting facility.

Talladega Superspeedway The 2.66-mile track was built on a former Air Force base in Lincoln.

ⓘ INSIDER INFO
Alabama A&M's football program has retired two numbers of alumni who made it big in the NFL: Hall of Fame receiver John Stallworth of the Pittsburgh Steelers, and Robert Mathis, who had 123 sacks in 14 seasons with the Indianapolis Colts.

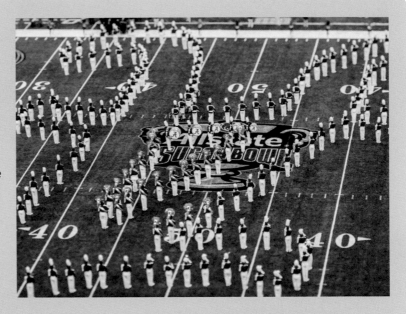

Alabama

Having decades of success and massive fan support means that you have time to develop some hard-core traditions. That's what has happened in Tuscaloosa, home of the University of Alabama. Traditions include singing along to the cheer "Rammer Jammer," accompanied by Alabama's 400-member Million Dollar Band. Houndstooth can be found on hats and clothes all over campus as a tribute to the hats worn by former coach Bear Bryant. The Crimson Tide nickname came from the school newspaper's description of the team after a 1907 game against Auburn in which the team's white sweaters became covered with red mud. The school's elephant mascot also came from a sportswriter. In 1930, the team's linemen were likened to a herd of elephants. That nickname lived on in Tuscaloosa, so in 1979, when the school was looking to add a mascot, an elephant was chosen.

Auburn

Auburn has its own traditions, the most famous centering on Toomer's Corner. The intersection of Magnolia Avenue and College Street is the site of pep rallies before games, and after wins fans celebrate by covering the trees with toilet paper. (In an ugly example of taking things too far, in 2010 an Alabama fan attempted to spoil this tradition by poisoning the Toomer's Corner oaks. He was caught, and new trees were planted.) Though the team's nickname is the Tigers, fans chant, "War Eagle!" The tradition is said to date back to an 1892 game between Auburn and Georgia, when a Civil War veteran's pet eagle began circling the field as Auburn mounted a critical drive. Now every home game begins with an eagle soaring above Jordan-Hare Stadium before landing on the field.

ALABAMA'S TROPHY SHELF

19 NCAA Football Championships Auburn claims two national football titles, in 1957 and in 2010. The second championship was won behind quarterback Cam Newton, with the Tigers defeating Oregon in the championship game. The rest of the hardware belongs to the Crimson Tide, including five since 2009 under coach Nick Saban. Bear Bryant's teams won three titles in the 1960s and three more in the 1970s. With the exception of one title won under coach Gene Stallings in 1992, the rest of the titles come from college football's early years, between 1925 and 1941. In basketball neither school has won a title. Auburn had an Elite Eight appearance in 1986; Alabama reached the Elite Eight in 2004.

BIG EVENT

Racing at Talladega

NASCAR's longest track, at 2.66 miles, is also its fastest and its most dramatic. Known for crazy finishes and big crashes, it is the first NASCAR track to see speeds of more than 200 miles per hour. It was also the site of the fastest qualifying lap ever (212.809 mph), set by Bill Elliott in 1987. (Cars have since been slowed down in the name of safety, so that record is secure.) The man who loved Talladega the most was Dale Earnhardt Sr., who won at the track 10 times.

HOMEGROWN HEROES

HANK AARON
From Mobile, Hammerin' Hank hit 755 career home runs, second best of all time, despite never hitting 50 in a season; he is also the career leader in RBIs and is third all time in hits.

WILLIE MAYS
Born in Westfield, the spectacular centerfielder known as the Say Hey Kid is fifth all time in home runs but is also remembered for dazzling catches. He was also known to play stickball with neighborhood kids.

OZZIE NEWSOME
The Muscle Shoals native helped redefine the tight end position with his pass-catching skills at Alabama and with the Cleveland Browns. He became the first African-American NFL general manager, with the Baltimore Ravens.

CHARLES BARKLEY
At Auburn, where he was close to 300 pounds despite being only 6' 6", the Leeds High grad was known as the Round Mound of Rebound. In the NBA the Hall of Famer averaged double digits in rebounds for 15 seasons.

ⓘ INSIDER INFO The Crimson Tide won 13 games in 2017, including a 56–0 rout of Mercer in which Irv Smith Jr. scored the game's first touchdown (right). It was the 10th straight season in which Bama won at least 10 games.

ALABAMA

MASCOT FACE-OFF

AL THE ELEPHANT
Alabama

 VS.

AUBIE
Auburn

AL THE ELEPHANT		AUBIE
Jan. 1, 1979	**BORN**	Feb. 28, 1979
Sugar Bowl	**DEBUT EVENT**	SEC basketball tourney
Beat Penn State	**RESULT**	Reached the semis
Short for an elephant	**SUSPICIOUSLY**	Tall for a tiger

THE NUMBERS

2

RANK in NFL career receiving yards for Terrell Owens of Alexander City, trailing only Jerry Rice.

25

TOTAL SACKS by future NFL All-Pros DeMarcus Ware and Osi Umenyiora when they played at Troy in 2002.

7

NBA TITLES won by Robert (Big Shot Bob) Horry, who starred at Andalusia High and for the Crimson Tide.

4

PRO FOOTBALL LEAGUES that had a team in Birmingham: the WFL, the USFL, the CFL, and the XFL.

ⓘ INSIDER INFO The only athlete ever to make All-Star teams in both the NFL and major league baseball, Bo Jackson won the Heisman Trophy as a running back at Auburn in 1985—the same year he batted .401 for the Tigers' baseball team. In track Jackson also qualified for the nationals in the 100 meters. At McAdory High, Jackson played every play for the football team. He even handled kicking and punting duties.

GREATEST MOMENT

NOVEMBER 30, 2013
The Kick Six

Many regard it as the greatest play in college football history. With one second left and the score tied 28–28, top-ranked Alabama lined up for a 57-yard field goal. The kick was short, and Auburn's Chris Davis caught it on the fly, which meant he could return it. Off he went, racing down the sideline for a game-ending 109-yard touchdown. The result, which put the Tigers in the SEC championship game, left Tide fans openmouthed as Auburn celebrated the most stunning win in the history of college football's biggest rivalry.

STATE-MENT

"Don't look back. Something might be gaining on you."

SATCHEL PAIGE, a Negro leagues legend from Mobile who pitched for the St. Louis Browns at age 46

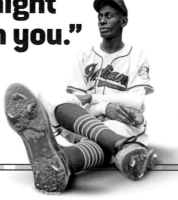

ENEMY OF THE STATE

LSU FOOTBALL

Auburn and Alabama are each other's greatest rival by far, but the school in Baton Rouge is the most consistent source of competition for supremacy in the SEC West.

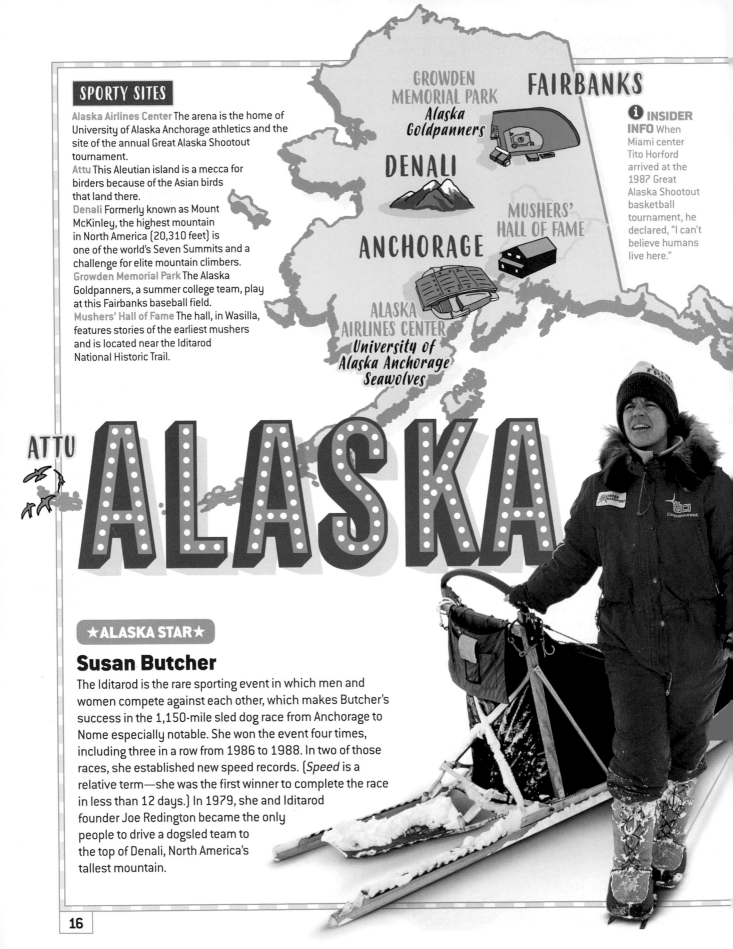

SPORTY SITES

Alaska Airlines Center The arena is the home of University of Alaska Anchorage athletics and the site of the annual Great Alaska Shootout tournament.

Attu This Aleutian island is a mecca for birders because of the Asian birds that land there.

Denali Formerly known as Mount McKinley, the highest mountain in North America (20,310 feet) is one of the world's Seven Summits and a challenge for elite mountain climbers.

Growden Memorial Park The Alaska Goldpanners, a summer college team, play at this Fairbanks baseball field.

Mushers' Hall of Fame The hall, in Wasilla, features stories of the earliest mushers and is located near the Iditarod National Historic Trail.

GROWDEN
MEMORIAL PARK
Alaska Goldpanners

FAIRBANKS

ⓘ INSIDER INFO When Miami center Tito Horford arrived at the 1987 Great Alaska Shootout basketball tournament, he declared, "I can't believe humans live here."

DENALI

MUSHERS' HALL OF FAME

ANCHORAGE

ALASKA AIRLINES CENTER
University of Alaska Anchorage Seawolves

ATTU

ALASKA

★ALASKA STAR★

Susan Butcher

The Iditarod is the rare sporting event in which men and women compete against each other, which makes Butcher's success in the 1,150-mile sled dog race from Anchorage to Nome especially notable. She won the event four times, including three in a row from 1986 to 1988. In two of those races, she established new speed records. (*Speed* is a relative term—she was the first winner to complete the race in less than 12 days.) In 1979, she and Iditarod founder Joe Redington became the only people to drive a dogsled team to the top of Denali, North America's tallest mountain.

16

BIG EVENT

Midnight Sun Baseball Game

Because Fairbanks is only 160 miles from the Arctic Circle, the sun is up nearly all day in the summer (and down all day in the winter). Each June 20–22 since 1960 the Alaska Goldpanners of Fairbanks have celebrated the longest days of the year with games that begin at 10:30 p.m. The games have run as late as 2 a.m., but they are always played in daylight.

ⓘ INSIDER INFO
The first girl in the United States to win a state wrestling title against boys was Michaela Hutchison of Skyview High in Soldotna. Hutchison won the 103-pound title in 2006.

THE NUMBERS

5
AGE at which Curt Schilling, the six-time MLB All-Star pitcher, moved from Anchorage to Arizona.

97
WEIGHT IN POUNDS of the world-record salmon caught by a fisherman on the Kenai River in 1985.

4
POINTS by which UA-Anchorage beat Michigan in basketball in 1988, during UM's title season.

GREATEST MOMENT

1994 WINTER OLYMPICS
Moe's Medals

"The coaching was tougher up there because everything is tougher up there." That's what Tom Moe Sr. said about how learning to ski in Alaska had influenced his son Tommy. The younger Moe won a gold and a silver in Lillehammer, Norway, becoming the first U.S. Alpine skier to win two medals in the same Winter Games.

HOMEGROWN HEROES

MARIO CHALMERS
The Anchorage native was cool under pressure in the 2008 NCAA title game. Chalmers hit a game-tying three-pointer for Kansas with 2.1 seconds left. (KU won in overtime.) In the NBA, he won two titles with LeBron James in Miami.

CARLOS BOOZER
From Juneau, Boozer won an NCAA title at Duke in 2001. The 6' 9" forward then played in the NBA for 13 seasons, making two All-Star teams.

MARK SCHLERETH
Born in Anchorage, the offensive lineman won three Super Bowls in 12 NFL seasons with the Washington Redskins and the Denver Broncos. He retired after the 2000 season and became a broadcaster.

SCOTT GOMEZ

The 1999–2000 NHL season was a good one for the Anchorage native. Gomez was named rookie of the year, and his New Jersey Devils won the Stanley Cup. The center, who is of Colombian and Mexican descent, also became the first Hispanic player to appear in an NHL game. He retired in 2016.

Larry Fitzgerald

The word *complete* comes up a lot when people talk about Fitzgerald. Through the 2017 season, Cardinals quarterbacks have completed 1,234 passes to him—the most career receptions for an active player, and the third most of all time. The 6' 3" Fitzgerald is also a complete receiver. He's a master of both deep and short routes, and he's adept at blocking on running plays. And *complete* also describes Fitzgerald as a person. In his off-season, he devotes himself to seeing the world. He's been to more

than 90 countries. He's had samurai sword lessons in Japan, walked the Great Wall of China, and seen the Pyramids in Egypt. He's also visited U.S. soldiers overseas. On and off the field, he's always learning.

STATE-MENT

"You'll be sorry you ever booed this young man."

Suns coach **COTTON FITZSIMMONS**, defending the selection of guard Dan Majerle *(left)*, who became a three-time All-Star for Phoenix

ARIZONA

SURPRISE STADIUM
Kansas City Royals and Texas Rangers spring training

TALKING STICK RESORT ARENA
Phoenix Suns
Phoenix Mercury

PHOENIX

UNIVERSITY OF PHOENIX STADIUM
Arizona Cardinals

SUN DEVIL STADIUM
Arizona State Sun Devils

GILA RIVER ARENA
Arizona Coyotes

CHASE FIELD
Arizona Diamondbacks

HANDBALL HALL OF FAME

MCKALE MEMORIAL CENTER
Arizona Wildcats

TUCSON

ARIZONA STADIUM
Arizona Wildcats

PRO TEAMS

NFL	Arizona Cardinals
MLB	Arizona Diamondbacks
NBA	Phoenix Suns
WNBA	Phoenix Mercury
NHL	Arizona Coyotes

Hockey legend **Wayne Gretzky** was both the owner and the (not very successful) coach of the Coyotes from 2005 to 2009.

SPORTY SITES

Handball Hall of Fame The Tucson hall also serves as the headquarters of the U.S. Handball Association.
McKale Memorial Center The Arizona basketball arena's Lute and Bobbi Olson Court is named after the championship-winning coach and his wife.
Sun Devil Stadium The Arizona State football stadium, which used to host the Fiesta Bowl, is undergoing a $256 million renovation.
University of Phoenix Stadium The Arizona Cardinals play in a stadium with the country's first fully retractable natural grass surface.

ⓘ INSIDER INFO
Andy Reid and Mike Shanahan were both assistant coaches for the University of Northern Arizona Lumberjacks before finding success as head coaches in the NFL.

ARIZONA

4 WINS in the 2001 postseason for the Diamondbacks by Curt Schilling, who was raised in Phoenix and pitched at Yavapai College in Prescott.

12 TRIPLE CROWN RACES won by horses trained by Bob Baffert of Nogales, who studied racetrack management at Arizona.

13 SACKS in the 2017 season by Minnesota Vikings defensive end Everson Griffen. It was a career high for the player from Avondale.

9 NCAA BASEBALL TITLES won by Arizona (4) and Arizona State (5). The Wildcats won the state's most recent title, in 2012.

FAN FAVORITES

DEVIN BOOKER
Suns guard

Booker is the chief reason that fans of the Phoenix Suns have cause to be optimistic. The shooting guard, selected with the 13th pick of the 2015 draft, is a tenacious shotmaker. In March 2017, he dropped 70 points on the Boston Celtics, making him the youngest player ever to score more than 60 in a game. At the 2018 All-Star Game he won the three-point contest in a field that included defending champ Klay Thompson. Because he plays on a weak team, opposing defenses can focus on stopping Booker. Still, his scoring average and shooting percentage have improved every season, a trend that is encouraging news in Phoenix.

PAUL GOLDSCHMIDT
Diamondbacks first baseman

The slugger has been the rock of the franchise in the 2010s. Goldschmidt finished in the top three in National League MVP voting three times in the past five years, and after only seven seasons he's first or second in Diamondbacks history in most offensive categories.

DAVID JOHNSON
Cardinals running back

In 2016, Johnson led the NFL in yards from scrimmage. (He had 1,239 rushing yards and 879 receiving yards.) He's so valuable that when he went down with a dislocated wrist in the first game of the 2017 season, the Cardinals went from Super Bowl hopefuls to the middle of the pack.

DIANA TAURASI
Mercury guard

Taurasi has won three WNBA titles in Phoenix, which isn't a surprise. The Mercury guard has been a winner everywhere she's played. Taurasi won four Olympic gold medals, six EuroLeague championships, and three college titles at Connecticut.

INSIDER INFO

Former Arizona State baseball players who have won MVP awards in major league baseball include Dustin Pedroia, Reggie Jackson, and Barry Bonds.

GREATEST MOMENT

MARCH 31, 1997

NCAA Championship

No team from the Grand Canyon State, college or pro, had ever won a major sports championship until the 1997 NCAA tournament. To bring home the elusive hardware, the University of Arizona, a No. 4 seed, had to knock off three No. 1 seeds (Kansas, North Carolina, and Kentucky). The Wildcats were carried by their backcourt stars: future NBA player Mike Bibby, and Miles Simon, who scored 30 points in the title game against Kentucky in Indianapolis and was named the tournament's Most Outstanding Player.

MASCOT FACE-OFF

GORILLA *Phoenix Suns*	VS.	SPARKY THE SUN DEVIL *Arizona State*
1980	**BORN**	1946
Trampoline dunk	**PET MOVE**	Trident jab
Man delivered singing telegram to arena in gorilla costume, found NBA gig	**HOW HE GOT THE JOB**	Students voted 819–196 to switch mascot from bulldog to sun devil

ARIZONA

COOL SCHOOLS

Arizona

Wildcats alumni have shown a knack for winning after moving on from Tucson. Steve Kerr, who made a ridiculous 57.3% of his three-pointers while at Arizona, won five NBA titles as an NBA shooting guard. (That included one in San Antonio with another former Wildcat, Sean Elliott.) Kerr has since coached the Golden State Warriors to a pair of championships; Arizona's Andre

Iguodala was Finals MVP for the first one. Tight end Rob Gronkowski has won two Super Bowls with the Patriots, and linebacker Tedy Bruschi helped the Patriots to another three. After winning a national title in softball at Arizona, Jennie Finch *(above)* pitched for the gold-medal-winning 2004 U.S. Olympic team. Terry Francona didn't have a great career as a baseball player, but in 2004, he managed the Boston Red Sox to their first World Series title since 1918. And don't forget about golfer Annika Sorenstam, who won 72 times on the LPGA tour.

Arizona State

No Sun Devil has been more influential than Pat Tillman. While he was a star on the field, his bigger contribution came

off it. Tillman's 1996 ASU team made the Rose Bowl, and he was later named Pac-10 defensive player of the year. In the NFL, the safety played four seasons for the Arizona Cardinals. But after the terror attacks on September 11, 2001, he left football to join the U.S. Army Rangers. In April 2004, he was killed in combat in Afghanistan. Each year Pat's Run, a 4.2-mile race through Tempe (his number was 42), raises education funds for service members and their families.

HOMEGROWN HEROES

PHIL MICKELSON

Mickelson, who learned to swing lefthanded by mirroring his father's golf swing, is from Scottsdale and attended Arizona State. He has won 43 PGA tournaments, including five major championships.

TY MURRAY

The nine-time world champion is as big a rodeo star as there is. Murray is the cofounder of Professional Bull Riders, and he appeared on Season 8 of the TV show *Dancing with the Stars*.

TERRELL SUGGS

The Chandler native had 24 sacks as a junior at Arizona State. As a Baltimore Ravens linebacker, Suggs was named NFL Defensive Player of the Year in 2011.

JIM PALMER

The Hall of Fame righthander won three Cy Young Awards and had a career ERA of 2.86. Palmer also had an 8–3 postseason record and played on World Series winners for the Baltimore Orioles in three different decades. At Scottsdale High, Palmer was all-state in football, basketball, and baseball. He turned down a UCLA basketball scholarship to sign with Baltimore in 1963.

ARIZONA'S TROPHY SHELF

1 World Series Championship To win the state's first pro title, in 2001, the Diamondbacks needed a ninth-inning comeback against one of the game's greatest closers, Mariano Rivera of the New York Yankees. With one out and a man on third, Luis Gonzalez's bloop single over a drawn-in infield brought home the winning run.

3 WNBA Championships The Mercury's first title came in 2007, behind the playoff MVP performance of Cappie Pondexter. The championship made Paul Westhead the first coach to lead both NBA and WNBA champions. The Mercury won again two years later, and they collected their third title in 2013, thanks to the addition of center Brittney Griner.

ⓘ INSIDER INFO
The Phoenix Suns teams coached by Mike D'Antoni from 2003 to 2008 never made it past the conference finals, but their philosophy of looking for quick shots, known as Seven Seconds or Less, has been widely imitated in the NBA.

BIG EVENT

Cactus League Spring Training
Spring training was once strictly a Florida phenomenon. The migration west started in 1946, when the Cleveland Indians and the New York Giants held their camps in Arizona. The flow increased greatly in the 1990s and 2000s, with new stadiums being built to lure teams. Perhaps the most stunning defection came in 2006, when the L.A. Dodgers abandoned their famed Dodgertown in Vero Beach, Florida, and moved to Glendale. By 2010, half of baseball's teams were training in Arizona.

ENEMY OF THE STATE

LOS ANGELES DODGERS
The Diamondbacks' stadium has a pool. In 2013, the Dodgers players jumped in that pool to celebrate winning a division title. Rivalry on.

SPORTY SITES

Bud Walton Arena In 1993, the Arkansas Razorbacks basketball team moved into its new home, where it went 16–0 on the way to an NCAA national championship.

Dickey-Stephens Park The Arkansas Travelers play in North Little Rock, just across the Arkansas River from downtown Little Rock.

Donald W. Reynolds Razorback Stadium A 2001 expansion increased the capacity of Arkansas's football stadium to 72,000.

First National Bank Arena The largest crowd at the Arkansas State arena was 10,892 for a basketball game between Arkansas State and Arkansas in the 2005 Women's NIT.

War Memorial Stadium This 54,000-seat Little Rock venue hosted the annual Delta Classic between Grambling State and Arkansas–Pine Bluff.

ⓘ INSIDER INFO Sonny Liston, the second youngest of 25 siblings and stepsiblings, grew up outside of Little Rock. He was the world heavyweight boxing champion for 17 months before losing to Muhammad Ali in 1964.

PRO TEAMS

Double A
Arkansas Travelers
Northwest Arkansas Naturals

The **Travelers**, founded in 1902 and now an affiliate of the Seattle Mariners, were the first sports team to use a state name as its geographic identifier.

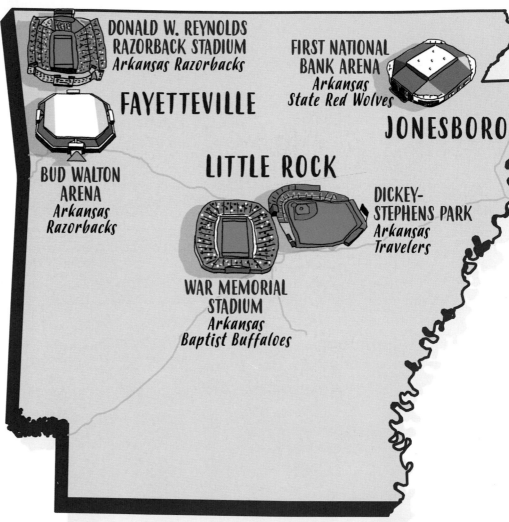

DONALD W. REYNOLDS
RAZORBACK STADIUM
Arkansas Razorbacks

FIRST NATIONAL
BANK ARENA
*Arkansas
State Red Wolves*

FAYETTEVILLE

JONESBORO

BUD WALTON
ARENA
*Arkansas
Razorbacks*

LITTLE ROCK

DICKEY-
STEPHENS PARK
*Arkansas
Travelers*

WAR MEMORIAL
STADIUM
*Arkansas
Baptist Buffaloes*

ARKANSAS

Scottie Pippen

It's amazing to think of what this kid from Hamburg achieved, considering how his college career began. He didn't have a scholarship to tiny Central Arkansas, so he also served as the team manager and worked as a welder to pay his tuition. As a freshman, he averaged only 4.3 points per game, but he developed so much in four years that he was the fifth overall pick of the 1987 NBA draft, by the Chicago Bulls. There he became the perfect complement to Michael Jordan. Pippen could fill every box on the stat

sheet. He scored, rebounded, passed, and made 10 NBA all-defensive teams. His Bulls teams won six NBA titles, and Pippen landed in the Hall of Fame.

STATE-MENT

"The doctors X-rayed my head and found nothing."

Lucas native **DIZZY DEAN**, after the Cardinals pitcher was hit by a thrown ball in the 1934 World Series

ARKANSAS

COOL SCHOOL

Arkansas

The school's teams were first called the Cardinals—ho-hum—but in 1909, football coach Hugo Bezdek compared his players to razorback hogs, and soon the team had its unique nickname. The Razorbacks' live mascot is a Russian boar named Tusk, and the school has a distinctive chant, too: "Wooooooooo. Pig. Sooie! Wooooooooo. Pig. Sooie! Wooooooooo. Pig. Sooie! Razorbacks!" The most dominant run of any Arkansas team came on the basketball court in the 1990s, when coach Nolan Richardson's squads made back-to-back NCAA finals appearances. (They won the title in 1994.) The teams played a suffocating defensive style known as 40 Minutes of Hell.

BIG EVENT

World Championship Duck Calling Contest

Since 1936, the world's best duck callers have converged on Stuttgart. While contestants traditionally use devices that are like small musical instruments, the winner of the original event used only his throat.

HOMEGROWN HEROES

PAUL (BEAR) BRYANT

An all-state lineman at Fordyce High, Bryant earned his nickname as a teenager when he wrestled a trained bear to impress a girl. He coached college football for 38 years, including 25 at Alabama, winning 323 games.

CLIFF LEE

The four-time All-Star won the 2008 American League Cy Young Award with the Cleveland Indians. Lee was born in Benton and played one season at Arkansas. The hard-throwing lefthander pitched 13 major league seasons, winning 143 games.

JOHN DALY

The long-driving golfer became an overnight sensation in 1991. After being given a spot in the PGA Championship because other players had withdrawn, Daly, who was the ninth alternate, won the tournament. Famous for his philosophy of "grip it and rip it," he also won the 1995 British Open.

MARK MARTIN

Martin, who grew up in Batesville, had 40 NASCAR wins and 453 top 10 finishes. He owns car dealerships in his hometown that display several of his race cars, helmets, and fire suits.

GREATEST MOMENT

JANUARY 1, 1965
Cotton Bowl

Arkansas defeated Nebraska 10–7 to complete an undefeated season and claim its only national championship. Arkansas also made a case for the title in 1977, when the Razorbacks went 11–1 and beat No. 2 Oklahoma in the Orange Bowl. But at the time college football didn't have a playoff, and the Hogs, though earning votes at No. 1, finished third.

ARKANSAS'S TROPHY SHELF

1 NCAA Football Championship
The 1964 title came under Frank Broyles, who coached Arkansas from 1958 to 1976.

1 NCAA Men's Basketball Championship
Arkansas knocked off Duke in the 1994 final behind 23 points from Corliss Williamson.

FAN FAVORITES

JOE JOHNSON
Houston Rockets forward

A seven-time NBA All-Star who grew up in Little Rock and played at Arkansas, Johnson soared as a member of the Atlanta Hawks. Beginning in 2005, he had five consecutive seasons in which he averaged more than 20 points per game. Johnson has impressed with his durability and adaptability, as the shooting guard has added a fierce inside game.

JERRY JONES
Dallas Cowboys owner

Jones was a guard and co-captain for the 1964 Arkansas title team, an experience that shaped his tenure as owner of the Dallas Cowboys. The first coach he hired was former college teammate Jimmy Johnson. After they won Super Bowls in 1993 and 1994, Jones replaced Johnson with Barry Switzer, an assistant on the 1964 Razorbacks squad.

THE NUMBERS

4 SEVEN-OVERTIME GAMES played in college football history. Arkansas was in two of them and won each time.

16 GOLD GLOVES won in 23 major league seasons by Baltimore third baseman Brooks Robinson, from Little Rock.

Serena Williams

Just when it seemed she'd accomplished everything a tennis star could, Williams added this feat in 2017: She won the Australian Open while pregnant with her first child. The win also happened to be her 23rd Grand Slam singles title. That's the most by any player, male or female, in the Open era. Serena has also won 14 Grand Slam doubles titles, all with her sister Venus. It's been quite a journey for Serena, who was born in Saginaw, Michigan, moved to Compton in Los Angeles as an infant, and began playing tennis at age four. When she won the U.S. Open in 1999 at age 17, she became the first African-American since Arthur Ashe in 1975 to win a Grand Slam event.

PRO TEAMS

NFL	**Los Angeles Chargers** **Los Angeles Rams** **Oakland Raiders** **San Francisco 49ers**
MLB	**Los Angeles Angels** **Los Angeles Dodgers** **Oakland Athletics** **San Diego Padres** **San Francisco Giants**
NBA	**Los Angeles Lakers** **Los Angeles Clippers** **Golden State Warriors** **Sacramento Kings**
WNBA	**Los Angeles Sparks**
NHL	**Anaheim Ducks** **Los Angeles Kings** **San Jose Sharks**
MLS	**L.A. Galaxy** **Los Angeles FC** **San Jose Earthquakes**

The **Kings** played in Rochester, Cincinnati, and Kansas City before arriving in Sacramento in 1985.

CALIFOR

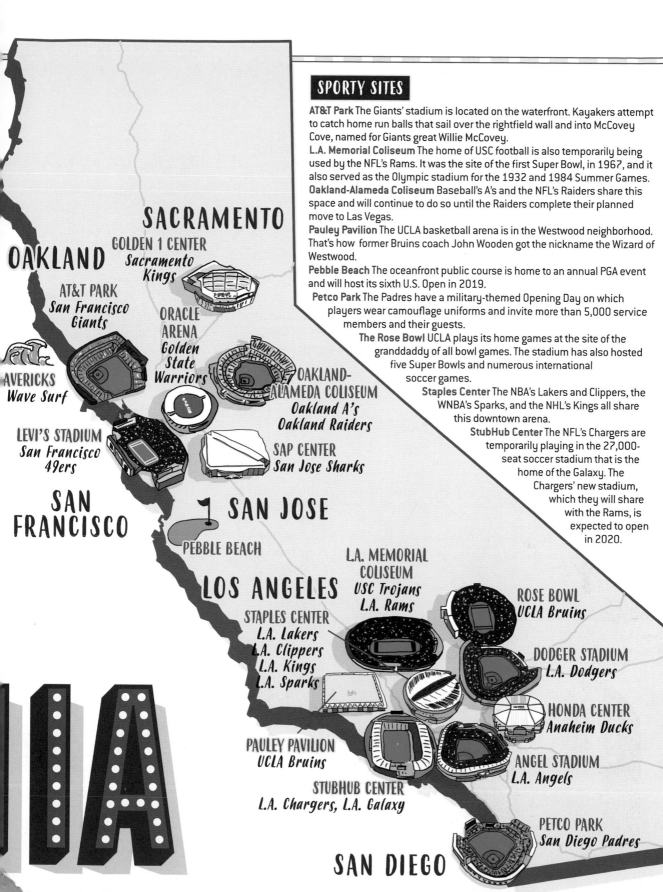

SPORTY SITES

AT&T Park The Giants' stadium is located on the waterfront. Kayakers attempt to catch home run balls that sail over the rightfield wall and into McCovey Cove, named for Giants great Willie McCovey.

L.A. Memorial Coliseum The home of USC football is also temporarily being used by the NFL's Rams. It was the site of the first Super Bowl, in 1967, and it also served as the Olympic stadium for the 1932 and 1984 Summer Games.

Oakland-Alameda Coliseum Baseball's A's and the NFL's Raiders share this space and will continue to do so until the Raiders complete their planned move to Las Vegas.

Pauley Pavilion The UCLA basketball arena is in the Westwood neighborhood. That's how former Bruins coach John Wooden got the nickname the Wizard of Westwood.

Pebble Beach The oceanfront public course is home to an annual PGA event and will host its sixth U.S. Open in 2019.

Petco Park The Padres have a military-themed Opening Day on which players wear camouflage uniforms and invite more than 5,000 service members and their guests.

The Rose Bowl UCLA plays its home games at the site of the granddaddy of all bowl games. The stadium has also hosted five Super Bowls and numerous international soccer games.

Staples Center The NBA's Lakers and Clippers, the WNBA's Sparks, and the NHL's Kings all share this downtown arena.

StubHub Center The NFL's Chargers are temporarily playing in the 27,000-seat soccer stadium that is the home of the Galaxy. The Chargers' new stadium, which they will share with the Rams, is expected to open in 2020.

SACRAMENTO

GOLDEN 1 CENTER
Sacramento Kings

OAKLAND

AT&T PARK
San Francisco Giants

ORACLE ARENA
Golden State Warriors

MAVERICKS
Wave Surf

OAKLAND-ALAMEDA COLISEUM
*Oakland A's
Oakland Raiders*

LEVI'S STADIUM
San Francisco 49ers

SAP CENTER
San Jose Sharks

SAN FRANCISCO

SAN JOSE

PEBBLE BEACH

L.A. MEMORIAL COLISEUM
*USC Trojans
L.A. Rams*

LOS ANGELES

ROSE BOWL
UCLA Bruins

STAPLES CENTER
*L.A. Lakers
L.A. Clippers
L.A. Kings
L.A. Sparks*

DODGER STADIUM
L.A. Dodgers

HONDA CENTER
Anaheim Ducks

PAULEY PAVILION
UCLA Bruins

ANGEL STADIUM
L.A. Angels

STUBHUB CENTER
L.A. Chargers, L.A. Galaxy

PETCO PARK
San Diego Padres

SAN DIEGO

CALIFORNIA

THE NUMBERS

0 **FOOTBALL TEAMS** with insignia on their helmets, until the Rams painted horns on their headgear in 1948.

7 **CALIFORNIA SCHOOLS** that have won an NCAA title in water polo. No school outside the state has ever won one in either men's or women's play.

.406 **BATTING AVERAGE** of Ted Williams in 1941. The Red Sox outfielder from San Diego is the last major leaguer to hit over .400.

17 **AGE** at which Chloe Kim of La Palma won Olympic gold in halfpipe in 2018 after hitting back-to-back 1080s.

FAN FAVORITES

STEPH CURRY
Warriors guard

From his pregame routine, in which he puts on a dazzling dribbling exhibition, to the seemingly impossible long-range shots he hits, Curry is both a great player and a topflight showman. At 6' 3" and 190 pounds, he is usually one of the slighter figures on the court. But with his quick trigger and lethal accuracy, he is as dangerous as any offensive player in the league. He won NBA MVP awards in 2015 and 2016, and his Warriors won NBA titles in 2015 and 2017. He and fellow guard Klay Thompson are known as the Splash Brothers.

CLAYTON KERSHAW
Dodgers pitcher

Fans in Los Angeles—or anywhere, for that matter—haven't seen a run of dominance like this since the days of Sandy Koufax. Kershaw, a 6' 4" lefthander, won three Cy Young Awards between 2011 and 2014, and he finished second in voting in 2012. He's had three seasons with a sub-2.00 ERA, and in his seven straight All-Star seasons (2011–2017), his record is a sterling 118–41.

BUSTER POSEY
Giants catcher

Good things started happening for the Giants right around the time that Buster Posey arrived behind the plate. In 2010, the catcher was the National League Rookie of the Year and San Francisco won the World Series. Two years later he led the league in hitting and was voted MVP as the Giants won another title. In 2014, Posey—one of the game's top defensive backstops—was behind the plate as the Giants won it all again.

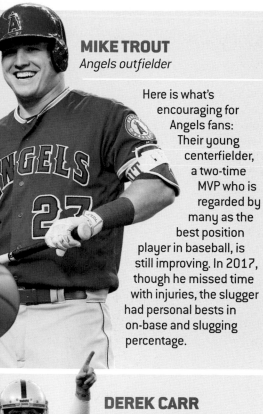

MIKE TROUT
Angels outfielder

Here is what's encouraging for Angels fans: Their young centerfielder, a two-time MVP who is regarded by many as the best position player in baseball, is still improving. In 2017, though he missed time with injuries, the slugger had personal bests in on-base and slugging percentage.

DEREK CARR
Raiders quarterback

Carr, a second-round pick out of Fresno State in 2014, has given the Raiders their best shot at long-term stability at quarterback since the 1970s. He showed his promise in 2016, when he threw 28 TDs and only six interceptions before a broken leg ended his season.

MAGIC JOHNSON
Lakers, Dodgers, Sparks

After leading the Lakers to five NBA championships from 1980 to 1988 as a 6' 9" point guard, Magic is now an outsized player off the field in the L.A. sports scene. He serves as the president of basketball operations for his former team, and he's also a part owner of the Dodgers and the WNBA's Sparks.

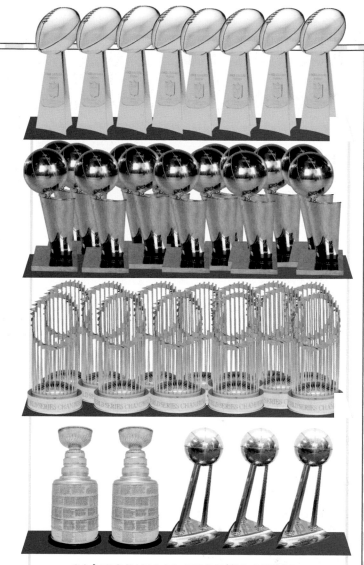

CALIFORNIA'S TROPHY SHELF

8 Super Bowl Wins The 49ers won five Super Bowls from 1982 to 1995 as their West Coast offense and Hall of Fame roster flummoxed the NFL. The Raiders won three Super Bowls in the 1970s and 1980s.

15 NBA Championships The Lakers have 11 NBA titles since moving from Minneapolis. The Warriors have four titles since coming from Philadelphia.

13 World Series Championships The Dodgers have won five World Series in L.A., while the Giants have taken three in San Francisco. The A's have four in Oakland, and the Angels won their first in 2002.

2 Stanley Cup Wins The Kings won their first Cup in 2012 and added another in 2014.

3 WNBA Championships The Sparks won titles in 2001, 2002, and 2016.

CALIFORNIA

USC

A costumed Trojan takes the field riding a white horse named Traveler while the band plays the *William Tell Overture*. Cheerleaders in old-school white sweaters cheer and the Trojan stabs his sword into the turf. This is how the games begin for USC football, a program rich in both success and tradition. The uniform number 55 was worn by such esteemed linebackers as Junior Seau, Willie McGinest, and Chris Claiborne. Now it is given only to a topflight linebacker. The school has turned out seven Heisman Trophy winners and 12 Pro Football Hall of Famers. It is also part of some of the sport's best rivalries. When the Trojans face UCLA, both teams wear their colored jerseys, so it's always the maroon and gold facing the blue and gold. USC also plays Notre Dame in an annual cross-country clash of two of the most vaunted programs in the sport.

FAMOUS TROJANS

RONNIE LOTT
Hall of Fame DB for 49ers, Raiders

MARCUS ALLEN
Hall of Fame RB for Raiders, Chiefs

TROY POLAMALU
All-Pro safety for Steelers

TYRON SMITH
All-Pro offensive tackle for Cowboys

CLAY MATTHEWS
All-Pro LB for Packers

UCLA

No college program ever succeeded as much as Bruins basketball under John Wooden. His teams, featuring Kareem Abdul-Jabbar and then Bill Walton, won 10 NCAA titles, including seven in a row. At one point his teams won 88 straight games.

Stanford

The Cardinal (it's singular—and it refers to the school color, not a bird) have succeeded in a broad range of sports. Going back to 1976, they've won an NCAA championship every school year. Across all sports they've won 115 titles—and counting.

Cal

The school that produced such diverse stars as Aaron Rodgers and Tony Gonzalez (NFL), Jason Kidd (NBA), Alex Morgan (women's soccer), and Natalie Coughlin (swimming) also has the nation's best rugby team, winner of 28 national championships.

BIG EVENT

Mavericks Challenge

When conditions are right and the swells a couple of miles offshore at Half Moon Bay in northern California rise to epic heights, the call goes out: Mavericks is on. And then some very brave surfers ride the very dangerous mountains of water. At their peak, the wave faces are as high as a five-story building.

ⓘ INSIDER INFO
Another extreme sporting event in California is the Badwater 135. It's billed as the World's Toughest Foot Race. The 135-mile trek begins below sea level in Death Valley and finishes 8,360 feet up on Mount Whitney.

ⓘ INSIDER INFO
Southern Cal has won 12 NCAA baseball titles, the most of any school. Noted alumni include Hall of Fame pitchers Tom Seaver and **Randy Johnson**.

MASCOT FACE-OFF

BOLTMAN *Los Angeles Chargers*	VS.	TREE *Stanford*
Muscular	DESCRIPTOR	Leafy
No, he's a fan	OFFICIAL?	No, he's part of the band
In 2017 police tried to remove his mask	FUN FACT	Inspired by sequoia on Palo Alto city seal
Sure, why not?	GET THEM TOGETHER?	Um, no, because that's how wildfires start

ⓘ INSIDER INFO Surfers in this competition don't hang 10—they hang 20. Dogs of all shapes and sizes show off their best board moves every year at the Surf Dog competition in Huntington Beach.

CALIFORNIA

GREATEST MOMENT

MAY 28, 1957
Dodgers and Giants Move to California

In the 1957 season there were three baseball teams in New York City and none in California. But in May, two of New York's franchises received permission to move to the West Coast the following season. The motives were financial: new stadiums and fresh markets. But the effect in California was cultural. The presence of these storied teams, with stars such as Willie Mays and Duke Snider, fundamentally shifted the American sports landscape westward. While the NFL's Rams had been in L.A. since 1946, the success of the Giants and Dodgers sparked a boom. California now has the most pro teams of any state.

DODGERS GO TO L.A. NEXT YEAR
Move Ends NL Ball in N.Y.

Dodger Double-Bill: Two Moving Pictures

MASCOT FACE-OFF

WILD WING *Anaheim Ducks*	VS.	S.J. SHARKIE *San Jose Sharks*
1993	BORN	1992
He's trying	MIGHTY?	He is, too
Suit once caught fire	LOW MOMENT	Got stuck while rappelling
Not him	WHO'D WIN IN A FIGHT?	No one wins a fight, really

HOMEGROWN HEROES

JACKIE ROBINSON

Before breaking the major league color barrier in 1947 with the Brooklyn Dodgers, Robinson, who grew up in Pasadena, was the first four-sport letterman at UCLA. He somehow found time to star in football, basketball, track, and baseball. He was the 1949 NL MVP.

BILL RUSSELL

Basketball's ultimate winner, he collected five NBA MVP awards while winning 11 championships in 13 seasons with the Boston Celtics. In college, Russell, who is from Oakland, led the University of San Francisco to 55 consecutive victories and the 1955 and 1956 national championships.

RICKEY HENDERSON

Baseball's greatest thief stole a record 1,406 bases. Henderson spent 14 of his 25 seasons with his hometown Oakland A's. In his prime, Henderson's steals were so automatic that a walk or a single might as well have been scored a double. He also played for the Padres, Angels, and Dodgers.

JOE DIMAGGIO

Joltin' Joe, whose 56-game hitting streak in 1941 remains one of baseball's most revered records, grew up in San Francisco and played for the minor league Seals. The graceful centerfielder won three MVP awards and played on nine New York Yankees title teams.

TIGER WOODS

Woods, the winner of 14 majors, single-handedly escalated the popularity of golf when he debuted in 1996. The Stanford alum from Cypress won four majors in a row in 2000 and 2001, a feat now known as a Tiger Slam. From 1998 to 2005, he went 142 tournaments without missing a cut, a PGA record.

STATE-MENT

"Willie Mays's glove is where triples go to die."

JIM MURRAY, Pulitzer Prize–winning *L.A. Times* sportswriter, on the Giants' outfielder

ENEMY OF THE STATE

BOSTON CELTICS

The top rivalry in the NBA began in the 1960s (Jerry West–Bill Russell), escalated in the 1980s (Magic Johnson–Larry Bird), and was renewed in the 2000s (Kobe Bryant–Paul Pierce).

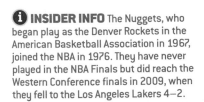

ⓘ INSIDER INFO The Nuggets, who began play as the Denver Rockets in the American Basketball Association in 1967, joined the NBA in 1976. They have never played in the NBA Finals but did reach the Western Conference finals in 2009, when they fell to the Los Angeles Lakers 4–2.

★COLORADO STAR★

John Elway

The most essential figure in Denver sports history might never have come to town at all if not for his skills in a second sport. Elway was the top player available in the 1983 NFL draft, but he didn't want to play for the Baltimore Colts, who owned the first pick. So the quarterback, who had also played baseball at Stanford, suggested that he might opt to play pro baseball if Baltimore selected him. The Colts made a deal with the Broncos, and Denver reaped the benefits for years. Elway was a dynamic quarterback with a flair for leading comebacks. (Ask fans in Cleveland about the Drive.) He took the Broncos to five Super Bowls, winning twice. After retirement, he returned to the team as an executive and made the deals that helped Denver win a third Super Bowl.

STATE-MENT

" "
_____

DIKEMBE MUTOMBO, former Nuggets center. Why use words when a finger wag says everything? The gesture, wordless but memorable, reminded countless shooters not to try to scale Mount Mutombo.

SPORTY SITES

Aspen The former mining town is now a ski resort that regularly hosts the Winter X Games.
Colorado Springs The city is the home of the U.S. Olympic Committee and the U.S. Olympic Training Center.
Coors Field Since baseballs travel farther in the high altitude, the Colorado Rockies' home park—located a mile above sea level—has been a slugger's dream.
Folsom Field The University of Colorado football stadium comes alive when Ralphie the Buffalo and her handlers charge across the turf before games.
Mile High Stadium The current version, which opened in 2001, replaced the original Mile High, built in 1948.
Pepsi Center In addition to hosting NBA and NHL games, the arena was the site of the 2008 NCAA Frozen Four hockey tournament.
Pikes Peak The Pikes Peak International Hill Climb is an annual motor race to the mountain's 14,115-foot summit.

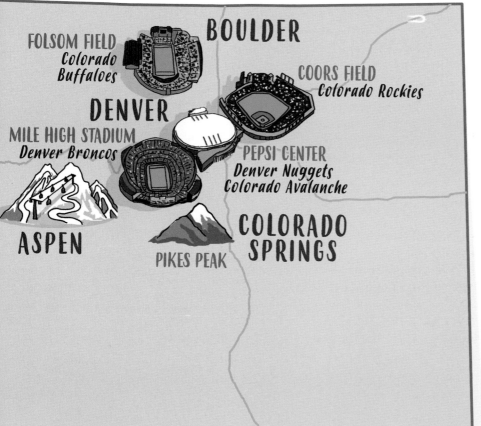

FOLSOM FIELD
Colorado Buffaloes

BOULDER

COORS FIELD
Colorado Rockies

DENVER

MILE HIGH STADIUM
Denver Broncos

PEPSI CENTER
Denver Nuggets
Colorado Avalanche

ASPEN

PIKES PEAK

COLORADO SPRINGS

PRO TEAMS

NFL	Denver Broncos
MLB	Colorado Rockies
NBA	Denver Nuggets
NHL	Colorado Avalanche
MLS	Colorado Rapids

The **Rapids**, a founding member of MLS, began play in 1996 and won their first (and, so far, only) MLS Cup in 2010.

COLORADO

COLORADO

THE NUMBERS

2

MILES that Glenn Morris of Simla would jog to school as a child. He set a world record in the decathlon at the 1936 Olympics.

3

U.S. OPENS won by golfer Hale Irwin of Boulder, who was also a two-time All—Big Eight defensive back at Colorado.

28.4

SCORING AVERAGE of Alex English in 1982—1983, the best in the NBA. He is the only Nugget ever to lead the league in scoring.

1

RANK IN RUNS SCORED at Coors Field in 2017, the sixth straight season it led the majors.

FAN FAVORITES

VON MILLER
Broncos defensive end

A college coach of Miller's at Texas A&M once told SPORTS ILLUSTRATED that the defensive end could limbo underneath a bar held only 18 inches above the floor. So, yes, he's flexible. Miller is also strong, and really, really fast. That's what makes the 6' 3", 237-pound Miller so confounding to blockers. In 104 regular-season games with the Broncos, he has 83½ sacks. His most memorable performance came in Super Bowl 50, when he had 2½ sacks and six tackles and forced a pair of fumbles. He was the key to neutralizing Carolina Panthers quarterback Cam Newton as the Broncos won 24—10.

NIKOLA JOKIĆ
Nuggets center

In a February 2018 game Jokić set an NBA record for the fastest triple double. He completed it with 1:54 left in the second quarter. That speaks to the versatility of the 6' 10" Serbian center, who is Denver's top rebounder and its best playmaker. His rare skills make the Nuggets a fun team to watch.

NOLAN ARENADO
Rockies third baseman

The offensive numbers for Arenado are impressive. In 2015 and 2016, he led the National League in home runs, RBIs, and total bases. But his defense might be even better. Fearless in the field, he has won a Gold Glove in all five of his major league seasons.

TIM HOWARD
Rapids goalkeeper

The longtime U.S. national team goalkeeper came back from Europe to join Colorado in 2016, his first MLS action since 2003. While Howard had to miss several games when called away for international duty, he still had 12 shutouts in 42 games for the Rapids in 2016 and 2017.

GREATEST MOMENT

JUNE 9, 2001

Stanley Cup Champs

The story of the 2001 Stanley Cup finals was, simply, Roy and Ray. Patrick Roy was magnificent in goal for the Avalanche, stopping 49 of 50 shots in Games 6 and 7 to top the New Jersey Devils. Then there was Ray Bourque, a wildly popular player for the Boston Bruins for 21 years who had come to Colorado to win a Cup. When he did, hockey fans all over rejoiced.

COLORADO'S TROPHY SHELF

3 Super Bowl Wins The Broncos lost in their first four Super Bowl appearances before getting the hang of it. They won in 1997 (over the Green Bay Packers), 1998 (Atlanta Falcons), and 2015 (Carolina Panthers).

2 Stanley Cup Wins On the other hand, why wait? After moving from Quebec, where they had been the Nordiques, the Avalanche won a Stanley Cup in their first year in Colorado. The Avs swept the Panthers in the 1996 finals and won their second Cup in 2001.

1 MLS Cup Win The Rapids came from behind to defeat Dallas 2–1 in 2010. Colorado won on an own goal in extra time.

ⓘ INSIDER INFO
The Broncos have sold out every home game since 1970. That's the longest such streak in the NFL.

COOL SCHOOLS

Colorado

The most successful season in school history, 1990, included one of college football's greatest officiating errors. At the end of a game against Missouri, the officials accidentally gave the Buffaloes an extra down, which Colorado used to score the game-winning touchdown. The 1990 squad featured many future pros, including senior running back Eric Bieniemy. Colorado finished the season 11–1 and beat Notre Dame 10–9 in the Orange Bowl, earning the No. 1 spot in the AP poll.

Colorado State

The two most accomplished athletes ever to compete for the Rams are both women. Becky Hammon, who made history as the NBA's first full-time female assistant coach, with the San Antonio Spurs, played her college ball at Colorado State. Then there's swimmer Amy Van Dyken, who was an All-America for the Rams and won six gold medals at the Olympics. In men's sports, the biggest game around is the Rocky Mountain Showdown football game against Colorado. In the series, which has been played in recent years at Mile High Stadium, the Rams have won just 22 of 89 meetings.

Denver

If the sport involves goals and sticks, the Pioneers are probably pretty good at it. That's been especially true on the ice. Denver won a national championship in hockey in 2017, the school's eighth since 1958. And in recent years, since hiring championship-winning coach Bill Tierney from Princeton, Denver has also become very competitive in lacrosse. That's unusual for a western school. In fact, the Pioneers actually compete in the Big East conference, but only in lacrosse. In 2015, Denver became the first school located outside the eastern time zone to win an NCAA title in the sport.

HOMEGROWN HEROES

MISSY FRANKLIN
A five-time Olympic gold medalist from Centennial, Franklin was a natural in the water. Her mother took her to a swim class when she was six months old, and while the other babies screamed when submerged, Franklin came up smiling.

JACK DEMPSEY
Dempsey's nickname, the Manassa Mauler, came from his hometown. After a storied boxing career that included 25 first-round knockouts, a 1950 poll named him the greatest fighter of the half century.

ℹ️ **INSIDER INFO** Colorado has 59 peaks that are at least 14,000 feet in elevation. Some have relatively easy trails that make them suitable for beginners, while others demand expert skill.

MASCOT FACE-OFF

RALPHIE THE BUFFALO *University of Colorado*	VS.	THUNDER *Denver Broncos*
1967	BORN	1993
American bison	BREED	Arabian
At the start of each half	APPEARS	Before the game and after touchdowns
Five handlers	TAKES FIELD WITH . . .	One rider

BIG EVENT

Leadville Trail 100 Ultramarathon

"The Race Across the Sky" is held in Leadville, a former mining town and America's highest incorporated city. The challenge is not just the distance of 100 miles but also the altitude and the ups and downs—from 9,200 to 12,600 feet. That makes the course chart look like a nervous person's heart rate chart. Speaking of which, this race is not for the faint of heart.

ENEMY OF THE STATE

OAKLAND RAIDERS

There's a long history of testiness between these AFC West foes. Several coaches have worked both sides of the rivalry, most notably Mike Shanahan, who won two Super Bowls in Denver after being fired by Oakland.

CONNECTICUT

INTERNATIONAL SKATING CENTER OF CONNECTICUT
SIMSBURY

STORRS
GAMPEL PAVILION
UConn Huskies

BRISTOL
ESPN HEADQUARTERS

UNCASVILLE
MOHEGAN SUN ARENA
Connecticut Sun

WIFFLE BALL INC.
SHELTON

PRO TEAMS

WNBA   **Connecticut Sun**

The **Sun** originally played in Orlando before moving in 2003 to a state filled with women's basketball fans.

CONNECTICUT'S TROPHY SHELF

4 NCAA Men's Basketball Championships The Huskies men's team won titles in 1999, 2004, and 2011 under coach Jim Calhoun. In 2014, coach Kevin Ollie, who had played for Calhoun in the 1990s, took the Huskies to the championship. That team triumphed as a No. 7 seed, behind guard Shabazz Napier.

11 NCAA Women's Basketball Championships After winning their first title in 1995, the women's team won four in a five-year span (2000–2004) and then six in eight years (2009–2016).

SPORTY SITES

ESPN The sports broadcasting behemoth is based in Bristol.

Gampel Pavilion With a capacity of 9,882, the University of Connecticut arena is the largest on-campus basketball arena in New England.

International Skating Center of Connecticut The Simsbury rink has been the training base for Olympic figure skating stars.

Mohegan Sun Arena The casino hosts WNBA and MMA action.

Wiffle Ball Inc. The plastic ball was invented in Fairfield in 1953, and the company is based in Shelton.

🛈 **INSIDER INFO** America's first college sports team was Yale's crew squad, launched in 1843. Harvard founded its team the next year, and in 1852 the squads met at Lake Winnipesaukee in New Hampshire for the first intercollegiate sporting event.

GREATEST MOMENT

APRIL 2, 1995
First Perfect Season

In 1995, the Connecticut women's basketball team didn't just win a championship—the Huskies set a standard. UConn completed its regular season undefeated and then swept through the Big East and NCAA tournaments, topping Tennessee in the national championship game to finish the season 35–0. It was Connecticut's first title but not its last. The Huskies have won 11 championships—and they've done it with a perfect record six times.

★CONNECTICUT STAR★

Geno Auriemma

The most successful coach in women's basketball was born in Italy and arrived in Norristown, Pennsylvania, as a second-grader who couldn't speak English. By 1985, at age 31, he had become the women's basketball coach at Connecticut, which in its 18 seasons of existence had had only one winning season. Now it's news when UConn loses a game. He is a nine-time Coach of the Year, and his teams have put together winning streaks of 90 and 111 games. In Storrs, Auriemma has built an empire.

HOMEGROWN HEROES

KRISTINE LILLY
Lilly, who grew up in Wilton, played for the U.S. women's national soccer team for 24 years. She holds the world record for appearances in international tournaments, with 352. Lilly played in five World Cups, the only woman to do so.

JOEY LOGANO
In 2009, Logano became the first teenager to win a race on NASCAR's top circuit. At age 19, the Middletown native finished first in the Lenox Industrial Tools 301 at the New Hampshire International Speedway.

BILL RODGERS
His wins in the Boston and New York Marathons helped inspire America's running boom in the 1970s. The Hartford native took up distance running as a Wesleyan student.

CHRIS DRURY
As a pitcher, he won the final game of the 1989 Little League World Series to give Trumbull the title. In hockey he won the Hobey Baker Award at Boston University in 1998 and took NHL rookie of the year honors with the Colorado Avalanche in 1999.

Elena Delle Donne

The University of Delaware women's basketball team had never won an NCAA tournament game until Delle Donne showed up on campus. The Wilmington native had committed to Connecticut, but after two days on the Storrs campus, she decided she wanted to be near her family—especially her older sister, Lizzie, who was born with cerebral palsy and is deaf and blind. As a senior Delle Donne led the Blue Hens to the Sweet 16 of the 2013 tourney, and in 2015 she was the WNBA MVP.

NEWARK

DELAWARE STADIUM
Delaware Blue Hens

DUPONT COUNTRY CLUB

BOB CARPENTER CENTER
Delaware Blue Hens

DOVER INTERNATIONAL SPEEDWAY

SPORTY SITES

Bob Carpenter Center The Philadelphia 76ers' G League affiliate, the Delaware 87ers, play at the Blue Hens basketball arena.

Delaware Stadium From 1999 to 2009, Delaware was the only FCS school to average more than 20,000 in home attendance for football.

Dover International Speedway The track hosts two NASCAR events each year.

DuPont Country Club The course was the site of the McDonald's LPGA Championship for 17 years.

PRO TEAMS

Class A   Wilmington Blue Rocks

The **Blue Rocks**, an affiliate of the Kansas City Royals, have three mascots, including the oddly popular Mr. Celery.

DELAWARE

GREATEST MOMENT

1972 SEASON
Delaware Blue Hens

In 1972, the Blue Hens won their games by an average of 26.8 points. They knocked off Bucknell 20–3 in the finale to finish 10–0 and clinch their second consecutive small-college championship, as determined by the polls. (The NCAA began its lower-division playoff system the following year.)

THE NUMBERS

3
UD COACHES in the College Football Hall of Fame: Bill Murray, Dave Nelson, and Tubby Raymond.

1
NHL PLAYER born in Delaware—Mark Eaton, who was a defenseman for four teams from 1999 to 2013.

8-0
DELAWARE'S RECORD vs. Delaware State in football. The schools didn't meet until 2007.

HOMEGROWN HEROES

RANDY WHITE

The 6' 4", 257-pound Hall of Fame defensive tackle and Wilmington native played in nine Pro Bowls in 14 years with the Dallas Cowboys. He was named co-MVP of Super Bowl XII and was the 1978 NFC Defensive Player of the Year. A two-sport star at Thomas McKean High, White won both the Outland Trophy and the Lombardi Award at Maryland in 1974.

JOHNNY WEIR
Born in Pennsylvania, Weir moved to Newark at age 12 to train. The figure skater, a three-time U.S. champion, competed in the Olympics in 2006 and 2010. For the last two Winter Olympics he has provided figure skating commentary for NBC.

FAN FAVORITE

JOE FLACCO
Blue Hens legend

Delaware quarterbacks have made their mark in the NFL. Matt Nagy is coach of the Chicago Bears. Rich Gannon was the 2002 NFL MVP and reached the Super Bowl that season with the Oakland Raiders. Joe Flacco elevated the Blue Hens' legacy when he was named MVP of Super Bowl XLVII for leading the Baltimore Ravens to their second championship. At Delaware, Flacco nearly led the Blue Hens to a title as well, but his team fell to Appalachian State in the FCS championship game. Flacco, a transfer from Pitt, played only two seasons at Delaware but holds many school records, including career completions (595) and yards passing in a season (4,263 in 2007). He is the only Blue Hen to be selected in the first round of the NFL draft.

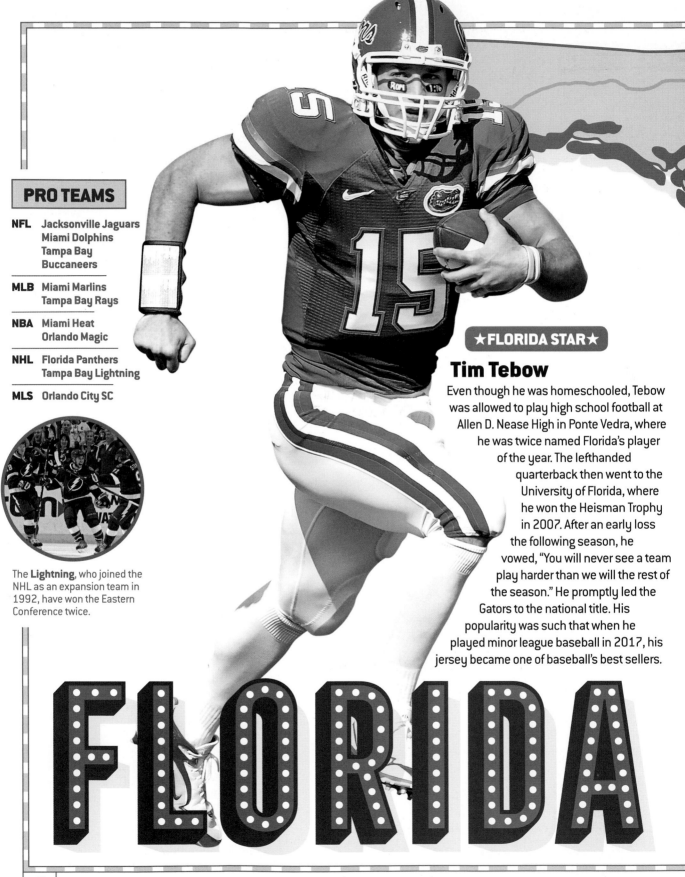

PRO TEAMS

NFL	Jacksonville Jaguars Miami Dolphins Tampa Bay Buccaneers
MLB	Miami Marlins Tampa Bay Rays
NBA	Miami Heat Orlando Magic
NHL	Florida Panthers Tampa Bay Lightning
MLS	Orlando City SC

The **Lightning**, who joined the NHL as an expansion team in 1992, have won the Eastern Conference twice.

★FLORIDA STAR★

Tim Tebow

Even though he was homeschooled, Tebow was allowed to play high school football at Allen D. Nease High in Ponte Vedra, where he was twice named Florida's player of the year. The lefthanded quarterback then went to the University of Florida, where he won the Heisman Trophy in 2007. After an early loss the following season, he vowed, "You will never see a team play harder than we will the rest of the season." He promptly led the Gators to the national title. His popularity was such that when he played minor league baseball in 2017, his jersey became one of baseball's best sellers.

FLORIDA

JACKSONVILLE

EVERBANK FIELD
Jacksonville Jaguars

TPC SAWGRASS

DAYTONA SPEEDWAY

ORLANDO

RAYMOND JAMES STADIUM
Tampa Bay Buccaneers

AMWAY CENTER
Orlando Magic

TAMPA

TROPICANA FIELD
Tampa Bay Rays

CHAMPION STADIUM
Atlanta Braves spring training

AMALIE ARENA
Tampa Bay Lightning

IMG ACADEMY

BB&T CENTER
Florida Panthers

FORT LAUDERDALE

HARD ROCK STADIUM
Miami Dolphins

INTERNATIONAL SWIMMING HALL OF FAME

MARLINS PARK
Miami Marlins

AMERICAN AIRLINES ARENA
Miami Heat

MIAMI

ⓘ INSIDER INFO
Warren Sapp—who was an All-America defensive tackle at Miami and the 1999 Defensive Player of the Year for the Tampa Bay Buccaneers—holds the Apopka High record for longest field goal.

SPORTY SITES

Champion Stadium The Braves hold spring training here, in ESPN's Wide World of Sports Complex. Overall, 15 teams train in Florida's Grapefruit League.

Everbank Field, Jacksonville In addition to being home of the Jaguars, the 67,164-seat stadium hosts the annual Georgia-Florida football showdown.

IMG Academy The boarding school was founded by tennis instructor Nick Bollettieri, but now it caters to athletes from many sports. Its famous alumni include Serena Williams (tennis), Cam Newton and Russell Wilson (football), and Paula Creamer (golf).

International Swimming Hall of Fame One display traces the history of swimming back to 3000 B.C.

◀ **Raymond James Stadium** Tampa Bay's football stadium features a 103-foot replica pirate ship that fires its cannon every time the Buccaneers score.

TPC Sawgrass The course is famous for its 17th hole, with an island green in the middle of a lake.

FLORIDA

COOL SCHOOLS

Florida

Florida fans celebrate big plays with the Gator Chomp. (To do it, hold your arms in front of you as if they are alligator jaws and bite away.) The faithful have waved their arms plenty over the years, because the Gainesville school excels in an impressive variety of sports. The Gators have won at least two national titles in—deep breath—football, basketball, softball, men's track and field (both indoor and outdoor), golf for both men and women, women's gymnastics, women's tennis, and swimming and diving for both men and women. In 1984 the Southeastern Conference began awarding a trophy for the school with the best all-around program. Florida has won it 27 times. In the Olympics, Florida athletes have won 60 gold medals. The best time to be a Gators fan had to be 2007, when Florida became the only school ever to hold the NCAA championships in both football and basketball at the same time.

FAMOUS GATORS

EMMITT SMITH
NFL's alltime
leading rusher

ABBY WAMBACH
Six-time U.S. Soccer
Athlete of the Year

AL HORFORD
All-Star center for the
Boston Celtics

DANTE FOWLER
Jacksonville Jaguars
defensive end

TRACY CAULKINS
Olympic swimmer,
three gold medals

Florida State

The Seminoles are known for their powerhouse football program, which won national titles in 1993, 1999, and 2013. It has produced three Heisman winners: Charlie Ward, Chris Weinke, and Jameis Winston. On the baseball field, Florida State's most notable alum is San Francisco Giants catcher Buster Posey. The school has also won national titles in soccer, softball, track, volleyball, and cheerleading.

University of Miami

The Hurricanes' football program swaggered its way to five national titles between 1983 and 2001, and it produced an amazing 15 NFL first-round picks from 2002 to 2004. Program traditions include the turnover chain. A necklace with the school's insignia in gold, it is presented on the sideline to a defensive player who has forced a turnover. Miami has also excelled in baseball, winning four national titles.

HOMEGROWN HEROES

VINCE CARTER
One of the NBA's all-time great dunkers financed a multimillion-dollar gym at his alma mater, Mainland High in Daytona Beach.

JOEY BOSA
The Chargers pass rusher went to St. Thomas Aquinas High in Fort Lauderdale. Other NFL players from the school include Geno Atkins and Giovani Bernard of the Cincinnati Bengals and two New England Patriots: James White and Phillip Dorsett.

DEVONTA FREEMAN
The Atlanta Falcons running back starred at Miami Central Senior High and Florida State, where he helped the Seminoles to the 2013 national title.

DALVIN COOK
Like Freeman, this Minnesota Vikings running back went to Central High and Florida State.

DEION SANDERS
From Fort Myers, the broadcaster was the ultimate shut-down cornerback at Florida State. The six-time NFL All-Pro is the only athlete to play in both the Super Bowl and the World Series.

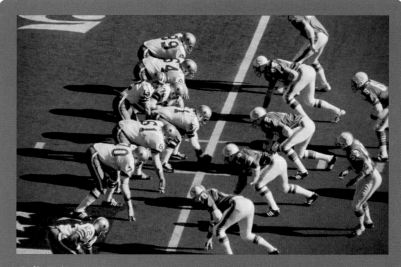

GREATEST MOMENT

1972 SEASON
Miami's Perfect Campaign
The 1972 Dolphins set a standard that NFL teams are still chasing. That year Miami went 17–0, making it the only team to ever complete a perfect season. Now every year after the last remaining undefeated team loses, members of the 1972 Dolphins pop champagne to celebrate the preservation of their status.

STATE-MENT

"Discipline is a lot more than saying, 'Don't throw your hands up in the air when you score a touchdown.' Discipline is when it's 110° in the Orange Bowl, no breeze, fourth quarter, a minute and a half left to play, fourth-and-three for the other team, you're dead tired, they come to the line, and the opposing quarterback gives you a hard count: HUT HUT. And you don't jump offsides. Because you're disciplined mentally and physically."**

MICHAEL IRVIN, former University of Miami wide receiver

FLORIDA

THE NUMBERS

11
NCAA FOOTBALL TITLES won by teams from the state. Miami has five, while Florida and Florida State each have three.

5
PGA TOUR EVENTS played in the state of Florida.

16
AGE at which Lexi Thompson of Coral Springs won her first LPGA tournament, in 2011.

13
CONSECUTIVE YEARS in which Chris Evert, from Fort Lauderdale, won at least one Grand Slam tennis title.

11
WORLD SURFING CHAMPIONSHIPS won by Cocoa Beach's Kelly Slater, the most decorated surfer in history.

FAN FAVORITES

STEVEN STAMKOS
Lightning center

The top pick of the 2008 NHL draft, Stamkos has since led the league in goals twice. The Lightning captain has suffered injuries in recent years (he now plays with a metal rod in his leg), but in 2017–2018 he showed classic form, leading the NHL's most-high-powered offense.

JALEN RAMSEY
Jaguars cornerback

The homegrown star was a 2015 All-America at Florida State, where he was the first true freshman to start at the position since Hall of Famer Deion Sanders. In 2017, he helped lead a Jags defense that gave up the second-fewest points—and fewest passing yards—in the NFL.

AARON GORDON
Magic forward

The 6' 9" power forward with big-time hops came into the NBA in 2014 known for his spectacular dunking ability. But Gordon has developed into a dangerous all-around player capable of draining three-pointers, grabbing rebounds, and playing suffocating defense.

UDONIS HASLEM
Heat center

Haslem was born in Miami and played his college ball at Florida. So after he went undrafted it made sense for him to sign with the Heat as a free agent in 2003. The tenacious rebounder has been a fixture in the frontcourt and is second in franchise history in games played.

BIG EVENT

The Daytona 500

In most sports the biggest event—think Super Bowl and World Series—comes at the end of the season. But since 1982, NASCAR has chosen to start things off with a bang, making its most prestigious race, the Daytona 500, the season opener. In 2018 the 500-mile event (which is 200 laps around Daytona International Speedway) was won by Austin Dillon.

FLORIDA'S TROPHY SHELF

3 Super Bowl Wins The Dolphins won Super Bowls in 1972 and 1973, while the Buccaneers soared in 2002 behind stars such as Warren Sapp (from the University of Miami) and Dexter Jackson (Florida State).

3 NBA Championships The Heat won their first title in 2006 with Dwyane Wade. They added two more in 2012 and 2013 after Wade was joined by LeBron James and Chris Bosh.

2 World Series Championships The Marlins, who began play in 1993, won their first title four years later. The Fish added a second in 2003.

1 Stanley Cup Win The Lightning electrified the NHL in 2004.

ENEMY OF THE STATE

GEORGIA FOOTBALL

Every year the Gators meet their SEC East foe on a neutral field in Jacksonville. The game is known as The World's Largest Outdoor Cocktail Party. The schools dispute when the first game was held, but they agree that Georgia holds a slight lead.

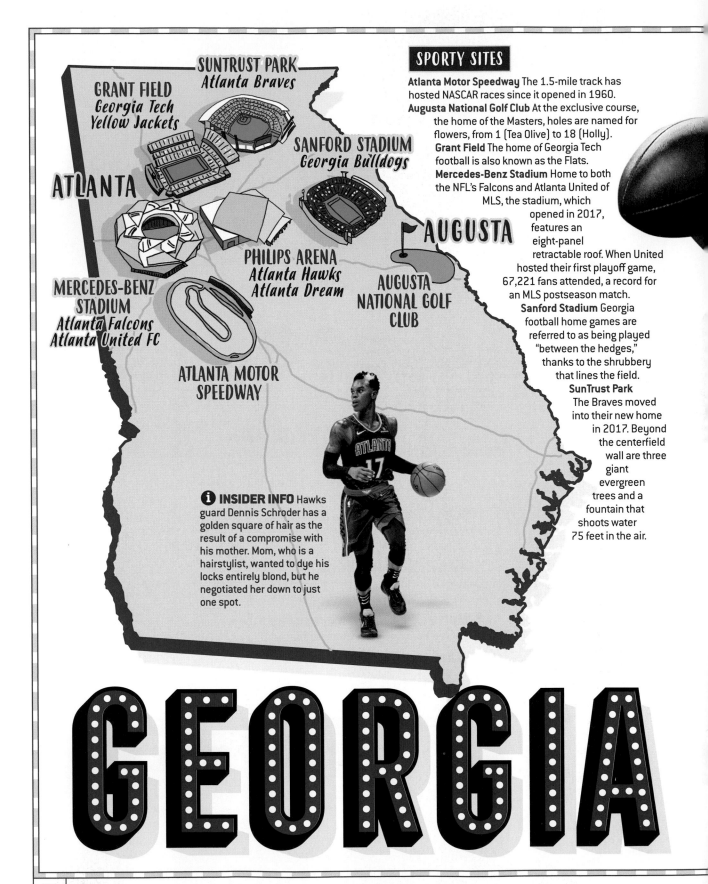

SUNTRUST PARK
Atlanta Braves

GRANT FIELD
*Georgia Tech
Yellow Jackets*

SANFORD STADIUM
Georgia Bulldogs

ATLANTA

AUGUSTA

PHILIPS ARENA
*Atlanta Hawks
Atlanta Dream*

AUGUSTA
NATIONAL GOLF
CLUB

MERCEDES-BENZ
STADIUM
*Atlanta Falcons
Atlanta United FC*

ATLANTA MOTOR
SPEEDWAY

SPORTY SITES

Atlanta Motor Speedway The 1.5-mile track has hosted NASCAR races since it opened in 1960.
Augusta National Golf Club At the exclusive course, the home of the Masters, holes are named for flowers, from 1 (Tea Olive) to 18 (Holly).
Grant Field The home of Georgia Tech football is also known as the Flats.
Mercedes-Benz Stadium Home to both the NFL's Falcons and Atlanta United of MLS, the stadium, which opened in 2017, features an eight-panel retractable roof. When United hosted their first playoff game, 67,221 fans attended, a record for an MLS postseason match.
Sanford Stadium Georgia football home games are referred to as being played "between the hedges," thanks to the shrubbery that lines the field.
SunTrust Park The Braves moved into their new home in 2017. Beyond the centerfield wall are three giant evergreen trees and a fountain that shoots water 75 feet in the air.

ℹ **INSIDER INFO** Hawks guard Dennis Schroder has a golden square of hair as the result of a compromise with his mother. Mom, who is a hairstylist, wanted to dye his locks entirely blond, but he negotiated her down to just one spot.

GEORGIA

PRO TEAMS

NFL	**Atlanta Falcons**
MLB	**Atlanta Braves**
NBA	**Atlanta Hawks**
WNBA	**Atlanta Dream**
MLS	**Atlanta United FC**

The **Braves** were at their best in the 1990s, behind Hall of Fame pitchers Greg Maddux, Tom Glavine, and John Smoltz.

★GEORGIA STAR★

Matt Ryan

Before Ryan was drafted in 2008, the Falcons had been to the playoffs just eight times in 42 years. Since Matty Ice took over under center, Atlanta has been to the postseason six times, including a Super Bowl berth in 2016, when Ryan was named the NFL's Most Valuable Player. Of course, Ryan isn't doing it alone; he's surrounded by outstanding talents, including All-Pro receiver Julio Jones. But with the cool and steady Ryan—who is the franchise leader in every major passing category—controlling the offense, Falcons fans enter every season feeling like contenders.

COOL SCHOOLS

Georgia

Located in Athens, the university has an outstanding football tradition that includes one national championship (1980), two Heisman Trophy winners (Frank Sinkwich in 1942 and Herschel Walker in 1982), and plenty of graduates who have made their NFL marks. Quarterback Fran Tarkenton and running back Terrell Davis are Hall of Famers, while QB Matthew Stafford and receiver A.J. Green are current fantasy stars. But the most successful team at Georgia is populated not by big men but by little (and ridiculously athletic) women. The Bulldogs' gymnastics team has won 10 national championships, including five in a row from 2005 to 2009. Women's swimming is strong, too, with seven national titles, including three since 2013. Georgia plays annual rivalry games with Georgia Tech. The football showdown is referred to as Clean, Old-Fashioned Hate. The Bulldogs lead the series 66-41-5.

Georgia Tech

You have to love a school whose teams are referred to not only as the Yellow Jackets but also as the Ramblin' Wreck from Georgia Tech. (It rhymes! We love rhymes!) Which sport is tops? On the gridiron Tech won a national championship in 1990 and has produced such standouts as receivers Calvin Johnson and Demaryius Thomas. The school has sent an impressive group of players (led by Chris Bosh and Stephon Marbury) to the NBA. And the baseball program has turned out stars Mark Teixeira, Nomar Garciaparra, and Jason Varitek. But the school may have had its greatest influence in golf. The list of former Yellow Jackets on the links includes British Open winners David Duval and Stewart Cink, 2010 money leader Matt Kuchar, and 13-time major winner Bobby Jones.

HOMEGROWN HEROES

EVANDER HOLYFIELD

Nicknamed the Real Deal, Holyfield was a four-time heavyweight boxing champion. The Atlanta native won two fights against Mike Tyson, including one in which Tyson bit off part of Holyfield's ear. Holyfield also won bronze at the 1984 Olympics.

HERSCHEL WALKER

From Wrightsville, the running back led Georgia to a national championship as a freshman in 1980. Two years later he won the Heisman Trophy. The exceptional athlete was also an Olympic bobsledder and an MMA fighter.

DOMINIQUE WILKINS

The Human Highlight Reel starred at Georgia and then became a nine-time All-Star and two-time NBA dunk champion with the Atlanta Hawks. He is now a Hawks broadcaster.

CHAMP BAILEY

Born in Folkston, the wildly athletic Bailey was the country's top defensive player at Georgia in 1998. He also played receiver and ran back punts and kicks. In the NFL, he made the Pro Bowl 12 times for the Washington Redskins and the Denver Broncos.

BIG EVENT

The Masters

Golf has four major championships, but only one takes place at the same course every year. The Masters, founded in 1934 by golfing legend and Atlanta native Bobby Jones, is held at Augusta National Golf Club during the first full week of April. Winners receive one of the most distinctive trophies in sports—the green jacket that is also worn by club members. Do you think 2017 champion Sergio García was thinking about what would look good with the jacket when he picked his final-round wardrobe (right)?

MASCOT FACE-OFF

UGA *Georgia*	VS.	BUZZ *Georgia Tech*
English bulldog	**SPECIES**	Yellow jacket
Yes	**REAL ANIMAL?**	No
Air-conditioned doghouse	**ACCESSORY**	Converse sneakers
Jumping at Auburn player	**HIGH POINT**	Unmasking at graduation
Ferocious, dignified	**PERSONALITY**	Not ferocious or dignified

GEORGIA'S TROPHY SHELF

1 World Series Championship

The Braves, who played in Boston and Milwaukee before moving to Atlanta in 1966, captured the only league title in Georgia history when they won the World Series in 1995. (Atlanta made four other World Series appearances in that decade.) The Falcons have lost two Super Bowls, while the Hawks have not been in the Finals since moving to Atlanta from St. Louis in 1968.

GEORGIA

THE NUMBERS

222-0

SCORE of Georgia Tech's win over Cumberland College in 1916, the most lopsided football game ever.

6
FCS CHAMPIONSHIPS won by the Georgia Southern Eagles.

$1
PRICE PER BUS of the two vehicles sold to the Georgia Southern football program by the Bulloch County Board of Education in 1981. The Eagles' program was starting up again and didn't have any money. The school still uses those buses today.

0
PLAYOFF GAMES WON by the NHL's Atlanta Thrashers in their 11 seasons of existence. The team qualified for the postseason only once, in 2007, when it was swept by the New York Rangers. In 2011 the Thrashers moved to Winnipeg and became the Jets.

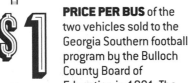

FAN FAVORITES

JULIO JONES
Falcons wide receiver

Had the nickname Human Highlight Reel not already been taken by Dominique Wilkins, Jones would have an excellent claim to it. The 6' 4", 220-pound wide receiver, who had a league-leading 136 receptions in 2015, is as tough to cover as anyone in the NFL because of his size, speed, and ability to make contested catches.

JULIAN GRESSEL
Atlanta United midfielder

How fitting that in 2017 a franchise in its first season also had the MLS Rookie of the Year. Gressel, who was born in Germany, was the eighth pick in the MLS SuperDraft, out of Providence College. He had five goals and nine assists, helping Atlanta make the playoffs.

KIRBY SMART
University of Georgia football coach

The former defensive back returned to his alma mater as head coach in 2016. The Bainbridge native took the Bulldogs to the College Football Playoff in his second season. Georgia rallied to a double-overtime comeback win in the semifinals but was nipped by Alabama in OT in the title game.

ENDER INCIARTE
Braves centerfielder

Inciarte's fourth major league season, in 2017, was also his best. Not only did he make his first All-Star team, but he also had 201 hits, the most by a Braves player since Marquis Grissom in 1996. The speedster also earned his second Gold Glove award in 2017.

GREATEST MOMENT

APRIL 8, 1974
Hank Aaron's 715th Home Run

This was the call by Milo Hamilton when Aaron came to the plate in the bottom of the fourth against the Dodgers at Atlanta–Fulton County Stadium: "Here's the pitch by [Al] Downing. Swinging. Here's a drive into left centerfield. That ball is gonna be . . . outta here! It's gone! It's 715! There's a new home run champion of all time, and it's Henry Aaron."

ENEMY OF THE STATE

FLORIDA FOOTBALL

The annual clash between Georgia and Florida football takes place at a neutral site with tickets split evenly between the schools. In a game where the outcome often decides the SEC East race, Georgia leads the series 50-43-2.

STATE-MENT

"I regret to this day that I never went to college. I feel I should have been a doctor."

TY COBB, known as the Georgia Peach and owner of the highest career batting average (.366) and second-most hits (4,189) in baseball history

SPORTY SITES

Aloha Stadium Home to the University of Hawaii's Rainbow Warrior football team, the stadium has hosted the NFL's Pro Bowl 35 times.

Banzai Pipeline The legendary surf spot on the North Shore of Oahu features huge waves near the shore that makes it look as if surfers are riding in a tube.

Ironman Triathlon Course The race began in Oahu in 1978 with just 15 competitors, but it moved to the less populated Big Island in 1981 to accommodate more competitors. In the October 2017 race, Patrick Lange of Germany set a course record of eight hours, one minutes, and 40 seconds.

Stan Sheriff Center Men's teams that play at the University of Hawaii sports arena are known as the Rainbow Warriors. Women's teams are called the Rainbow Wahine. (*Wahine* is Hawaiian for "woman.")

BANZAI PIPELINE

ALOHA STADIUM
University of Hawaii Rainbow Warriors

OAHU

STAN SHERIFF CENTER
University of Hawaii Rainbow Warriors

IRONMAN TRIATHLON COURSE

HAWAII

KONA

THE NUMBERS

2,352 **MILES**, at a minimum, that a University of Hawaii sports team must fly to play a game on the United States mainland.

1 **RANK** of the Virginia Cavaliers in 1982 when they lost 77–72 to the Chaminade Silverswords of Honolulu. It was college basketball's biggest regular-season upset ever.

551 **WEIGHT IN POUNDS** of Chad Rowan of Waimānalo, the first American to earn the title of *yokozuna* (grand champion) in sumo.

★HAWAII STAR★

Marcus Mariota

When Marcus Mariota was growing up in Honolulu, the University of Hawaii's football coach was June Jones, inventor of the run-and-shoot offense. Many nearby high schools, including Mariota's, were soon using quick-pass schemes. This helped Mariota develop into the quarterback who starred at the University of Oregon and now leads the Tennessee Titans. Mariota, in a nod to island culture, wore leis to the 2014 Heisman Trophy ceremony. After winning that award, he thanked people back home. "In Hawaii," he said, "if one person is successful, the entire state is successful."

HAWAII

HOMEGROWN HEROES

MICHELLE WIE

The 2014 U.S. Women's Open champion excelled from an early age. At 10 the Honolulu native was the youngest golfer ever to qualify for a USGA amateur event. At 13 she made her first cut in a pro tournament.

BETHANY HAMILTON

Hamilton was 13 years old in 2003 when she was attacked by a tiger shark while surfing. She lost her left arm but returned to the water a month later and won a major competition in 2004. That year she also published her memoir, *Soul Surfer*, and in 2011 a movie based on the book was released.

SHANE VICTORINO

The Flyin' Hawaiian, born and raised in Wailuku, whipped around the bases for 12 major league seasons. The two-time All-Star outfielder earned World Series rings with the Philadelphia Phillies in 2008 and the Boston Red Sox in 2013.

SUNNY GARCIA

Hawaii is home to many great competitive surfers; you can become really good at water sports when you go to the beach every day. Garcia, from Wai'anae, won the Triple Crown of Surfing six times. (All three legs take place on Hawaii beaches.) He was the second surfer to top $1 million in career earnings.

STATE-MENT

"Swim 2.4 miles. Bike 112 miles. Run 26.2. Brag for the rest of your life."

JOHN COLLINS, Ironman triathlon cofounder

FAN FAVORITE

THE ROCK
Football player, wrestler, movie star

Dwayne Johnson moved plenty as a kid. Born in California, he also lived in New Zealand and Pennsylvania. But the son of a Samoan mother and an African-American father spent part of his youth in Hawaii before going on to play football at Miami, win WWE belts as the Rock, and become a movie star. In the Disney movie *Moana* he leaned on his island roots for his role as the demigod Maui.

IDAHO

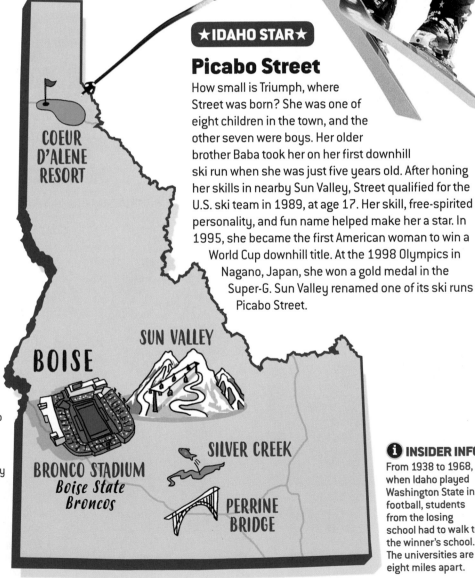

PRO TEAMS

Class A Boise Hawks

Rookie Idaho Falls Chukars

The **Chukars** are an affiliate of the Kansas City Royals. A chukar is a kind of partridge found in the western U.S.

SPORTY SITES

Coeur d'Alene Resort The golf course includes a floating green that players can reach only by boat.

Perrine Bridge Daredevil alert! This span across the Snake River Canyon attracts a great many BASE jumpers, who parachute 486 feet to the watery, rocky bottom.

Silver Creek Author Ernest Hemingway is among the many who have been lured here by the fly-fishing.

Sun Valley With 65 runs for skiers and snowboarders, the resort area has long attracted celebrities, from actor Clark Gable to Mark Zuckerberg.

COEUR D'ALENE RESORT

SUN VALLEY

BOISE

BRONCO STADIUM
Boise State Broncos

SILVER CREEK

PERRINE BRIDGE

★ IDAHO STAR ★

Picabo Street

How small is Triumph, where Street was born? She was one of eight children in the town, and the other seven were boys. Her older brother Baba took her on her first downhill ski run when she was just five years old. After honing her skills in nearby Sun Valley, Street qualified for the U.S. ski team in 1989, at age 17. Her skill, free-spirited personality, and fun name helped make her a star. In 1995, she became the first American woman to win a World Cup downhill title. At the 1998 Olympics in Nagano, Japan, she won a gold medal in the Super-G. Sun Valley renamed one of its ski runs Picabo Street.

ℹ INSIDER INFO

From 1938 to 1968, when Idaho played Washington State in football, students from the losing school had to walk to the winner's school. The universities are eight miles apart.

HOMEGROWN HEROES

JERRY KRAMER
The Green Bay guard was a key blocker on the sweep running plays that the Packers used to dominate the NFL in the 1960s. The five-time All-Pro and Hall of Famer was raised in Sandpoint and played at the University of Idaho.

HARMON KILLEBREW
The stoic slugger from Payette hit 573 career home runs, the 12th most in major league history. The longtime Minnesota Twin made 13 All-Star teams and was the 1969 American League MVP.

JAKE PLUMMER
After starting at quarterback for 10 seasons for the Arizona Cardinals and Denver Broncos, Plummer walked away from the NFL. He returned to his native Idaho, where he funneled his competitive urges into handball.

GREATEST MOMENT

JANUARY 1, 2007
Fiesta Bowl
The game stands as a classic not just for the David vs. Goliath aspect of upstart Boise State knocking off mighty Oklahoma, but also because of the way the Broncos did it. After tying the game on a last-minute 50-yard hook-and-lateral play, Boise State triumphed in overtime with a two-point conversion on another trick play, the Statue of Liberty.

ⓘ INSIDER INFO
Cincinnati Bengals coach Marvin Lewis began his coaching career working with linebackers at his alma mater, Idaho State—where the mascot happens to be the Bengals.

STATE-MENT

"They know it's not grass, so there's really no reason it needs to be green."

GENE BLEYMAIER, Boise State AD, on why he installed blue artificial turf

THE NUMBERS

15
BOISE STATE ALUMS in the NFL in 2017, including Jay Ajayi, Doug Martin, and DeMarcus Lawrence.

13
AGE of Michelle Wie when she competed against men at the Boise Open; she missed the cut by 12 shots.

9
WINS in Triple Crown races by jockey Gary Stevens of Caldwell. His father trained horses.

ℹ INSIDER INFO
Candace Parker of the WNBA's Los Angeles Sparks grew up in Naperville and was named national high school player of the year by *USA Today* in both 2003 and 2004. She is the only player to win the award twice.

PRO TEAMS

NFL	Chicago Bears
MLB	Chicago Cubs
	Chicago White Sox
NBA	Chicago Bulls
WNBA	Chicago Sky
NHL	Chicago Blackhawks
MLS	Chicago Fire

The **Blackhawks**, after going nearly a half century without a Stanley Cup, have picked up three since 2010.

★ILLINOIS STAR★

Michael Jordan

Few players have had as big an impact on their sport as His Airness. Jordan burst onto the scene as a high-scoring, high-flying rookie for the Chicago Bulls in 1984. Shortly after his debut, Nike introduced the Air Jordan line, which launched the craze of personalized shoes. To an entire generation of fans who never saw him play, Jordan is recognizable as the silhouetted figure in Nike's Jumpman logo. To those lucky enough to see him in action, he was simply peerless. Jordan led the NBA in scoring 10 times, including seven seasons in a row. His Bulls won six NBA championships between 1991 and 1998, thanks largely to his clutch performances. During Jordan's heyday, there was a commercial that featured the jingle, "I want to be like Mike." Indeed, countless current NBA stars—including LeBron James—admit that they modeled their games on Jordan's, and with good reason. His Airness redefined what it means to be a superstar.

ILLINOIS

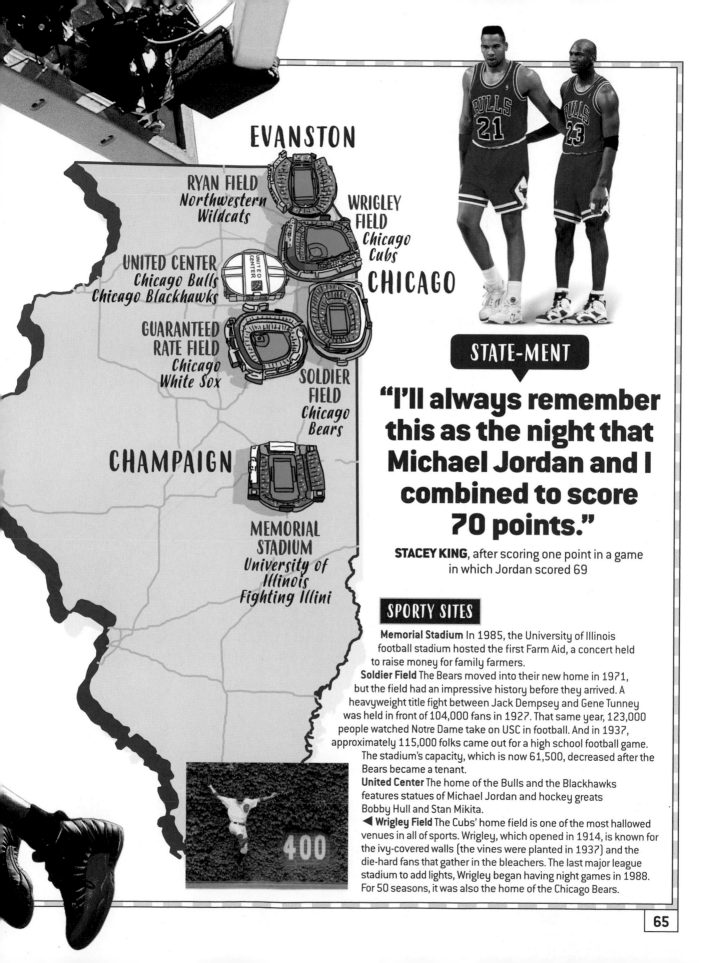

EVANSTON

RYAN FIELD
*Northwestern
Wildcats*

WRIGLEY
FIELD
*Chicago
Cubs*

UNITED CENTER
*Chicago Bulls
Chicago Blackhawks*

CHICAGO

GUARANTEED
RATE FIELD
*Chicago
White Sox*

SOLDIER
FIELD
*Chicago
Bears*

CHAMPAIGN

MEMORIAL
STADIUM
*University of
Illinois
Fighting Illini*

400

STATE-MENT

"I'll always remember this as the night that Michael Jordan and I combined to score 70 points."

STACEY KING, after scoring one point in a game
in which Jordan scored 69

SPORTY SITES

Memorial Stadium In 1985, the University of Illinois
football stadium hosted the first Farm Aid, a concert held
to raise money for family farmers.

Soldier Field The Bears moved into their new home in 1971,
but the field had an impressive history before they arrived. A
heavyweight title fight between Jack Dempsey and Gene Tunney
was held in front of 104,000 fans in 1927. That same year, 123,000
people watched Notre Dame take on USC in football. And in 1937,
approximately 115,000 folks came out for a high school football game.
The stadium's capacity, which is now 61,500, decreased after the
Bears became a tenant.

United Center The home of the Bulls and the Blackhawks
features statues of Michael Jordan and hockey greats
Bobby Hull and Stan Mikita.

◀ **Wrigley Field** The Cubs' home field is one of the most hallowed
venues in all of sports. Wrigley, which opened in 1914, is known for
the ivy-covered walls (the vines were planted in 1937) and the
die-hard fans that gather in the bleachers. The last major league
stadium to add lights, Wrigley began having night games in 1988.
For 50 seasons, it was also the home of the Chicago Bears.

ILLINOIS

THE NUMBERS

5
NBA TITLES won by center George Mikan of Joliet, the best player from the earliest days of the NBA. He is the most notable athlete to come out of DePaul University in Chicago.

48
YEARS in which the University of Chicago competed in the Big Ten, from 1892 to 1939. Then the school's president, who opposed football, discontinued the program.

50
AMOUNT IN DOLLARS that Ben Zobrist of Eureka paid to be in a showcase for high school seniors. He was impressive enough to receive a scholarship offer and is now an All-Star infielder with the Cubs.

27
AVERAGE MARGIN OF VICTORY in the playoffs for the Bears' 1985 Super Bowl team. In the regular season their average margin was 16.1 points per game.

FAN FAVORITES

KRIS BRYANT
Cubs third baseman

Kris Bryant's father's job is "hitting instructor," so perhaps it's not a surprise that the 6' 5", 230-pound Bryant has one of the sweetest swings in the majors. Bryant began his pro career as a highly touted prospect; as a junior in college, he outhomered 223 of the other 296 Division I teams. (He stroked 31.) Since being drafted by the Cubs, he has been named the 2015 National League Rookie of the Year and the MVP in 2016, when the Cubs won the World Series.

JORDAN HOWARD
Bears running back

The 2016 and 2017 seasons were rough for the Bears, but Howard was a bright spot. As a rookie in 2016, the fifth-round pick out of Indiana finished second in the league in rushing with 1,313 yards. He avoided the sophomore slump by rushing for 1,122 yards and nine touchdowns in 2017.

JONATHAN TOEWS
Blackhawks center

Since Toews became captain of the Blackhawks in 2008, good things have happened. When he won the first of his three Stanley Cups, in 2010, Toews became the second-youngest player to be named playoff MVP, after scoring 29 points in 22 games.

GREATEST MOMENT

OCTOBER 2016
Cubs Win!
Cubs Win!

To appreciate how big this win was, you have to consider the wait: more than a century. Entering the 2016 season, the Cubs had last won a World Series in 1908, and the drought had fans feeling jinxed. After they lost the 1945 World Series, people started blaming a billy goat. A tavern owner named William Sianis had attempted to bring his pet goat to a game and was turned away. He then supposedly placed a curse on the Cubs. Then in 1969 came the black cat. That season, the Cubs looked to be on their way to a division title, when the unlucky cat came onto the field during a September game and—whaddya know? Chicago went into a tailspin and missed the playoffs. There were more strange happenings in 2003. In the NLCS, fan Steve Bartman reached out from the stands and touched a ball before it could be caught by a Cubs player. That gave the Marlins an extra out, and they used it to start a game-winning rally.

But 2016 was different. Chicago got back to the World Series and fell behind three games to one. The Cubs battled back, and for once everything went right. They won three in a row, took the title, and vanquished a curse. This is why five million people took to the streets of Chicago for the victory parade.

ILLINOIS

COOL SCHOOLS

Illinois

The Champaign school produced some of the biggest names from the early days of the NFL. Three-time All-America Red Grange was the sport's biggest star in the 1920s, and Hall of Fame linebacker Ray Nitschke anchored the Green Bay Packers' defense in the 1960s. The Fighting Illini basketball program had its best run in 2005, when point guard Deron Williams *(left)* led the team to the NCAA championship game. Men's gymnastics is a strong sport, with 10 NCAA titles.

Northwestern

Wildcats are known for writing and talking about sports as much as for playing them. Notable alumni include ESPN figures Michael Wilbon, Mike Greenberg, and J.A. Adande; the NFL Network's Rich Eisen; and longtime broadcaster Brent Musberger. The football program has had ups (Big Ten titles in 1995, 1996, and 2000) and downs (an FBS-record 34-game losing streak from 1979 to 1982). The Wildcats excel in women's lacrosse—the school won seven NCAA titles between 2005 and 2012.

HOMEGROWN HEROES

DICK BUTKUS

The Bears' defense has long been known as the Monsters of the Midway, and Butkus was the scariest of them all. Known for his vicious hits and his quickness at middle linebacker, the snarling Bears great was named to NFL All-Decade teams for both the 1960s and the 1970s. Before coming to the NFL the Chicago native was a two-time All-America at Illinois.

BONNIE BLAIR

Raised in Champaign, Blair began speedskating at age four, and by the time her career ended, she had become the most dominant woman ever to compete in the sport. In four Olympic appearances from 1984 through 1994, she won five gold medals and one bronze. In 1994, after winning the 1,000-meter race by the largest margin ever, she shared the SPORTS ILLUSTRATED Sportsperson of the Year award.

JACKIE JOYNER-KERSEE

The East St. Louis native is one of the greatest all-around athletes ever to compete. She twice won Olympic gold in the heptathlon, in which athletes are scored in seven grueling events. She also won Olympic gold in the long jump. Her older brother, Al Joyner, won Olympic gold in the triple jump in 1984.

RED GRANGE

The Illini quarterback scored four touchdowns in the first 12 minutes of a 1924 game against Michigan. (He later added two more.) The performance still stands as one of the greatest in college football history. After college, the Galloping Ghost, who grew up in Wheaton, led the Bears to NFL titles in 1932 and 1933.

ILLINOIS'S TROPHY SHELF

1 Super Bowl Win The Bears have won only one Super Bowl, in 1985. But that team, coached by Mike Ditka, went 15–1 and is regarded as one of the best squads in NFL history.

6 NBA Championships The Bulls won three in a row from 1991 to 1993. Then Michael Jordan took off nearly two seasons to play baseball. After his return, the Bulls started another threepeat in 1996.

6 World Series Championships Before their 2016 title, the Cubs won in 1907 and 1908. The White Sox also collected two early trophies (1906, 1917) before a long drought (which ended in 2005).

6 Stanley Cup Wins What is it about Chicago and droughts? The Blackhawks, an Original Six NHL franchise, won the Cup in 1934, 1938, and 1961—and then didn't raise the trophy again for 49 years.

ⓘ INSIDER INFO Eastern Illinois University QBs have a strong NFL presence. Jimmy Garoppolo of the San Francisco 49ers, former Dallas Cowboy Tony Romo, and New Orleans Saints head coach Sean Payton all played under center for the Panthers.

MASCOT FACE-OFF

BENNY THE BULL *Chicago Bulls*	**VS.**	**SALUKI** *Southern Illinois*
Male cow	**WHAT IS IT?**	Egyptian dog
NBA mascot	**WAS THE FIRST . . .**	NCAA Saluki mascot
No	**ARENA STATUE**	Yes
Was once round bellied	**FITNESS NOTE**	Real salukis are very quick
Michael Jordan	**FAMOUS PAL**	Hall of Famer Walt Frazier

ENEMY OF THE STATE

GREEN BAY PACKERS

The NFL's oldest rivalry is also one of its tightest. The Bears held the lead in the series from 1932 until 2017, when their NFC North foes in green and gold pulled ahead.

INSIDER INFO
Wrigley Field was the site of a hockey game on New Year's Day 2009. The Blackhawks fell to the Detroit Red Wings 6–4 on a day when the windchill made it feel like it was around 15°F.

INDIANA

Peyton Manning won four NFL MVP awards and a Super Bowl while playing quarterback for the Colts from 1998 to 2010.

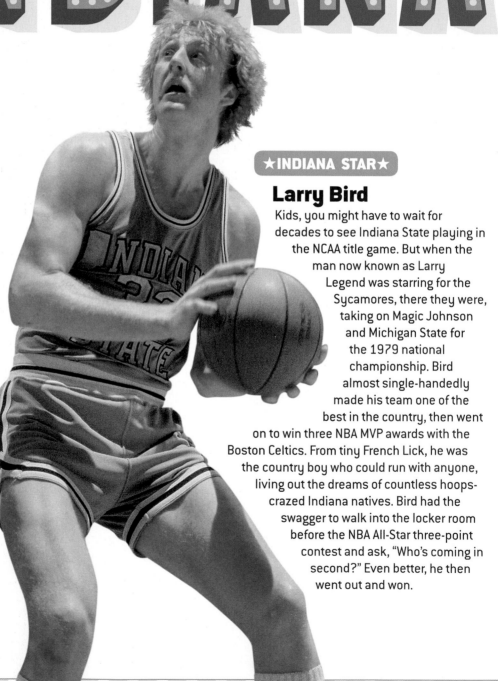

★ INDIANA STAR ★

Larry Bird

Kids, you might have to wait for decades to see Indiana State playing in the NCAA title game. But when the man now known as Larry Legend was starring for the Sycamores, there they were, taking on Magic Johnson and Michigan State for the 1979 national championship. Bird almost single-handedly made his team one of the best in the country, then went on to win three NBA MVP awards with the Boston Celtics. From tiny French Lick, he was the country boy who could run with anyone, living out the dreams of countless hoops-crazed Indiana natives. Bird had the swagger to walk into the locker room before the NBA All-Star three-point contest and ask, "Who's coming in second?" Even better, he then went out and won.

ⓘ INSIDER INFO

Scott Rolen, the seven-time All-Star third baseman from Jasper, didn't get picked until the second round of the baseball draft. He explained, "Everybody figured, 'He's from Indiana. He's going to play college basketball.' " The 6' 4" Rolen did, in fact, have a hoops scholarship offer from the University of Georgia.

WEST
LAFAYETTE

NOTRE DAME
STADIUM
*Notre Dame
Fighting Irish*

MACKEY ARENA
Purdue Boilermakers

INDIANAPOLIS

INDIANAPOLIS
MOTOR
SPEEDWAY

HINKLE
FIELDHOUSE
Butler Bulldogs

LUCAS OIL
STADIUM
*Indianapolis
Colts*

BANKERS LIFE
FIELDHOUSE
*Indiana Pacers
Indiana Fever*

BLOOMINGTON

ASSEMBLY
HALL
*Indiana
Hoosiers*

SPORTY SITES

Hinkle Fieldhouse The Butler University basketball arena, constructed in 1928, is one of the most cherished venues in the sport. It has been declared a National Historic Landmark.

▼ **Indianapolis Motor Speedway** Opened in 1909, the track was originally paved with 3.2 million bricks. By 1937, it was covered with asphalt, but a three-foot strip of brick remains at the start/finish line. Winners of the Indianapolis 500 and the Brickyard 400 traditionally kneel to kiss the bricks after taking the checkered flag.

Lucas Oil Stadium The home of the Indianapolis Colts is a major site for college sports. The Big Ten football title game has been held there since the game's inception in 2011. And the NCAA men's basketball tournament was held there in 2010 and 2015. It will return in 2021.

Mackey Arena The Purdue basketball arena sits on John Wooden Drive, which was named for Purdue basketball's most famous graduate. The Boilermakers opened the arena in 1967 with a game against UCLA—which was coached by none other than Wooden. The Bruins won by two.

Notre Dame Stadium The stadium gives fans a view of great football and also of Touchdown Jesus, the nickname of the mural on the school library tower that overlooks the stadium.

STATE-MENT

"Be quick, but don't hurry."

JOHN WOODEN, the legendary UCLA coach and Martinsville native

Indiana

In an area as basketball mad as this one, you know the hoops program at the state's biggest school has to be a big deal. The Hoosiers, who warm up in distinctive red-and-white striped pants and play their home games in historic Assembly Hall, have won five national titles. The last three (1976, 1981, and 1987) came under coach Bob Knight, whose face would match the color of his red sweater when he was angered by what he saw on the court. The 1976 team was the last one to complete its season undefeated. While basketball is king, Indiana is also a men's soccer powerhouse, having won eight national championships between 1982 and 2012. The swim team produced Mark Spitz, who set the standard for Olympic dominance until Michael Phelps came along. Oh, and if you're wondering why Indiana didn't make the mascot face-off on the next page, it's because the school doesn't have one.

FAMOUS HOOSIERS

KYLE SCHWARBER
Hit .412 for the Cubs in 2016 World Series

ISIAH THOMAS
NCAA and NBA champion

MARK SPITZ
Seven swim golds at 1972 Olympics

Notre Dame

For a century, Notre Dame has had an outsized influence on the history of college football. Legendary coach Knute Rockne built the school into the first national power, taking his team all over the country to meet the best schools. The Fighting Irish have won 11 national titles. Their golden helmets are among the most iconic in football, and no matter where you are, when you hear the opening notes of Notre Dame's famed "Victory March," you'll feel like it's fall and you're in a football stadium.

FAMOUS FIGHTING IRISH

JOE MONTANA
Four-time Super Bowl winner

SKYLAR DIGGINS
Three-time WNBA All-Star

JEFF SAMARDZIJA
All-America WR turned pitcher

Purdue

The nickname Boilermakers was adopted by Purdue in 1891. A headline in the Wabash paper called Purdue players BOILER MAKERS, which was supposed to be a mean reference to the students' working-class backgrounds. Purdue has produced a pair of Super Bowl–winning quarterbacks, Drew Brees and Bob Griese. And the West Lafayette school has sent hoopsters Glenn (Big Dog) Robinson, the top pick of the 1994 draft, and Caleb Swanigan, a 2017 first-round pick of the Portland Trail Blazers, to the NBA.

BIG EVENT

Indianapolis 500

Do you like to drink milk? Drivers in this race do, because it means they finished first. Winners have traditionally celebrated with the dairy drink, since Louis Meyer requested a glass of buttermilk after emerging from his car in 1935. The race, which dates to 1911 and takes place on Memorial Day, is attended by 300,000 people. In 2005, Danica Patrick made history when she led the race for 19 laps, the first woman ever to lead the field.

MASCOT FACE-OFF

PURDUE PETE *Purdue*	VS.	LEPRECHAUN *Notre Dame*
1965	**BORN**	1965
Carbon-fiber head	**ACCESSORY**	Irish country hat
Hammer carrying	**SKILL**	Jig dancing
1940 bookstore ad	**ORIGIN**	Irish folklore
Boilermaker Special locomotive	**SEEN WITH . . .**	Selfie-taking celebs

HOMEGROWN HEROES

OSCAR ROBERTSON

The Big O's team at Crispus Attucks High in Indianapolis was the first team from an all-black school to win a state title. As a member of the NBA's Cincinnati Royals, Robertson averaged a triple double (30.8 points, 11.4 assists, and 12.4 rebounds) in 1961–1962.

JEFF GORDON

At age 16, Gordon became the youngest person ever licensed to drive in USAC races. His family moved from Florida to Pittsboro to further his racing career. The prom king at his high school in 1989, he won four NASCAR season titles between 1995 and 2001.

TONY STEWART

Stewart won a world go-kart title while he was still in high school in Columbus. It wasn't his last championship. Stewart topped the Indy Racing League in 1997 and is a three-time NASCAR season champion. He twice won the Brickyard 400 in Indianapolis.

ⓘ **INSIDER INFO** Takuma Sato (26) made history in 2017 when he became the first driver from Asia to take the checkered flag at the Indianapolis 500. The native of Tokyo took the lead with five laps remaining and won by just .2011 of a second.

INDIANA

5 NBA TITLES won by coach Gregg Popovich of the San Antonio Spurs. Pop was born in East Chicago and went to Merrillville High.

3 DREW FAMILY MEMBERS who coached Valparaiso basketball from 1988 to 2011: Homer and sons Bryce and Scott. (The boys also played for their father.)

8 WINS in the Governors Cup for Indiana University in its all-around sports competition with Purdue. The Boilermakers have won six times since the annual program began in the fall of 2001.

8 POINTS scored in nine seconds by Pacers guard Reggie Miller, in his historic game-closing outburst to defeat the New York Knicks in Game 1 of the 1995 Eastern Conference semifinals.

FAN FAVORITES

ANDREW LUCK
Colts quarterback

Luck likes to hand out compliments on the field—not just to his teammates, but also to his opponents. If the quarterback is sacked, he'll tell the player who got him, "Great hit, well done." This positive disposition is just one of Luck's admirable qualities. The first overall pick in 2012, the former Stanford star made it to the Pro Bowl in each of his first three seasons. In his third year he led the NFL in touchdown passes with 40. A good decision-maker blessed with a strong arm and speed (he has 14 career rushing touchdowns), Luck possesses everything fans could want in a quarterback—except good health. A shoulder injury has limited him in recent years. He missed much of 2015 and all of 2017 because of it.

VICTOR OLADIPO
Pacers guard

It can be good to go home again. Oladipo first gained the attention of the nation while playing for the Indiana Hoosiers. The 6' 4" guard steadily improved during his three seasons in Bloomington, and as a junior he won several national awards, including co–Defensive Player of the Year. He was taken by the Orlando Magic with the second pick of the 2013 draft. But Orlando traded him to the Oklahoma City Thunder in 2016, and then OKC dealt him to the Indiana Pacers in 2017. That second trade was a boon for the high-energy Oladipo. Since returning to the state of his college heroics, he has been playing the best basketball of his career. He made his first All-Star team in 2018.

GREATEST MOMENT

MARCH 20, 1954
The *Hoosiers* Game

Before 1998, Indiana had one statewide basketball tournament for all teams, instead of grouping schools by size as is done now. The current format produces more winners, but the old tournament resulted in one of the most memorable high school games ever. In 1954, tiny Milan (enrollment: 162) faced Muncie Central, which had 10 times as many students. Milan won the game 32–30 to claim the state title. The legend of the game was such that it inspired the classic 1986 movie *Hoosiers* (right).

The movie takes a few liberties with the facts. The real-life coach was not a grizzled veteran starting over at the school. And the team was no ragtag crew. Milan had made it to the state semifinals the year before its title. The player who hit the game-winner was not named Jimmy Chitwood, but Bobby Plump. Still, the movie gets the most important part right—the wonder of the moment.

INDIANA'S TROPHY SHELF

1 Super Bowl Win The Colts, who moved to Indiana in 1984, defeated the Chicago Bears 29–17 in Super Bowl XLI.

1 WNBA Championship In 2012, the Fever defeated the Minnesota Lynx behind series MVP and franchise star Tamika Catchings.

ⓘ **INSIDER INFO** Morten Andersen was visiting Indianapolis as an exchange student from Denmark when he tried kicking a football for the first time. He wound up being a six-time NFL All-Pro.

ENEMY OF THE STATE

NEW ENGLAND PATRIOTS

Peyton Manning and the Colts met Tom Brady's Patriots in the playoffs three times. The first two times New England ended Indy's season. But in January 2007, the Colts came back from a 21–6 halftime deficit for a dramatic 38–34 win. Brady has also met current QB Andrew Luck twice in the postseason, including in the infamous Deflategate game that took this rivalry to the courtroom.

DYERSVILLE

AMES

JACK TRICE STADIUM
Iowa State Cyclones

CARVER-
HAWKEYE
ARENA
*Iowa
Hawkeyes*

FIELD OF DREAMS

IOWA CITY

DES MOINES

DRAKE STADIUM
Drake Relays

KINNICK
STADIUM
*Iowa
Hawkeyes*

KNOXVILLE RACEWAY

Drake Stadium Since 1910, the Drake University campus has been home to the Drake Relays, a track event that draws 40,000 spectators and athletes from 220 schools. In honor of the school mascot, relay week also features the Beautiful Bulldog Contest.

▼ *Field of Dreams* In the 1989 baseball movie, the supernatural whisper, "If you build it, he will come," inspired a farmer to build a baseball diamond in a cornfield. A working diamond now exists at the movie's site in Dyersville.

Jack Trice Stadium Iowa State's football stadium is named for Trice, the second African-American major college player, who died after being injured in a 1923 game.

Knoxville Raceway The half-mile dirt oval at the Marion County Fairgrounds in Knoxville is also the site of the National Sprint Car Hall of Fame & Museum.

GREATEST MOMENT

1939
The Ironmen

The 1939 Iowa football team stood out for its endurance. Even in an age when players often played both offense and defense, the Hawkeyes took it to an extreme, usually using just 14 to 17 players in a game. In Iowa's game against an undefeated Notre Dame team, Nile Kinnick *(above)* scored the lone touchdown on a four-yard run, then kicked the extra point for a 7–6 win. The next week Kinnick threw two touchdowns against rival Minnesota. He sealed the win by making a last-minute interception on defense. Kinnick became the first Hawkeye to win the Heisman Trophy, and the team now plays in a stadium named for him.

STATE-MENT

"We look a lot like the Pittsburgh Steelers. Until the ball is snapped."

Iowa football coach **HAYDEN FRY** in 1979, after the Hawkeyes switched to black-and-gold uniforms

The **Iowa Cubs** were once an affiliate of the Chicago White Sox. (But they weren't called the Cubs then—that would have been awkward.)

IOWA

★IOWA STAR★

Kurt Warner

One of the most unlikely origin stories for a Pro Football Hall of Fame quarterback belongs to Warner. Born in Burlington, he played college ball at Northern Iowa, where he started for the Panthers only as a senior. After college Warner played for the Iowa Barnstormers of the Arena Football League and stocked grocery shelves in Cedar Rapids, among other jobs. He finally caught on as a backup with the St. Louis Rams in 1998. After an injury to starter Trent Green, Warner stepped up and directed a high-scoring offense all the way to victory in Super Bowl XXXIV. He threw for 414 yards and was named the MVP. Wow.

ⓘ INSIDER INFO

Here's one sign that wrestling is a big deal in Iowa: In 2017, Northern Iowa, which is a member of the Missouri Valley Conference, joined the Big 12 for wrestling only. The Panthers moved so they could compete against the likes of Iowa State, Oklahoma, and Oklahoma State.

IOWA

COOL SCHOOLS

Iowa

Iowa's tough football team has become known in recent years for knocking off Big Ten giants. Under coach Kirk Ferentz, the Hawkeyes clobbered Ohio State 55–24 in 2017 to keep the Big Ten–champion Buckeyes out of the playoffs. A year earlier Iowa gave a 9–0 Michigan team its first loss. Notable Hawkeyes football alums include Hall of Fame linebacker Andre Tippett and Marshal Yanda, a six-time Pro Bowl tackle with the Baltimore Ravens. The Stoops brothers—Bob, Mark, and Mike—all played on the Iowa defense before becoming successful college coaches. But the most outstanding sport on the Iowa City campus is wrestling. Iowa won 23 NCAA team championships between 1975 and 2010. The team's home meets draw huge crowds to 15,500-seat Carver-Hawkeye Arena.

Iowa State

In 1895, the farmers of Iowa were hit by a series of brutal storms. That fall, the Iowa Agricultural College—as the school was known then—walloped Northwestern 36–0, and a sportswriter opined that Northwestern "might as well have tried to play football with an Iowa cyclone." The nickname stuck. (It isn't easy to make a recognizable cyclone outfit, which is why the school's mascot is Cy the Cardinal.) Basketball alums include current Chicago Bulls coach Fred Hoiberg and former New York Knicks coach Jeff Hornacek. The Cyclones won eight national titles in wrestling, most recently in 1987. Cael Sanderson went undefeated as a Cyclone before coaching the team from 2007 until 2009.

HOMEGROWN HEROES

DAN GABLE

The wrestling great took gold at the 1972 Olympics without surrendering a single point. As a wrestler at Iowa State, he went 117–1, losing only in his final match as a senior. He coached at Iowa, where his teams won 15 NCAA titles between 1976 and 1997. He also coached the U.S. Olympic team three times.

NICK COLLISON

While at Kansas, Collison was voted the national college player of the year by coaches in 2003, and he was drafted in the first round by the Seattle SuperSonics. The 6' 10" forward from Iowa Falls became one of the most enduring players in the history of his franchise, staying with the team for 15 seasons, through its move to Oklahoma City, before retiring in 2018.

BOB FELLER

A pitcher from Van Meter, Feller made his major league debut at age 17. He struck out 15 batters for the Cleveland Indians, the beginning of a Hall of Fame career. Feller was the first active MLB player to volunteer for World War II, enlisting in the Navy.

45

POINTS by which Iowa's Chuck Long lost the Heisman vote to Bo Jackson (1,509 to 1,464), the second-closest margin ever.

4

SEASONS in which Kyle Korver, who went to high school in Pella, has led the NBA in three-point percentage.

43

WINS for Iowa in the Iowa–Iowa State football rivalry; the Cyclones have won 22 times. Iowa leads in basketball 44–27.

75

CAREER HOME RUNS by Jeff Clement of Marshalltown, a national high school record.

ZACH JOHNSON
PGA golfer

The two-time major winner triumphed in the 2007 Masters and the 2015 British Open. Raised in Cedar Rapids, Johnson was one of those kids who was good at all sports. In high school he was an all-city soccer player, and at Drake he won a campus-wide contest by hitting 19 of 25 three-point shots in basketball. He has 12 PGA Tour wins.

① INSIDER INFO

In 1935, Jay Berwanger of Dubuque became the first winner of the Heisman Trophy. After leaving the University of Chicago, he was the top overall pick of the 1936 draft, by the Philadelphia Eagles. But Berwanger decided he would rather become a businessman and never played pro football.

FRED HOIBERG
Chicago Bulls coach

Hoiberg is nicknamed the Mayor because of his popularity in Ames, where he led his high school team to the 1991 state title and then became the greatest player in Iowa State Cyclones history. After a 10-year NBA career, Hoiberg returned to Ames and coached the Cyclones for five seasons, leading them to four NCAA tournament berths before being hired as the Bulls' coach in 2015.

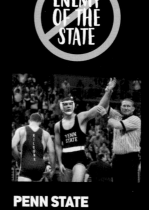

ENEMY OF THE STATE

PENN STATE WRESTLING

Penn State earned the enmity of both Iowa state schools and became a true rival to Big Ten foe Iowa by hiring coach Cael Sanderson from Iowa State in 2009.

KANSAS

★KANSAS STAR★

Bill Self

Since the Kansas basketball program was founded in 1898, the school has had just seven head coaches. Included in that group are giants such as James Naismith (who invented basketball) and Phog Allen (who led the Jayhawks to 590 wins). Self took the position in 2003, and since then he has won a national title in 2008 and twice been named coach of the year. He knows how to deal with the high expectations that come with leading a program so prominent in basketball history. He has told recruits, "Look, I am never going to be the greatest coach at Kansas. And you are never going to be the greatest player. So we might as well get that straight right off the bat."

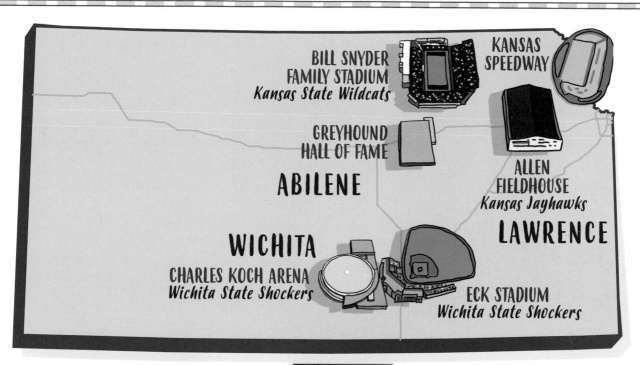

BILL SNYDER
FAMILY STADIUM
Kansas State Wildcats

KANSAS
SPEEDWAY

GREYHOUND
HALL OF FAME

ABILENE

ALLEN
FIELDHOUSE
Kansas Jayhawks

LAWRENCE

WICHITA

CHARLES KOCH ARENA
Wichita State Shockers

ECK STADIUM
Wichita State Shockers

SPORTY SITES

Allen Fieldhouse The basketball arena in Lawrence, with an official capacity of 16,300, is named for Phog Allen, who coached Kansas basketball for 39 years.

Bill Snyder Family Stadium The building opened in 1968 as KSU Stadium, but in 2005 it was renamed for the Wildcats coach.

Eck Stadium At the Wichita State baseball field, fans can take in the games from the stands or bring blankets and set up on Coleman Hill, beyond the outfield wall.

Greyhound Hall of Fame Visitors to the museum, which is across the street from the Dwight D. Eisenhower Presidential Library in Abilene, are greeted by retired racing dogs.

Kansas Speedway The 1.5-mile tri-oval track in Kansas City, built in 2001, hosts two NASCAR races every year.

STATE-MENT

"That's the best arena in the whole world."

Former Jayhawk **JOEL EMBIID**, on Allen Fieldhouse, when his NBA team, the Philadelphia 76ers, practiced there in 2017

GREATEST MOMENT

APRIL 7, 2008
Mario's Miracle

Taking on Derrick Rose's Memphis Tigers in the 2008 national title game, Kansas trailed by three points as the clock approached zero. Guard Mario Chalmers took a pass, dribbled to the left, and swished a three-pointer from the top of the key with 2.1 seconds remaining to tie the game. The Jayhawks rolled in overtime to win 75–68 and claim the school's third national championship.

KANSAS

Kansas

James Naismith invented basketball in Massachusetts in 1891. But his creation took hold in Kansas, where he founded and coached the KU team in 1898. Fans have chanted, "Rock! Chalk! Jayhawk!"—the cheer actually predates basketball—to urge on basketball greats from Wilt Chamberlain *(right)* to Danny Manning to Paul Pierce to 2017 national player of the year Frank Mason III. Oh, and the Jayhawks play football, too. Noted alums include two Hall of Fame running backs (Gale Sayers and John Riggins) and current All-Pro cornerback Aqib Talib.

Kansas State

The 2012–2013 school year wasn't a bad one for the Wildcats. Kansas State won Big 12 conference regular-season titles in football, basketball, and baseball. On the football field, quarterback Collin Klein led the team to a 10–0 start and a brief stay at No. 1 in the polls. In basketball, coach Bruce Weber, in his first season in Manhattan, led the Wildcats to their first conference title since 1977. On the diamond, the baseball team set a school record by winning 45 games. Speaking of baseball, perhaps the most notable Wildcats alum in that sport is Earl Woods, a catcher who raised a golfer named Tiger.

Wichita State

The school's athletes are called the Shockers—a delightful nickname given in the days when many students also worked harvesting (or "shocking") wheat. The baseball team won the national title in 1989 and has made six other College World Series appearances. The basketball team has been a steady presence in the NCAA tournament, making the Big Dance every year from 2012 to 2018.

HOMEGROWN HEROES

JORDY NELSON

Even though Nelson is a Pro Bowl receiver, the former Kansas State star still comes home to his family's farm in Riley to work 12-hour days during the offseason. (He says his favorite farm task is working with cattle.) Nelson, who recently joined the Oakland Raiders, led the NFL with 14 touchdown receptions in 2016, when he was a member of the Green Bay Packers.

BARRY SANDERS

Perhaps the toughest runner to tackle in football history, Sanders began his career at Wichita North High before going on to Oklahoma State. As the face of the Detroit Lions, he dodged NFL defenders for 10 seasons. Sanders led the league in rushing four times.

DEAN SMITH

One of Kansas coach Phog Allen's former players became his most notable coaching disciple. Smith, who was born in Emporia, played on Allen's 1952 championship team and then joined Allen's staff as an assistant for three years. Smith eventually moved on to North Carolina, where he won 879 games and retired in 1997 as basketball's winningest coach, as well as one of its most respected gentlemen.

KANSAS'S TROPHY SHELF

3 NCAA Men's Basketball Championships

Kansas won it all in 1952, 1988, and 2008, under coaches Phog Allen, Roy Williams, and Bill Self. The Jayhawks have made it to nine title games, most recently in 2012.

ⓘ INSIDER INFO Jim Ryun of Wichita was the first high school runner to break the four-minute mile, in 1964. The second-place finisher was 20 seconds behind him. As a Kansas Jayhawk, Ryun set a world record for the mile in 1966.

ENEMY OF THE STATE

MISSOURI TIGERS

Kansas and Missouri haven't played hoops since the Tigers moved to the Southeastern Conference in 2012, but the animosity lingers.

THE NUMBERS

417
GAMES won by Hall of Fame pitcher Walter (Big Train) Johnson of Humboldt, the second most ever.

110
HIGH SCHOOLS in Kansas with eight-man football teams; only Nebraska has more.

1920
YEAR that the first world horseshoe competition was held, in Bronson.

FAN FAVORITES

DARREN SPROLES
Philadelphia Eagles running back

The 5' 6" Sproles is proof that size doesn't matter. At Kansas State he led the nation in rushing yards and all-purpose yards and finished fifth in Heisman Trophy voting. After being drafted in the fourth round by San Diego in 2005, he has been brilliant for 12 NFL seasons, excelling as a running back, a receiver, and one of the league's most dangerous kick returners.

ANDREW WIGGINS
Minnesota Timberwolves forward

The son of an NBA player and an Olympic sprinter, Wiggins was dubbed the Maple Jordan while growing up in Canada. An All-America in his only season at Kansas, Wiggins was selected first overall by the Cleveland Cavaliers and traded to Minnesota. He was Rookie of the Year in 2015, and in 2017–2018 he helped the Timberwolves to their first winning record since the 2004–2005 season.

★KENTUCKY STAR★

Muhammad Ali

Cassius Clay's road to becoming the Greatest began when he was a 12-year-old in Louisville and his bike was stolen. The man who would later change his name to Muhammad Ali went to a police officer who ran a local gym. He was looking to fill out a report about the bike—and also vowing revenge. The officer told him, "You better learn to fight before you start fighting." The policeman became Clay's first boxing instructor. The young pugilist became an Olympic gold medalist, a heavyweight champion, and sport's most magnetic personality. He could spout funny rhymes, and he could also take a moral stand at a high personal cost. When he refused to enlist for the Vietnam War, Ali was stripped of his title and banned from fighting for three years. But he came back and regained his heavyweight title, his star burning brighter than ever, respected as an athlete and—more so—as a man.

STATE-MENT

"Impossible is nothing."

MUHAMMAD ALI,
who was also known as the Louisville Lip

KENTUCKY

JOHN CALIPARI
Kentucky men's basketball coach

The Wildcats have been a perennial championship contender since Calipari came to Lexington in 2009. The former coach of UMass, Memphis, and the NBA's New Jersey Nets has taken the Wildcats to the Final Four four times, winning the title in 2012. His rosters are always loaded with high school All-Americas, and he has produced three NBA top draft picks.

SPORTY SITES

Churchill Downs More than 165,000 people attend the Kentucky Derby at this 1½-mile track that is also home to the Kentucky Oaks and many other races.
Louisville Slugger Museum & Factory Outside, leaning against the building, is the world's largest bat. It is 120 feet long, made of steel, and weighs 68,000 pounds. Inside, visitors can see regular wood bats being made.
Rupp Arena The Kentucky basketball arena, which opened in 1976 in Lexington, is named for coach Adolph Rupp, who led the Wildcats to 876 wins from 1930 to 1972.
Valhalla Golf Club The course in Louisville has hosted three PGA Championships and the 2008 Ryder Cup.

PRO TEAMS

Triple A
Louisville Bats
Lexington Legends

Class A
Bowling Green Hot Rods

Former players for the **Bats**, a Cincinnati Reds farm club, include Joey Votto and Billy Hamilton.

LOUISVILLE

VALHALLA GOLF CLUB

LOUISVILLE SLUGGER MUSEUM

RUPP ARENA
Kentucky Wildcats

LEXINGTON

CHURCHILL DOWNS

CARDINAL STADIUM
Louisville Cardinals

KFC YUM! CENTER
Louisville Cardinals

KENTUCKY

COOL SCHOOLS

Kentucky

At Kentucky basketball games, cheerleaders take to the Rupp Arena court and spell out the name of the school, with a famous alum coming out to make a Y with his or her arms. It's a long-standing tradition, and with the Wildcats' history of success, they have plenty of former stars to choose from. The basketball program, which has the most wins of any NCAA team, has produced current NBA stars Anthony Davis, John Wall, Karl-Anthony Towns, Devin Booker, DeMarcus Cousins, Eric Bledsoe, and Jamal Murray, to name just a few. (Actually, that's more than a few.) The football team, though not as elite, was coached by Paul (Bear) Bryant for eight seasons, winning a Sugar Bowl and a Cotton Bowl before Bryant moved to Alabama. The Wildcats have made seven bowl games in the past 12 years and have sent several players to the NFL, including Randall Cobb, Bud Dupree, and Danny Trevathan. The baseball team's most successful player is Brandon Webb, the Ashland native who won the 2006 Cy Young Award with the Arizona Diamondbacks.

Louisville

Men's basketball is the main event at Louisville. The school has cut down the nets at the Final Four three times (though the Cardinals were stripped of their most recent title for using ineligible players). Alumni include Hall of Famer Wes Unseld, 1980 college Player of the Year Darrell Griffith, and 2017–2018 rookie sensation Donovan Mitchell of the Utah Jazz. But the Cardinals aren't only about basketball. The baseball team has been to four College World Series, including in 2017. The football program has been exciting in recent years, thanks to quarterback Lamar Jackson. He's the latest in a line of impressive Cardinals signal-callers. Teddy Bridgewater was a first-round pick of the Minnesota Vikings in 2014, and NFL legend Johnny Unitas is honored with a statue outside of Cardinal Stadium.

THE NUMBERS

6 **SWEET 16 APPEARANCES** by the Western Kentucky Hilltoppers, who have been to the NCAA tournament 23 times.

1 **PERSON** elected to both the Baseball Hall of Fame and the U.S. Senate: Jim Bunning, of Southgate.

3 **NBA ASSIST TITLES** for Rajon Rondo, who was born in Louisville and played at Kentucky. (He's also a master at Connect Four and a great roller skater.)

3 **GOLD MEDALS** won by swimmer Mary T. Meagher, from Louisville, in the 1984 and 1988 Olympics. She also set seven world records. Her nickname was Madame Butterfly.

HOMEGROWN HEROES

PHIL SIMMS

Simms, from Springfield, played at FCS school Morehead State before leading the New York Giants to a win in Super Bowl XXI. In that game, he completed 22 of 25 passes and was named the Super Bowl MVP. Simms is now an analyst with CBS Sports.

PEE WEE REESE

The Hall of Fame shortstop for the Dodgers is remembered for his play and for a gesture of solidarity. In 1947 his teammate Jackie Robinson became the first African-American player in the majors. When he was jeered by fans, Reese, from Ekron, crossed the infield and placed an arm around Robinson's shoulders.

DARRELL AND MICHAEL WALTRIP

The brothers from Owensboro are the only siblings to win the Daytona 500. Michael won it twice before retiring in 2017. Big bro Darrell also won three NASCAR season championships and 84 races. They are now broadcasters.

BIG EVENT

Kentucky Derby

The first Saturday in May is horse racing's biggest day of the year. Known as the Run for the Roses because of the blanket of flowers placed on the winning horse, the Kentucky Derby is the first leg of the Triple Crown. The race, which was first run in 1875 and takes place at Churchill Downs in Louisville, is quite a spectacle—on and off the track. From the big hats worn by women to the band performing "My Old Kentucky Home" before the race, the event is filled with pageantry and tradition.

KENTUCKY'S TROPHY SHELF

10 NCAA Men's Basketball Championships

Kentucky has made it to 17 Final Fours and won eight national titles, most recently in 2012. Louisville also has an impressive collection of hardware. The Cardinals have won a pair of NCAA championships and made it to the Final Four 10 times.

ENEMY OF THE STATE

DUKE BASKETBALL

The Blue Devils regularly battle Kentucky and Louisville for supremacy; ex-Dukie Christian Laettner has joked that when he drives through the state, he's afraid to get out of the car.

Drew Brees

One of the most prolific passers in NFL history, Brees brought respectability to a franchise that had, for decades, been considered one of the sorriest in the NFL. (Saints fans famously wore paper bags over their heads to hide their shame during a particularly futile period.) But Brees has also been a Hall of Fame citizen of New Orleans. He signed with the Saints in 2006, the year after the city was devastated by Hurricane Katrina, and he made generous donations to rebuilding efforts. In 2010, he gave the city a reason to smile as he led the Saints to their first Super Bowl in franchise history. That year Sports Illustrated named Brees its Sportsperson of the Year. One teammate told the magazine, "People come up to Drew and don't say, 'Congratulations.' They say, 'Thank you. Thank you for coming here.' "

STATE-MENT

"Everything I've done, I think I dreamed of it first."

EDDIE ROBINSON,
legendary Grambling
football coach

FAN FAVORITE

ANTHONY DAVIS
Pelicans forward

As a high school sophomore, Anthony Davis was 6' 2" and played guard. Then came the growth spurt. By his senior year he was 6' 10", and suddenly recruiters were very interested. After a season at Kentucky, he was drafted first overall by New Orleans in 2012. Known as the Brow for his trademark unibrow, the five-time All-Star combines a wing player's skills with a center's body.

INDEPENDENCE STADIUM
SHREVEPORT

SPORTY SITES

Independence Stadium
The Shreveport stadium, which opened in 1925 and seats 50,459, hosts the Independence Bowl.

The Superdome The home of the Saints is also the site of the annual Bayou Classic between Southern and Grambling. The Superdome has seen its share of big events, including seven Super Bowls, five NCAA Final Fours, and nearly every Sugar Bowl since the stadium opened in 1975.

Tiger Stadium Known as Death Valley, the LSU stadium, which seats 102,321, began hosting night games in 1931. The Tigers play a majority of their home games after the sun has gone down.

TIGER STADIUM
LSU Tigers
BATON ROUGE

THE SUPERDOME
New Orleans Saints

SMOOTHIE KING CENTER
New Orleans Pelicans

NEW ORLEANS

PRO TEAMS

NFL   New Orleans Saints

NBA   New Orleans Pelicans

The **Pelicans** were called the Hornets when they arrived from Charlotte but took a new name in 2013.

LOUISIANA

COOL SCHOOLS

LSU

Louisiana State is the home of not only the Tigers, but also a real live tiger. His name is Mike, and he lives on campus in a habitat that includes a stream, a waterfall, and a tower in the style of the university's architecture. Like seemingly everyone else in Baton Rouge, Mike comes out for LSU football games. The school has won three national championships, most recently in 2007. While the Tigers have never won an NCAA basketball title, the school has produced a pair of legendary players. Guard Pete Maravich averaged a record 44.2 points for his college career, and Shaquille O'Neal is a four-time NBA champion. Ben Simmons, the 2016 No. 1 NBA overall draft pick, by the Philadelphia 76ers, doesn't look too shabby either.

Louisiana Tech

For the lesser football power in the state, the Bulldogs are doing pretty well for themselves. The Ruston school has produced three NFL Hall of Famers: QB Terry Bradshaw, defensive end Fred Dean, and offensive lineman Willie Roaf. Louisiana Tech also won a Division II national championship in 1973 before graduating to college football's highest tier in 1988. The Bulldogs have produced impressive basketball stars as well. NBA Hall of Famer Karl Malone and current All-Star forward Paul Millsap are former Bulldogs, as are WNBA stars Teresa Weatherspoon and Cheryl Ford.

THE NUMBERS

34-5

RECORD of Isidore Newman School in New Orleans while Peyton Manning (son of Saints great Archie) was their QB.

5

200-YARD GAMES that future NFL Pro Bowl running back Matt Forte had as a senior at Tulane in 2007.

938

STOLEN BASES by Lou Brock, who grew up in Mer Rouge and played at Southern. That's the second most in MLB history.

HOMEGROWN HEROES

SEIMONE AUGUSTUS

The Baton Rouge native was a two-time national player of the year at LSU before being taken first overall in the 2006 WNBA draft by the Minnesota Lynx. The franchise has won four league championships since her arrival.

ODELL BECKHAM JR.

Before dazzling with his one-handed catches as a wide receiver with the New York Giants, the Baton Rouge native deployed his speed and skill for his hometown team, LSU.

TERRY BRADSHAW

The quarterback for four Super Bowl winners with the Pittsburgh Steelers played college ball at Louisiana Tech and grew up in Shreveport (where he rooted for the closest NFL team and his future nemesis, the Dallas Cowboys).

EDDIE ROBINSON

The titan of black college football won 408 games at Grambling State University, the second most for a college coach at any level. While building the tiny program into a powerhouse, the Jackson native sent more than 200 players to the NFL.

GREATEST MOMENT

SEPTEMBER 25, 2006

First Saints Home Game After Katrina

The Superdome was closed for the 2005 season because of damage from Hurricane Katrina, forcing the Saints to play their "home" games in Baton Rouge, San Antonio, and even New York. But the Saints were able to come back to the Superdome the following season, and their first home game, against the Atlanta Falcons, was scheduled for *Monday Night Football*. The night was a celebration from the moment the Saints came through the tunnel, as the city welcomed back its team. Then, 90 seconds into the game, Saints special-teamer Steve Gleason blocked a Falcons punt that was recovered by teammate Curtis Deloatch for a touchdown, and the fans gave out a roar for the ages. The party continued as the Saints rolled to a 23–3 victory.

ⓘ INSIDER INFO The Pelicans are the mascot of the NBA franchise in New Orleans, but the name was also used by minor league baseball teams that played in the city between 1887 and 1997. New Orleans's current minor league baseball team has an even more unusual nickname: the Baby Cakes.

LOUISIANA'S TROPHY SHELF

1 Super Bowl Win The Saints were five-point underdogs against Peyton Manning's Indianapolis Colts in 2010. But cornerback Tracy Porter returned an interception 74 yards for a touchdown to seal the 31–17 upset.

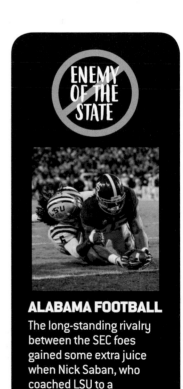

ENEMY OF THE STATE

ALABAMA FOOTBALL
The long-standing rivalry between the SEC foes gained some extra juice when Nick Saban, who coached LSU to a national title in 2003, took over at Alabama and started racking up championships there.

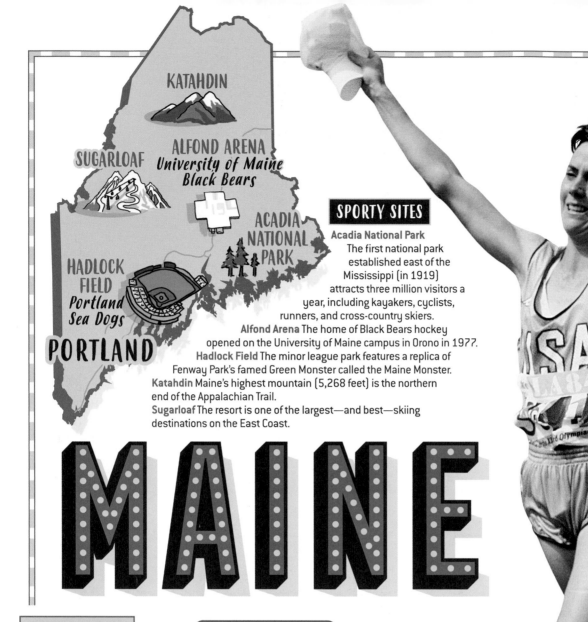

KATAHDIN

SUGARLOAF

ALFOND ARENA
University of Maine Black Bears

ACADIA NATIONAL PARK

HADLOCK FIELD
Portland Sea Dogs

PORTLAND

SPORTY SITES

Acadia National Park The first national park established east of the Mississippi (in 1919) attracts three million visitors a year, including kayakers, cyclists, runners, and cross-country skiers.

Alfond Arena The home of Black Bears hockey opened on the University of Maine campus in Orono in 1977.

Hadlock Field The minor league park features a replica of Fenway Park's famed Green Monster called the Maine Monster.

Katahdin Maine's highest mountain (5,268 feet) is the northern end of the Appalachian Trail.

Sugarloaf The resort is one of the largest—and best—skiing destinations on the East Coast.

MAINE

PRO TEAMS

Double A Portland Sea Dogs

The **Sea Dogs** were a Miami Marlins farm team, but since 2003 they have been an affiliate of the Boston Red Sox.

★ MAINE STAR ★

Joan Benoit Samuelson

When Joan Benoit was growing up, it was unusual for girls and women to go out for long jogs. She says, "When I first started running, I was so embarrassed, I'd walk when cars passed me. I'd pretend I was looking at the flowers." Eventually she embraced her passion for running. She was the only girl to compete in cross-country at Cape Elizabeth High. And as a Bowdoin College senior she set an American record at the Boston Marathon, in 1979, crossing the finish line in a Red Sox cap she had been handed at the 23rd mile. She then took gold in the first women's Olympic marathon, in 1984, making it clear that her running was something to celebrate.

FAN FAVORITES

PAUL KARIYA
Hockey Hall of Famer

In 2017, Kariya, a five-time NHL All-Star, became the first former University of Maine player to be elected to the Hockey Hall of Fame. As a Black Bear, Kariya won the Hobey Baker Award—which goes to the best college player—in 1993, when he starred on Maine's first NCAA championship team.

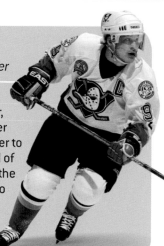

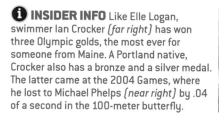

ELLE LOGAN
Rower

From Boothbay Harbor, the 6' 2", 175-pound Logan won gold medals in women's eight at three consecutive Olympics from 2008 to 2016, making her the first American rower ever to do so. She has also won three golds at the rowing world championships.

BIG EVENT

U.S. National Toboggan Championships

If you're looking for fast fun in February, the place to be is Camden. Since 1991, racers have gathered to rocket down a 440-foot, ice-slicked wooden chute on sleds that can reach 45 miles per hour. The event, which is open to anyone but dominated by Maine residents, attracts 400 teams annually.

ⓘ INSIDER INFO Sportswriting great Shirley Povich, from Bar Harbor, met the owner of The *Washington Post* while caddying for him at a country club. The owner brought Povich to the *Post*, where he wrote for 75 years, until his death in 1998.

ⓘ INSIDER INFO Like Elle Logan, swimmer Ian Crocker *(far right)* has won three Olympic golds, the most ever for someone from Maine. A Portland native, Crocker also has a bronze and a silver medal. The latter came at the 2004 Games, where he lost to Michael Phelps *(near right)* by .04 of a second in the 100-meter butterfly.

ENEMY OF THE STATE

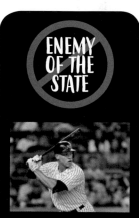

NEW YORK YANKEES

Like most people in New England, Maine fans root for Boston teams, which means that the sight of pinstripes boils the blood.

THE NUMBERS

115
CAREER WINS by Bob (the Steamer) Stanley, the most by an MLB pitcher who was born in Maine.

5
UFC TITLES won by Tim (the Maine-iac) Sylvia, the 6' 8", 255-pound fighter from Ellsworth.

2
MAINE NATIVES who have become NBA coaches: Brett Brown *(right)* of the 76ers and Steve Clifford of the Magic.

INSIDER INFO The University of Maryland's two NCAA basketball championships came within four years of one another. In 2002, the men's team took the title behind the play of guards Juan Dixon and Steve Blake. In 2006, the women captured their crown, led by tournament Most Outstanding Player Laura Harper.

INSIDER INFO The original Orioles team played in Baltimore for two seasons, in 1901 and 1902, before moving to New York and eventually changing its name to the Yankees.

PRO TEAMS

NFL Baltimore Ravens

MLB Baltimore Orioles

Today's **Orioles** began play in 1954, after the St. Louis Browns were sold and moved to Baltimore under their new name.

★MARYLAND STAR★

Michael Phelps

They call him the Baltimore Bullet, and his hometown's pride was on display in 2008. As Phelps was competing in his final race at the Olympics, 59% of homes in Baltimore were tuned in—plus the stadium jumbotron at a Ravens preseason game. Phelps did not disappoint, winning his eighth gold medal of those Games. Not bad for a kid who took up swimming in part to control his attention deficit disorder. While Phelps initially amazed fans with his speed, he has also impressed with his staying power. In 2016, he competed in his fifth Olympics and capped off a career that saw him win 28 medals (including 23 gold). That's a whopping 10 more than the next-highest total.

MARYLAND

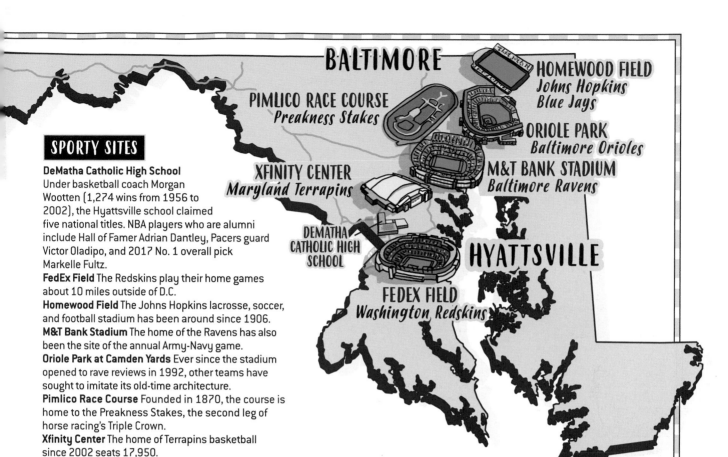

BALTIMORE

PIMLICO RACE COURSE
Preakness Stakes

HOMEWOOD FIELD
Johns Hopkins Blue Jays

ORIOLE PARK
Baltimore Orioles

XFINITY CENTER
Maryland Terrapins

M&T BANK STADIUM
Baltimore Ravens

DEMATHA CATHOLIC HIGH SCHOOL

HYATTSVILLE

FEDEX FIELD
Washington Redskins

SPORTY SITES

DeMatha Catholic High School Under basketball coach Morgan Wootten (1,274 wins from 1956 to 2002), the Hyattsville school claimed five national titles. NBA players who are alumni include Hall of Famer Adrian Dantley, Pacers guard Victor Oladipo, and 2017 No. 1 overall pick Markelle Fultz.

FedEx Field The Redskins play their home games about 10 miles outside of D.C.

Homewood Field The Johns Hopkins lacrosse, soccer, and football stadium has been around since 1906.

M&T Bank Stadium The home of the Ravens has also been the site of the annual Army-Navy game.

Oriole Park at Camden Yards Ever since the stadium opened to rave reviews in 1992, other teams have sought to imitate its old-time architecture.

Pimlico Race Course Founded in 1870, the course is home to the Preakness Stakes, the second leg of horse racing's Triple Crown.

Xfinity Center The home of Terrapins basketball since 2002 seats 17,950.

GREATEST MOMENT

DECEMBER 28, 1958
The Greatest Game Ever Played

When tracing the rise of football's popularity in America, many people look back to this game between the Colts (whose home was then Baltimore) and the New York Giants. To understand how different the sports landscape was back then, consider this: 1958 was the first year the NFL title game was televised to a national audience. With 45 million people watching, the teams delivered the kind of show that left the public wanting more. Seventeen future Hall of Famers played in this game, including Colts quarterback Johnny Unitas, who led a last-minute drive for a field goal that sent the game into overtime. In the extra period, Unitas led a 13-play, 80-yard drive that was capped by Alan Ameche's one-yard touchdown run, giving Baltimore the 23–17 win. It has been called the greatest game ever played (that was the SPORTS ILLUSTRATED headline at the time), and it paved the way to new TV contracts for the NFL and the Super Bowl hoopla we know today.

MARYLAND

THE NUMBERS

9 NCAA LACROSSE TITLES won by Johns Hopkins. The Blue Jays, who won their most recent title in 2007, have been runners-up nine times.

150 MEMBERS (including equipment staff) of Baltimore's Marching Ravens, making it the largest marching band in the NFL.

0 HOLES in the grapefruit-sized ball used in duckpin bowling, a variation of the sport that was invented in Baltimore and continues in the city today.

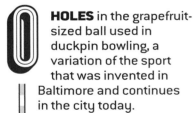

5 NFL TITLES won by coach Bill Belichick, who was first exposed to coaching when he attended practices at the Naval Academy in Annapolis, where his dad was an assistant.

FAN FAVORITES

TERRELL SUGGS
Ravens linebacker

When Ravens opponents have the ball in their hands, they better watch out for Suggs. The outside linebacker and 2011 NFL Defensive Player of the Year holds the team record for forced fumbles, with 34. He is also Baltimore's all-time sacks leader, with 125½. And somebody needs to tell Suggs that players are supposed to slow down as they age. In 2017, when he was 35 years old, Suggs had 11 sacks and made his seventh Pro Bowl.

MANNY MACHADO
Orioles shortstop

The four-time All-Star infielder delivers on both offense and defense. The winner of Gold Gloves at third base in 2013 and 2015 (before he moved to shortstop), Machado has the ability to throw out runners while on the move or from crazy angles. At the plate, he has hit at least 33 home runs every season from 2015 to 2017.

ADAM JONES
Orioles outfielder

Jones has been a rock in centerfield since 2008. That was when the Orioles acquired the young prospect from Seattle in what now looks like a very lopsided trade. Jones has been a complete player, with five All-Star selections, four Gold Gloves, and countless pie-related celebrations.

BIG EVENT

Jousting Championship

Believe it or not, the official state sport of Maryland is jousting. The government declared it so in 1962. (In 2004, an act was passed that made lacrosse, more representative of what kids actually play, the state's official *team* sport.) But jousting in Maryland has a history that dates back to the 1600s, when settlers brought it over from England. In modern competitions, jousters aren't trying to knock each other off their horses (which would hurt). Instead, they ride courses and compete to collect the most rings on their lances.

MARYLAND'S TROPHY SHELF

3 Super Bowl Wins The Baltimore Ravens have won both of their trips to the Super Bowl, in 2002 and 2013. The Colts also won a Super Bowl for Baltimore in 1970, before moving to Indianapolis in 1984.

3 World Series Championships Between 1966 and 1983, the Baltimore Orioles went to the World Series six times, winning in half of those appearances. Recently, the Orioles reached the AL Championship Series in 2014 but were swept in four games.

ENEMY OF THE STATE

PITTSBURGH STEELERS

This AFC North rivalry features hard-hitting defenses and annual games of consequence. When the teams meet late in the season, one or both are usually vying for a playoff spot.

HOMEGROWN HEROES

CAL RIPKEN, JR.

The Hall of Fame shortstop for the Orioles played in a record 2,632 consecutive games, becoming a hero to those who recognize the underappreciated value of putting in a hard day's work—every day.

BABE RUTH

The Baltimore-born Bambino redefined sports celebrity—and also changed the game of baseball. Before Ruth, the record for home runs in a season was 27. The Bambino hit 60 in 1927 for the New York Yankees and 714 in his career.

TRAVIS PASTRANA

The motocross legend and X Games star began driving a one-speed Honda when he was a four-year-old in Annapolis. As an adult, he developed stunts on a 20-acre course he built behind his home there.

DOMINIQUE DAWES

From Silver Spring, the gymnast competed on the U.S. national team for 10 years. Dawes was the first African-American to win an Olympic gold in the sport, when she was part of the victorious U.S. team in 1996. She also won three bronze medals in her three Games.

MASSACHUS

PRO TEAMS

NFL	New England Patriots
MLB	Boston Red Sox
NBA	Boston Celtics
NHL	Boston Bruins
MLS	New England Revolution

The **Bruins'** logo represents the idea that Boston is the "hub," as the city calls itself, to which all roads lead.

Tom Brady

When Brady was a rookie who had yet to play a down for the Patriots, he ran into team owner Robert Kraft in a hallway. Brady told him, "I'm the best decision this organization has ever made." What's amazing is not how confident this unheralded sixth-round pick was but how right he was. An injury elevated Brady to starter that year, and thus began a run of seemingly automatic division titles and five Super Bowl wins. Generally, when teams go on runs like this, they do so with multiple Hall of Fame players, but Brady and coach Bill Belichick have been the Patriots' only constants. Brady is fanatical about his diet—he's a guy who eats his vegetables—which is one reason why, at age 40, he looks better than most ever would.

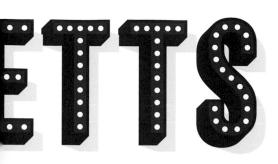

ETTS

ℹ INSIDER INFO The Cape Cod summer league is the oldest in baseball, dating back to 1885; team names that reflect local history include the Cotuit Kettleers. The term comes from colonists who traded kettles to the Native Americans for corn.

ERNATIONAL
LEYBALL HALL
OF FAME

HOLYOKE

SPRINGFIELD

NAISMITH MEMORIAL
BASKETBALL HALL
OF FAME

TD GARDEN
Boston Celtics
Boston Bruins

FENWAY PARK
Boston Red Sox

THE COUNTRY CLUB

BOSTON

CHARLES RIVER

FOXBOROUGH

GILLETTE STADIUM
New England Patriots

SPORTY SITES

Charles River The annual Head of the Charles Regatta attracts 11,000 participants and tens of thousands of spectators for the two-day competition in October.

The Country Club The golf club in Brookline was the site of the dramatic 1913 U.S. Open (re-created in the 2005 movie *The Greatest Game Ever Played*) and the U.S. team's comeback win in the 1999 Ryder Cup.

▶ **Fenway Park** Opened in 1912, the park is known for its Green Monster: the 37-foot wall in leftfield. With a capacity of only 37,731, Fenway is one of the true cathedrals of baseball.

Gillette Stadium The home of the Patriots is 28 miles southwest of downtown Boston.

Naismith Memorial Basketball Hall of Fame The game's best are honored in the city where James Naismith invented basketball in 1891 while working at Springfield College.

TD Garden The home of the Bruins and the Celtics opened in 1995 as the replacement for the old Boston Garden. As in the old facility, the parquet floor for basketball games is a signature look. Bobby Orr's iconic leaping goal from the 1970 Stanley Cup finals is memorialized in a statue outside the arena.

International Volleyball Hall of Fame The sport was invented in Holyoke by William G. Morgan in 1895 for people who didn't like the physical contact and exertion of basketball.

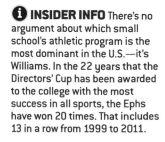

ℹ INSIDER INFO There's no argument about which small school's athletic program is the most dominant in the U.S.—it's Williams. In the 22 years that the Directors' Cup has been awarded to the college with the most success in all sports, the Ephs have won 20 times. That includes 13 in a row from 1999 to 2011.

"IT'S GOOD TO BE KING"

-TOM PETTY

ⓘ INSIDER INFO What does the inside of a monster look like? At Fenway Park, the area behind the Green Monster (the 37-foot-high leftfield wall) houses all of the equipment necessary to operate the fence's manual scoreboard.

MASSACHUSETTS

COOL SCHOOLS

Boston College

One of the most popular Boston College traditions was borrowed from the Boston Red Sox. At Alumni Stadium, fans love to sing along as the band plays the song "Sweet Caroline" during football games. They also love following the exploits of former Eagles in the NFL, including Atlanta Falcons quarterback Matt Ryan and Carolina Panthers linebacker Luke Kuechly. Hockey is the Eagles' best sport, though. BC has won five NCAA hockey championships, most recently in 2012.

Boston University

BU's sports teams are called the Terriers, and they have a mascot who is named Rhett, after the character in the book and movie *Gone with the Wind*. (Rhett is in love with a woman named Scarlett, and scarlet is a BU color. Make sense?) Like BC, the Terriers have won five national titles in hockey, most recently in 2009. BU has a series-leading 30 wins in the Beanpot tournament, a two-day battle for city hockey supremacy that also includes BC, Harvard, and Northeastern.

Massachusetts

Basketball is the sport in which the Minutemen have made their greatest mark. Julius Erving, one of the most iconic stars in the sport, went to UMass. One of his teammates was future NCAA championship–winning coach Rick Pitino. The high point of the program came when the Minutemen—coached by John Calipari and led by NBA future No. 1 overall pick Marcus Camby—went to the 1996 Final Four.

Harvard

Harvard traces its athletic history back to an 1852 boat race with Yale, and the annual football game between the schools is one of the sport's oldest rivalries. Harvard also has the strongest NFL representation of any Ivy League school, with Ryan Fitzpatrick and Cameron Brate of the Tampa Bay Buccaneers and Kyle Juszczyk of the San Francisco 49ers.

HOMEGROWN HEROES

ALY RAISMAN

She got her start in gymnastics when she was two years old and her mother took her to "mommy and me" classes. Raisman, who grew up in Needham, became the captain of the U.S. gymnastics teams that won gold medals at the 2012 and 2016 Olympics. She also won a gold, two silvers, and a bronze for her individual performances at those Games.

ROCKY MARCIANO

His first love was baseball, but after a failed tryout with the Chicago Cubs, the kid from Brockton went into boxing. Doubters said Marciano's reach wasn't long enough, but he became the only heavyweight champion to finish his career undefeated, with a record of 49–0.

DOUG FLUTIE

The Natick High grad won the Heisman Trophy at Boston College in 1984. He made one of the greatest plays in college football history that year with his last-second, 48-yard touchdown pass to Gerard Phelan to defeat Miami. Many questioned whether Flutie, at 5' 10", could succeed as a professional, but he played 20 seasons in the CFL and NFL. He won six CFL MVP awards, and his NFL time included two stints with the Patriots.

BIG EVENT

Boston Marathon

The first Boston Marathon, held in 1897, drew 15 participants. Now about 30,000 people compete in the race held annually on the third Monday in April, better known in Boston as Patriots' Day—a holiday commemorating the start of the Revolutionary War. The Red Sox are part of this tradition, too. The team plays a home game with an early start time of 11:05 a.m., and the marathon course goes past Fenway's leftfield fence.

MASSACHUSETTS'S TROPHY SHELF

5 Super Bowl Wins After decades of futility, the Patriots now have more Super Bowl wins than every team except the Pittsburgh Steelers.

17 NBA Championships From 1957 to 1969, Bill Russell's Celtics won 11 titles in 13 seasons, one of the most dominant runs in any sport.

8 World Series Championships The Red Sox won five World Series between 1903 and 1918. Their other three have come since 2004.

6 Stanley Cup Wins The Bruins won three in the early years of the NHL, two in the 1970s, and their most recent in 2011.

MASSACHUSETTS

THE NUMBERS

1

RANK of Harvard Stadium on the list of oldest college football stadiums. The home of the Crimson opened in 1903.

15

NUMBER, IN THOUSANDS, of fans who came to celebrate when beloved longtime Bruin Ray Bourque brought the Stanley Cup he won with the Colorado Avalanche to Boston in 2001.

2

NATIONAL TITLES claimed by Holy Cross, in baseball (1952) and basketball (1947). The basketball championship team featured future Celtics great Bob Cousy.

29

FORMER CELTICS PLAYERS who have been inducted into the Basketball Hall of Fame.

GREATEST MOMENT

OCTOBER 27, 2004
Red Sox Break the Curse

Before 2004, the Red Sox had not won a World Series since 1918, and over the decades the team's fans had come to believe the team was cursed. Witness Bill Buckner's stunning error in the 1986 World Series, or Boston's blowing a 5–2 lead to the New York Yankees in Game 7 of the 2003 AL Championship Series. But the Red Sox got revenge on the Yankees the next year, coming back from a three-game deficit to beat the Yanks and then sweeping the St. Louis Cardinals in the World Series.

ⓘ **INSIDER INFO** The first American hockey player to jump directly from high school to the NHL was Bobby Carpenter of Peabody. The Washington Capitals selected him third overall from St. John's Prep in the 1981 draft. Carpenter scored 53 goals in the 1984–1985 season, then a record for a U.S.-born player. He played 18 NHL seasons, winning a Stanley Cup with the New Jersey Devils in 1995.

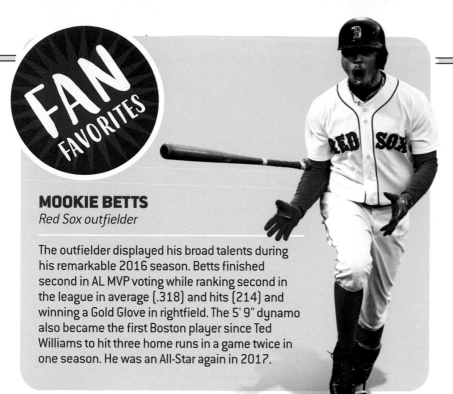

FAN FAVORITES

MOOKIE BETTS
Red Sox outfielder

The outfielder displayed his broad talents during his remarkable 2016 season. Betts finished second in AL MVP voting while ranking second in the league in average (.318) and hits (214) and winning a Gold Glove in rightfield. The 5' 9" dynamo also became the first Boston player since Ted Williams to hit three home runs in a game twice in one season. He was an All-Star again in 2017.

KYRIE IRVING
Celtics guard

Acquired in a trade with Cleveland in the summer of 2017, Irving quickly took command of the Celtics' offense. Irving showed the confidence and shotmaking ability on drives and three-pointers that had helped him win a championship with the Cavs.

PATRICE BERGERON
Bruins center

The career Bruin has won the NHL's Frank J. Selke Trophy as the forward with the best defensive abilities four times. That's tied for the most in NHL history. Bergeron was at his best in Game 7 of the 2011 finals, when he scored two goals to help Boston win the Stanley Cup.

ROB GRONKOWSKI
Patriots tight end

Gronk is a tight end who excels at blocking, and he may also be Tom Brady's best downfield threat. The fun-loving Gronkowski has averaged 15 yards a reception for his career, and in his first 100 games he had 75 touchdown catches.

ENEMY OF THE STATE

NEW YORK YANKEES

Whether it's Joe DiMaggio vs. Ted Williams or Mookie Betts vs. Aaron Judge, the Red Sox and the Bronx Bombers have for decades been thwarting one another's postseason dreams.

Magic Johnson

Earvin Johnson was given the nickname Magic at age 15 by a sportswriter who was wowed by the Lansing kid's dazzling moves. Earvin's mother, a school custodian and a Christian, found the nickname blasphemous, but it stuck. It also fit him very well. At Michigan State, Magic led the Spartans to the 1979 national title, defeating Larry Bird's Indiana State team in a matchup that led to a huge bump in popularity for the college game. Magic and Bird similarly invigorated the NBA. Johnson, a 6' 9" point guard who always seemed to be smiling, won five championships and three MVP Awards with the Los Angeles Lakers. Since retiring he has found great success as a businessman and franchise owner.

ISHPEMING
U.S. SKI AND SNOWBOARD HALL OF FAME

ⓘ **INSIDER INFO**
Also known as the Motor City, Detroit hosted a Formula One Grand Prix race in the 1980s. The course sent cars zooming through downtown streets. The city now puts on an IndyCar race on Belle Isle, which is an island in the Detroit River. The 2017 event attracted 100,000 spectators.

STATE-MENT

"If I don't talk to the ball, who will?"

MARK FIDRYCH,
the famously quirky Tigers pitcher who became a sensation in 1976 for winning 19 games—and having conversations with the baseball

SPORTY SITES

◀ **Comerica Park** Attractions here include not only Detroit Tigers baseball but also a carousel and the Fly Ball Ferris Wheel. Fans can take a whirl inside giant baseballs.

Crisler Center The University of Michigan plays its basketball games in an arena named for a football coach. Fritz Crisler led the Wolverines to the 1947 national championship and introduced the team's famed winged football helmets.

Ford Field In 2003 the Lions' home stadium accommodated 78,129 basketball fans. The largest crowd in college hoops history watched Michigan State take on Kentucky in the Basketbowl. The Wildcats won 79–74.

Little Caesars Arena The luxurious venue, which opened in 2017, lured the Pistons back downtown. The team had played in the suburbs since 1978.

Michigan Stadium With a seating capacity of 107,601, the home of the Michigan Wolverines has earned the nickname the Big House.

Oakland Hills Country Club The course in Bloomfield Hills has been the site of six U.S. Opens, three PGA Championships, and the Ryder Cup.

U.S. Ski and Snowboard Hall of Fame The hall is located on the Upper Peninsula, in Ishpeming. That's where local businessmen and skiers organized the National Ski Association, which was officially formed in 1905.

PRO TEAMS

NFL	Detroit Lions
MLB	Detroit Tigers
NBA	Detroit Pistons
NHL	Detroit Red Wings

The **Pistons** played their first nine seasons in Fort Wayne, Indiana, before moving to Detroit in 1957.

DETROIT

OAKLAND HILLS COUNTRY CLUB

LITTLE CAESARS ARENA
Detroit Pistons
Detroit Red Wings

FORD FIELD
Detroit Lions

ANN ARBOR

MICHIGAN STADIUM
Michigan Wolverines

COMERICA PARK
Detroit Tigers

CRISLER CENTER
Michigan Wolverines

MICHIGAN

MICHIGAN

COOL SCHOOLS

Michigan

The school's fight song is considered the best college march by many, including famous composer John Philip Sousa. "The Victors" was written in 1898, and its appeal has endured. Look around on YouTube and you'll find versions with ukuleles, bagpipes, and glee clubs, as well as the conventional marching band rendition. The song has the lyric, "Hail! Hail! to Michigan, the champions of the West." That hints at the depth of Wolverines tradition, because "the West" refers to the Western Conference, which is what the Big Ten was called in the 19th century. The school claims 11 national football titles (though only one has come since 1948). The Wolverines also won a title in men's basketball in 1989, but the school's most famous squads, led by the Fab Five, lost in the final in 1992 and 1993. The nickname came from the five players—Chris Webber, Jalen Rose, Juwan Howard, Jimmy King, and Ray Jackson—who changed the look of the sport with their baggy shorts and black socks, turning tradition on its head.

FAMOUS WOLVERINES

TOM BRADY
Three-time
NFL MVP

GERALD FORD
Football star, 38th
U.S. president

JIM HARBAUGH
NF L quarterback,
Wolverines coach

BARRY LARKIN
Baseball Hall of
Famer

Michigan State

Here's a close call: When MSU students voted on a nickname in 1925, they chose the very bland Michigan Staters. (Aren't college kids supposed to be crazy?) But local sports editor George S. Alderton intervened and persuaded the school to go with another entry: Spartans. The Spartans are at their best on the basketball court, winning national titles in 1979 and 2000 and sending Los Angeles Lakers legend Magic Johnson and Golden State Warriors big man Draymond Green to the NBA. The football team has six national titles, all of which were won between 1951 and 1966. Plenty of MSU alums are in the NFL, including the league's highest-paid player, Minnesota Vikings QB Kirk Cousins.

HOMEGROWN HEROES

JOE LOUIS

The Brown Bomber, one of the greatest heavyweight champions ever, was born Joeseph Louis Barrow. He began fighting under the shortened name as an amateur because he didn't want his mom to find out he was boxing.

TOM IZZO

Since taking over as Michigan State basketball coach in 1995, the Iron Mountain native has always been busy in March. His teams have made 21 straight NCAA tournament appearances, advancing to the Final Four seven times.

DEREK JETER

The iconic shortstop signed a letter of intent to play college baseball for Michigan, but the Kalamazoo kid decided to sign with the New York Yankees instead. He's still a Wolverines fan, though.

DAVE BING

Bing became so popular as a high-scoring guard with the Pistons that after a successful post-NBA business career, he was elected mayor of Detroit in 2009.

JEROME BETTIS

The powerful Steelers running back had a storybook ending to his career when in 2006 he won a Super Bowl in his hometown of Detroit.

BIG EVENT

Michigan vs. Michigan State

The intrastate series has produced many exciting moments, the wildest of which came in 2015. The Wolverines were up by two points with 10 seconds left, needing only to get off a punt to seal the game. But then the Wolverines' punter fumbled the snap and Michigan State ran the ball in for a touchdown as time expired. The result gave the Spartans a key Big Ten victory,

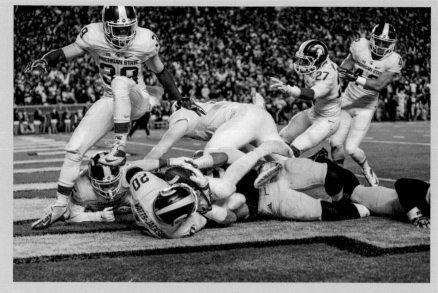

bragging rights, and a cool trophy. Each year the winner takes possession of the Paul Bunyan Trophy, a four-foot-tall statue of the legendary lumberjack. It was first presented in 1953, the year the Spartans joined the Big Ten.

MASCOT FACE-OFF

SPARTY Michigan State	VS.	AL THE OCTOPUS Detroit Red Wings
Student in costume	IS A . . .	Giant arena decoration
Muscular	ARMS	Numerous
At every game	SHOWS UP . . .	For the playoffs
Can't put a price on him	WORTH . . .	Sold for $7,700 when Joe Louis Arena closed in 2017

MICHIGAN

THE NUMBERS

3

ALL-AMERICA TEAMS made by Dave DeBusschere at the University of Detroit. As a pro he made seven NBA All-Star teams, including three for his hometown Pistons.

2

CONSECUTIVE MVP AWARDS won by the Tigers' Hal Newhouser, in 1944 and 1945. He is the only major league pitcher ever to accomplish that feat.

57

FEET that Rick (Pellet Gun) Krause spit a cherry pit to win the 2017 International Cherry Pit-Spitting Championship in Eau Claire.

786

GOALS scored as a Red Wing by Gordie Howe; it is the NHL record for goals scored by a player with a single franchise.

FAN FAVORITES

MIGUEL CABRERA
Tigers first baseman

Cabrera has twice won baseball's MVP award, including in 2012, when he led the American League in home runs (44), RBIs (139), and batting average (.330). That made the slugger the first player to win a Triple Crown since Carl Yastrzemski of the Boston Red Sox in 1967. Cabrera has won four batting titles for the Tigers.

DYLAN LARKIN
Red Wings center

When Larkin was 13 years old, he made a video of himself playing hockey in his basement and calling himself D-Boss. After the video surfaced in 2016, the Red Wings gave fans a D-Boss bobblehead—a way to honor the speedy skater who went on to lead the team in points in 2017–2018.

MATTHEW STAFFORD
Lions quarterback

Two alumni of Highland Park High in Dallas (Bobby Layne and Doak Walker) have become Pro Football Hall of Famers with the Lions. Stafford would like to become the third. The top pick of the 2009 NFL draft has thrown for more than 34,000 yards and led Detroit to three playoff appearances.

ⓘ **INSIDER INFO** Only two Lions have ever led the NFL in rushing: Barry Sanders, who did it four times in the 1990s (including a career-best 2,053 yards in 1997) and Byron (Whizzer) White, who had 514 yards in 1940. White became a U.S. Supreme Court justice.

GREATEST MOMENT

JUNE 13, 1989

Bad Boys Topple the Lakers

The 1989 NBA Finals featured a matchup of two teams with opposite styles. The Los Angeles Lakers played a fast-breaking style of basketball known as Showtime. The Pistons, on the other hand, were a rough-and-tumble bunch known as the Bad Boys. The series was a rematch of the 1988 Finals, in which the Lakers had narrowly beaten Detroit. But in 1989, Los Angeles was missing guards Magic Johnson and Byron Scott due to injury. Led by guards Isiah Thomas and Joe Dumars and big men Bill Laimbeer, Rick Mahorn, and Dennis Rodman, the Pistons rolled to a sweep. The next season the Bad Boys proved that their title was no fluke when they took care of the Portland Trail Blazers in five games for back-to-back titles.

MICHIGAN'S TROPHY SHELF

3 NBA Championships In addition to back-to-back wins in 1989 and 1990, the Pistons took home another title in 2004 behind the team-oriented play of Chauncey Billups, Richard Hamilton, and Ben Wallace.

4 World Series Championships The Tigers' most recent win came in 1984, when the team featured former Michigan State baseball and football star Kirk Gibson.

11 Stanley Cup Wins The Red Wings' wins include four in the 1950s behind Gordie Howe. Only two NHL teams (the Montreal Canadiens and the Toronto Maple Leafs) have lifted the trophy more times.

ENEMY OF THE STATE

OHIO STATE FOOTBALL

You know a sporting event is a big deal if it's simply called the Game. The matchup between Michigan and OSU has decided the Big Ten championship 22 times.

MINNESOTA

PRO TEAMS

NFL	**Minnesota Vikings**
MLB	**Minnesota Twins**
NBA	**Minnesota Timberwolves**
WNBA	**Minnesota Lynx**
NHL	**Minnesota Wild**
MLS	**Minnesota United FC**

The **North Stars** were Minnesota's NHL team from 1967 to 1993; the Wild began play in 2000.

SPORTY SITES

3M Arena at Mariucci The 10,000-seat home of Minnesota Golden Gophers hockey has also been home to NCAA tournaments, the women's Frozen Four, and lunchtime open skates.

National Sports Center The Blaine facility, billed as the world's largest amateur sports complex, hosts all sorts of competitions with its 54 grass fields, eight-rink ice complex, golf course, and cycling velodrome.

Target Center The basketball arena features a green rooftop that is covered with grass and plants.

U.S. Bank Stadium The 66,655-seat stadium, which opened in 2016, was the site of the 2018 Super Bowl and will host the 2019 NCAA Final Four.

U.S. Hockey Hall of Fame Museum Minnesota is a hockey hotbed, and a Hall of Fame dedicated to the game in the United States is located in Eveleth.

EVELETH
U.S. HOCKEY HALL OF FAME

BRAINERD ICE FISHING EXTRAVAGANZA

NATIONAL SPORTS CENTER

MINNEAPOLIS
TARGET FIELD
Minnesota Twins

TARGET CENTER
Minnesota Timberwolves
Minnesota Lynx

U.S. BANK STADIUM
Minnesota Vikings

ST. PAUL
XCEL ENERGY CENTER
Minnesota Wild

3M ARENA AT MARIUCCI
University of Minnesota Gophers

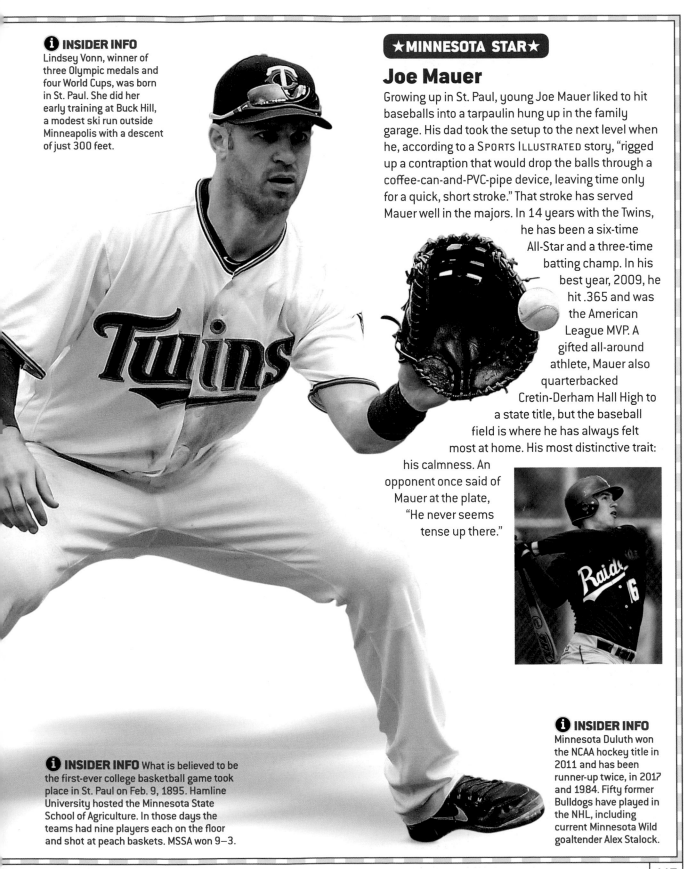

ⓘ INSIDER INFO
Lindsey Vonn, winner of three Olympic medals and four World Cups, was born in St. Paul. She did her early training at Buck Hill, a modest ski run outside Minneapolis with a descent of just 300 feet.

★MINNESOTA STAR★

Joe Mauer

Growing up in St. Paul, young Joe Mauer liked to hit baseballs into a tarpaulin hung up in the family garage. His dad took the setup to the next level when he, according to a SPORTS ILLUSTRATED story, "rigged up a contraption that would drop the balls through a coffee-can-and-PVC-pipe device, leaving time only for a quick, short stroke." That stroke has served Mauer well in the majors. In 14 years with the Twins, he has been a six-time All-Star and a three-time batting champ. In his best year, 2009, he hit .365 and was the American League MVP. A gifted all-around athlete, Mauer also quarterbacked Cretin-Derham Hall High to a state title, but the baseball field is where he has always felt most at home. His most distinctive trait: his calmness. An opponent once said of Mauer at the plate, "He never seems tense up there."

ⓘ INSIDER INFO What is believed to be the first-ever college basketball game took place in St. Paul on Feb. 9, 1895. Hamline University hosted the Minnesota State School of Agriculture. In those days the teams had nine players each on the floor and shot at peach baskets. MSSA won 9–3.

ⓘ INSIDER INFO
Minnesota Duluth won the NCAA hockey title in 2011 and has been runner-up twice, in 2017 and 1984. Fifty former Bulldogs have played in the NHL, including current Minnesota Wild goaltender Alex Stalock.

MINNESOTA

489

CAREER WINS by John Gagliardi of Division III St. John's University, the most by a football coach at any level. The famously easygoing (for a coach) Gagliardi won four national titles.

0

GAMES that St. Paul's Dave Winfield played in the minor leagues. He went straight from the University of Minnesota to the San Diego Padres' outfield. The Hall of Famer played 22 seasons, including two with the Twins.

5

NBA TITLES won by the Lakers in the 12 seasons they spent in Minneapolis. The team moved to Los Angeles in 1960.

10

PERCENT of Minnesotans who have a boat registration, according to the 2010 Census. That's the most of any state.

FAN FAVORITES

KARL-ANTHONY TOWNS
Timberwolves center

Towns was named the NBA's Rookie of the Year in 2015–2016, and his game has only grown since then—which is saying something, given Towns's rare versatility. Towns's father pushed him to be able to do everything on the court, playing five hours a day, learning all the positions, not just the big man. This is why the athletic 7-footer not only is one of the league's best scorers around the rim but can also sink three-pointers at a rate that a wing player could build a career around. He found a professional mentor in Timberwolves great Kevin Garnett. Towns says KG's best advice was, "You'll be great when you find out exactly what your routine is."

MAYA MOORE
Lynx forward

Since they drafted the former UConn star in 2011, the Lynx have won four WNBA titles. Moore has been the driving force, making first-team all-league in each of the last five seasons. She is one of two WNBA players to be named MVP of the regular season, Finals, and All-Star Game.

ADAM THIELEN
Vikings wide receiver

The Detroit Lakes native was an NFL long shot after going undrafted out of Division II Minnesota State. Not only has he made it, but he's also become a Pro Bowl performer. In 2017 he had 1,276 receiving yards, which was good for fifth in the NFL, as the Vikings went 13–3.

ZACH PARISE
Wild forward

Minnesota hockey is in his blood. Parise's father, J.P., played for the North Stars, the state's former NHL franchise. Zach, who was born in Minneapolis, signed a 10-year contract with the Wild in 2012. He was also captain of the 2014 U.S. Olympic hockey team.

BIG EVENT

Brainerd Ice Fishing Extravaganza

If you can't handle cold weather, this event is not for you. Every January, about 10,000 anglers take to the frozen waters of Hole in the Day Bay on Gull Lake. More than 20,000 holes are predrilled, and fishermen compete for $150,000 in cash and prizes.

MINNESOTA'S TROPHY SHELF

2 World Series Championships The Twins, who came to Minnesota from Washington, D.C., in 1961, have been to three World Series. They won in 1987 (a year after finishing 21 games under .500) and 1991.

4 WNBA Championships The Lynx, who began play in 1999, have dominated recent WNBA history. All four trophies have been won since 2011.

"This team isn't talented enough to win on talent alone."

Coach **HERB BROOKS**, on his Miracle on Ice 1980 U.S. Olympic hockey team. Brooks, who grew up in St. Paul, also coached the University of Minnesota.

MINNESOTA

ⓘ INSIDER INFO
Only one WNBA player has won five championships: Rebekkah Brunson (32). The power forward has won four with the Lynx, including in 2017. Brunson won her first ring back in 2005 as a member of the Sacramento Monarchs—a team that doesn't exist any longer.

MINNESOTA

GREATEST MOMENT

OCTOBER 27, 1991
Epic World Series Game 7

The stakes couldn't have been any higher—and neither could the quality of the pitching. In the winner-take-all matchup between the Twins and the Atlanta Braves, Jack Morris and John Smoltz hung up zero after zero on the Metrodome scoreboard. Smoltz finally left the game with one out in the eighth inning, and after nine innings neither team had scored. Morris continued into the 10th and blanked the Braves again. In the bottom of the inning Dan Gladden led off with a double. He advanced to third on a bunt and scored when unheralded pinch hitter Gene Larkin drove a hit into left centerfield. With that the Twins had won their second World Series, and Morris had cemented his reputation as one of the game's great clutch pitchers.

HOMEGROWN HEROES

PAUL MOLITOR

The 2017 American League Manager of the Year with the Twins is a St. Paul native and a Minnesota alum. He spent most of his Hall of Fame career playing with the Milwaukee Brewers, but his final three seasons were spent with the Twins. He is one of just three players with at least 3,000 hits, 500 stolen bases, and a career average above .300.

LARRY FITZGERALD

The son of a Minneapolis sportswriter, young Larry was a Vikings' ball boy, which gave him an up-close look at receivers such as Randy Moss and Cris Carter. Fitzgerald went on to become a pretty good wideout himself: He's made 11 Pro Bowls and at the end of the 2017 season was third on the all-time receptions list.

KEVIN MCHALE

McHale entered Hibbing High as a 5' 11" hockey fanatic and left as a 6' 10" basketball standout. After playing at Minnesota, he was drafted by the Boston Celtics, forming a fearsome frontcourt with Larry Bird and Robert Parish. With his long arms and low-post moves, McHale twice led the NBA in field goal percentage. He was a seven-time All-Star and a three-time NBA champion.

Minnesota

If you want to know how hockey-mad the state is, consider this: Minnesota is one of only two schools where the men and women each have their own hockey rink. The men and women have each claimed seven national titles. That's the same number of championships won by the Gophers' football program. The most recent was in 1960, and five came between 1934 and 1941. The school's greatest player was 1920s star Bronko Nagurski, the only man ever to be a consensus All-America at two positions (fullback and tackle). Minnesota has also turned out coaches Bud Grant, who led the Vikings, and Tony Dungy, the first African-American coach to win a Super Bowl.

ENEMY OF THE STATE

GREEN BAY PACKERS

The Vikings have taken four of the last five matchups against their hated NFC North rivals, but the Packers still lead the overall series 60-53-2.

MASCOT FACE-OFF

RAGNAR *Minnesota Vikings*	VS.	VIKTOR *Minnesota Vikings*
1994–2015	**YEARS**	2007–present
Unofficial mascot	**STATUS**	Official mascot
Clearly	**HUMAN?**	Probably
Joe Juranitch	**REAL NAME**	Could be anyone
Asked for $20,000 a game	**FATAL ERROR**	Time will tell

OXFORD

VAUGHT-HEMINGWAY STADIUM
Ole Miss Rebels

DAVIS WADE STADIUM
Mississippi State Bulldogs

STARKVILLE

RICHBURG

SPORTY SITES

Davis Wade Stadium at Scott Field The home of the Mississippi State Bulldogs opened in 1914 under its original name: New Athletic Field.
Richburg The town has a historic marker for the 1889 heavyweight title bout between John L. Sullivan and Jake Kilrain. They fought without gloves, and bare-knuckle boxing was illegal. So the bout took place on a farm for secrecy. Both men were arrested after the fight, which lasted 75 rounds.
Vaught-Hemingway Stadium The Ole Miss stadium opened in 1915 with a capacity of 24,000. After numerous renovations, it now seats 64,038.

THE NUMBERS

1 **PUNTER** in the Pro Football Hall of Fame: Ray Guy of Southern Mississippi.

64 **WINS** for Mississippi in the annual Egg Bowl game against Mississippi State. Ole Miss has 41 losses, and there have been six ties.

5 **200-YARD RECEIVING GAMES**, an NFL career record, by Lance Alworth of Hog Chain.

★ MISSISSIPPI STAR ★

Brett Favre

After he retired in 2010, the NFL's alltime leader in passing yards and touchdowns became the offensive coordinator at Oak Grove High, where he had worked out during the off-season. When Oak Grove won the 6A state title in 2013, Favre jumped up and down like a kid. Which explains why the Green Bay Packers great endeared himself to fans all over the country. In a game where so many quarterbacks are cool and methodical, the Southern Mississippi alum always played the game with the exuberance of a youngster running around the sandlot.

PRO TEAMS

Double A Biloxi Shuckers
Mississippi Braves

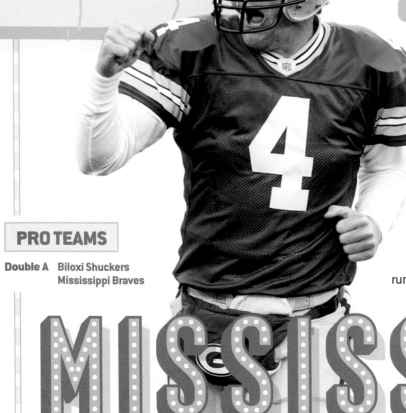

MISSISSIPPI

HOMEGROWN HEROES

JERRY RICE

The receiver with the NFL records for most catches (1,549), receiving yards (22,895), and touchdowns (197) in NFL history, Rice was born in Starkville and went to Mississippi Valley State. Playing in a pass-heavy offense that was ahead of its time, Rice had 112 receptions, 1,845 yards, and 27 touchdowns as a senior for the Delta Devils.

WALTER PAYTON

The Chicago Bears running back scored 110 NFL touchdowns and ran for 16,726 yards, which was an NFL record when he retired. The man called Sweetness grew up in Columbia and played at Jackson State. In 2006, the school opened the Walter Payton Recreation and Wellness Center.

ⓘ INSIDER INFO Walter Payton is one of four Jackson State Tigers in the Pro Football Hall of Fame, along with cornerback Lem Barney, offensive tackle Jackie Slater, and linebacker Robert Brazile. That's more than SEC schools Ole Miss (two) and Mississippi State (zero).

ENEMY OF THE STATE

ALABAMA FOOTBALL

Mississippi and Mississippi State are each other's biggest rivals, but wins against the Crimson Tide, the pigskin superpower of the SEC West, are both rare and treasured.

Ole Miss

When it comes to a football game-day experience, Ole Miss can compete with any school in the country. The Grove, a 10-acre plot in the middle of the Oxford campus, hosts very refined tailgating. Men wear ties, women are in hats and dresses, and food is eaten off china plates. Football is revered enough that the campus speed limit used to be 18 miles per hour, in honor of former quarterback Archie Manning, who wore number 18. Archie's son Eli went here, too, before winning two Super Bowls with the Giants.

Mississippi State

You know you're at a Bulldogs football game when you hear the cowbells. The tradition dates back to the 1930s, when a cow wandered onto the field. The SEC banned the noisemakers in 1974, but in 2010 the rules were relaxed to allow fans to ring them in timeouts, at halftime, and after scores. One notable NFL star who inspired fans to ring bells in Starkville is Dallas Cowboys quarterback Dak Prescott. The Bulldogs baseball team has won 11 SEC titles and produced MLB stars Rafael Palmeiro and Will Clark.

STATE-MENT

"Cool Papa Bell was so fast he could get out of bed, turn out the lights across the room, and be back in bed under the covers before the lights went out."

JOSH GIBSON, on his fellow Hall of Famer and Negro leagues star, who hailed from Starkville

MISSOURI

PRO TEAMS

NFL Kansas City Chiefs

MLB Kansas City Royals
St. Louis Cardinals

NHL St. Louis Blues

MLS Sporting Kansas City

Though the club is still based in Missouri, **Sporting Kansas City** plays its home games just across the border in Kansas.

ARROWHEAD STADIUM
Kansas City Chiefs

NEGRO LEAGUES BASEBALL MUSEUM

COLUMBIA

ENTERPRISE CENTER
St. Louis Blues

ST. LOUIS

BELLERIVE COUNTRY CLUB

KAUFFMANN STADIUM
Kansas City Royals

FAUROT FIELD
University of Missouri Tigers

KANSAS CITY

BUSCH STADIUM
St. Louis Cardinals

SPORTY SITES

Arrowhead Stadium One of the noisiest stadiums in the NFL, the Chiefs' home is a sea of red on game days. It has also hosted five Big 12 championship games and a 2010 soccer friendly between the Kansas City Wizards (now known as Sporting Kansas City) and English superpower Manchester United.

Bellerive Country Club Located in Town and Country (that's really the name of the place), the course will host the 2018 PGA Championship, its third major.

Busch Stadium The current version of the Cardinals' home opened in 2006. The Redbirds settled in nicely, becoming the first modern-day team to win a World Series in their first season in a new stadium.

▶ **Negro Leagues Baseball Museum** The Kansas City museum, which tells the story of Negro leagues teams from the late 1800s to the 1960s, shares a complex with the American Jazz Museum.

Enterprise Center The home of the Blues opened in 1994 on the site of their old home, Kiel Auditorium.

Yadier Molina

In the Molina family, catching is a way of life. Yadier is the younger brother of Bengie and José, both of whom had fine major league careers behind the plate. As a teenager, Yadier, who is eight years younger than Bengie and seven years younger than José, followed his brothers' exploits from Puerto Rico, learning what he could from news clippings and brief phone calls. He hoped one day to join them in the big leagues. He got his chance in 2004, when the Cardinals called him up from the minors. Yadier became one of the game's greatest defensive catchers, winning eight Gold Gloves. He's not a bad hitter, either, slugging his way to eight All-Star teams and picking up a pair of World Series rings.

ⓘ INSIDER INFO

The Rawlings brothers, George and Alfred, opened a sporting goods store in St. Louis in 1887. They later became equipment manufacturers and invented the webbed baseball mitt. They also started the tradition of awarding a Gold Glove to the top fielders in the major leagues.

ⓘ INSIDER INFO

The University of Missouri's Memorial Stadium features a giant *M* made out of rocks. The letter is 90 feet by 95 feet. In 1957, the night before a game against Nebraska, mischievous Cornhuskers fans changed the *M* to an *N*, but the whitewashed rocks were back in their proper place before kickoff.

MISSOURI

COOL SCHOOL

University of Missouri

After decades in the Big 12 (previously known as the Big Eight, Big Seven, and Big Six), Missouri jumped to the SEC in 2012. The Tigers landed a few good punches in the early rounds in college football's heavyweight division, wowing home crowds at Faurot Field and making it to the SEC title game in 2013 and 2014. (One downside of the conference switch is that Mizzou no longer has annual visits from its most bitter rival, the University of Kansas.) Mizzou basketball has made five trips to the Elite Eight and produced a steady stream of NBA players, including the Cleveland Cavaliers' Jordan Clarkson. Since no other SEC schools field wrestling teams, Mizzou competes in the Mid-American Conference in that sport. That program has turned out a pair of Olympians.

STATE-MENT

"A heckuva lot better than being the shortest player in the minor leagues."

The Kansas City Royals'
5' 4" **FREDDIE PATEK**, when
asked in 1971 how it felt to
be the shortest player
in the major leagues

HOMEGROWN HEROES

YOGI BERRA

The longtime New York Yankees catcher, who was from St. Louis, won the most World Series rings of any player, with 10. He is also baseball's most quoted star, with such memorable lines as "It ain't over till it's over" and "When you come to a fork in the road, take it."

ALBERT PUJOLS

Pujols was born in the Dominican Republic but grew up in Independence. He played for the Cardinals from 2001 to 2011, winning three National League MVP awards.

DAVID FREESE

The native of the St. Louis suburbs earned his place in Cardinals lore during the 2011 World Series. In Game 6, he hit a two-out, two-run triple to tie the game in the ninth inning and won it with a walk-off home run in the 11th. St. Louis then beat the Texas Rangers in Game 7 for the championship.

TOM WATSON

The Kansas City native won four Missouri state amateur golf titles. As a professional, he won 39 PGA Tour events and eight major championships, including two victories at the Masters.

GREATEST MOMENT

OCTOBER 1985
I-70 Series

The seven-game thriller between Missouri's two major league teams (they are connected by Interstate 70) is remembered for an infamous umpiring error. St. Louis led Kansas City three games to two and was up by one run in the bottom of the ninth inning of Game 6. Three outs away from elimination, the Royals got their leadoff man on when Jorge Orta was called safe at first on a slow ground ball. He was clearly out, but baseball did not use instant replay to review calls in those days. The Royals went on to score two runs to win the game. The next night they blew out the Cardinals in Game 7, as pitcher Bret Saberhagen tossed an 11–0 shutout that gave Kansas City its first World Series victory.

MASCOT FACE-OFF

BILLIKEN *St. Louis University*	VS.	FREDBIRD *St. Louis Cardinals*
A doll that was popular in the early 20th century	**WHAT IS IT?**	Common bird
Supposedly resembles former coach John R. Bender	**LOOKS LIKE . . .**	No one. It's a bird.
Around 1911	**BORN**	1979
Unique to SLU	**COMMON?**	Quite
Yes	**FREAKY?**	No. Well, maybe a little.

MISSOURI

10 — NCAA MEN'S SOCCER TITLES
won by the St. Louis Billikens, all between 1959 (the first official championship) and 1973.

18 — YEARS that Bill Bradley of Crystal City served in the U.S. Senate. After twice being named a high school basketball All-America, he starred at Princeton and won two NBA titles with the New York Knicks.

3 — STANLEY CUP FINALS
reached by the St. Louis Blues in their first three seasons, from 1968 to 1970. The team lost all three finals and hasn't been back since.

2 — NBA FRANCHISES
that have left Missouri: the St. Louis (now Atlanta) Hawks in 1968 and the Kansas City (now Sacramento) Kings in 1985. The Hawks were the 1958 NBA champs.

FAN FAVORITES

TRAVIS KELCE
Kansas City Chiefs tight end

The Chiefs star grew up always playing—and competing—with his older brother, Jason, who is now an All-Pro center with the Eagles. Once, after a game of basketball, the two got into a scrap that led to the family's oven being destroyed. (The casserole that was cooking in it was lost as well.) That feistiness is noticeable when Kelce is on the field. He is an essential weapon in the Chiefs' offense, racking up more than 1,000 receiving yards in both 2016 and 2017. He's also the rare tight end who has been handed the ball on running plays.

VLADIMIR TARASENKO
Blues forward

The high-scoring winger, who grew up in Siberia and was raised by grandparents while his father, Andrei, played professional hockey, has found a home in St. Louis since arriving in 2012. Tarasenko has made three All-Star teams and finished in the top 10 in goals three times.

ALEX GORDON
Royals leftfielder

When the Royals drafted Gordon in 2005, they were one of the worst teams in the league, but the slugger was a big piece of their turnaround. The three-time All-Star has won five Gold Gloves, and his ninth-inning, game-tying home run in Game 1 helped Kansas City win the 2015 World Series.

MISSOURI'S TROPHY SHELF

2 Super Bowl Wins The Jets' upset of the Colts in 1969 was the first time an AFL team beat an NFL squad in the Super Bowl. Not as famous but just as impressive was Kansas City's rout of the Minnesota Vikings the next year, which gave the Chiefs their only Super Bowl championship. The Rams won a Super Bowl for St. Louis in 2000. Sixteen years later the team left town to return to Los Angeles.

13 World Series Championships The Cardinals have won 11 World Series; only the New York Yankees have won more. St. Louis won its first title in 1926, and its most recent title came in 2011. The Royals' two championships were won in 1985 and 2015.

ⓘ INSIDER INFO The Rams led the NFL in scoring for three consecutive years, from 1999 to 2001. The Greatest Show on Turf featured quarterback Kurt Warner, running back Marshall Faulk, and receivers Isaac Bruce and Torry Holt.

ⓘ INSIDER INFO
St. Louis was once home to the International Bowling Museum and Hall of Fame (most famous visitor: Homer Simpson). In 2008, the hall moved from its home near Busch Stadium to Arlington, Texas.

BIG EVENT

The Show-Me State Games

Since 1985, Missourians have been staging their own version of the Olympics. Athletes of all ages gather in Columbia each summer to compete in 40 events, from archery to wrestling, shooting to softball. It is the largest in-state event of its type in the country.

ENEMY OF THE STATE

CHICAGO CUBS

If familiarity breeds contempt, watch out for these two. The Cards and Cubs have been meeting since 1892, and more than 300 players have appeared for both teams.

GREATEST MOMENT

JULY 4, 1923

Jack Dempsey vs. Tommy Gibbons

Epic fail alert! A 40,208-seat stadium was built in Shelby so the town could host a heavyweight title fight. Dempsey won a 15-round decision in an exciting bout, but fewer than 12,000 tickets were sold. So much money was lost that four area banks closed.

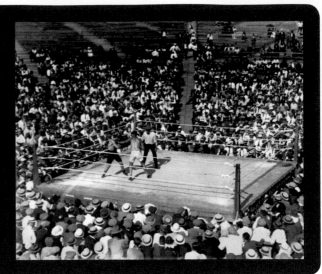

PRO TEAMS

Rookie Billings Mustangs
Great Falls Voyagers
Helena Brewers
Missoula Osprey

The four teams make up a division of the **Pioneer League**, whose players are mostly in their first or second years.

GLACIER NATIONAL PARK

MISSOULA

WASHINGTON-GRIZZLY STADIUM
University of Montana Grizzlies

BOZEMAN

BOBCAT STADIUM
Montana State Bobcats

SPORTY SITES

Bobcat Stadium Montana State has been playing football in the 17,777-seat stadium since 1973.
Glacier National Park The park features more than 700 miles of hiking trails.
Washington-Grizzly Stadium University of Montana Grizzlies enthusiasts regularly pack the 25,217-seat stadium.

MONTANA

18
CAREER INTERCEPTIONS by N.Y. Jets cornerback and Montana alum Trumaine Johnson.

2
FCS NATIONAL TITLES won by Montana, in 1995 and 2001.

3

NATIONAL TITLES in football for Montana State: 1956 (NAIA), 1976 (Division II), and 1984 (Division I-AA).

ⓘ **INSIDER INFO** Norwegian-born Jan Stenerud came to Montana State on a skiing scholarship and didn't join the football team until he was a junior. Still, he went on to play 19 NFL seasons, including 13 with the Kansas City Chiefs. In 1991, he became the first kicker elected to the Pro Football Hall of Fame.

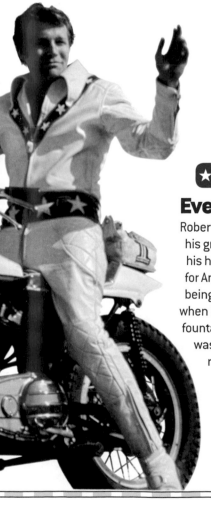

★ MONTANA STAR ★

Evel Knievel

Robert Knievel found his calling as a boy when his grandparents took him to a car stunt show in his hometown of Butte. But the vehicle of choice for America's most famous daredevil ended up being a motorcycle. The nation gasped in 1967 when he attempted to jump 141 feet over the fountains at a Las Vegas casino. He crashed and was in a coma for 29 days. As soon as he recovered, though, the jumps continued—over rows of cars and double-decker buses. He tried to jump the Snake River Canyon in Idaho, but the parachute on his "Skycycle" deployed early. In his career, Knievel broke 35 different bones at least once. In short: Kids, don't try this at home.

HOMEGROWN HEROES

BRENT MUSBURGER
His phrase "You are looking live . . ." welcomed countless fans to Sunday football in his years hosting *The NFL Today* on CBS in the 1970s. Raised in Billings, his broadcast résumé includes baseball, the NBA, and seven NCAA football title games. He retired from announcing in 2017.

DAVE MCNALLY
The three-time All-Star from Billings was a starting pitcher on two World Series winners for the Baltimore Orioles. He threw a 1–0 shutout to clinch the 1966 Series against the Dodgers. Because of Montana's short springs and the distance between schools, McNally's high school did not have a baseball team, but he played American Legion ball in the summer.

BROCK OSWEILER
The 6' 7" quarterback, raised in Kalispell, replaced an injured Peyton Manning for the Broncos in 2015. The team went 5–2 in games he started and won the Super Bowl after Manning returned. Osweiler, who also played for the Texans, joined the Dolphins in 2018.

SPORTY SITES

Las Vegas Motor Speedway The 1.5-mile track hosts two NASCAR events per season.

Mackay Stadium Colin Kaepernick played his college ball at the University of Nevada stadium in Reno, which seats 30,000.

MGM Grand Arena Among the boxers to compete here: Mike Tyson, Evander Holyfield, Oscar De La Hoya, Floyd Mayweather, and Manny Pacquiao.

National Bowling Stadium The 78-lane facility in Reno is where the big competition in the 1996 comedy *Kingpin* was filmed.

T-Mobile Arena The home of the Golden Knights features a store called the Armory, which sells team gear.

Thomas & Mack Center The UNLV basketball arena also hosts the NBA Summer League.

PRO TEAMS

WNBA   Las Vegas Aces

NHL   Vegas Golden Knights

In 2017 the **Golden Knights** became the first major pro sports team to call Las Vegas home; the Aces arrived in 2018.

MACKAY STADIUM
University of Nevada Wolf Pack

RENO

NATIONAL BOWLING STADIUM

LAS VEGAS

T-MOBILE ARENA
Vegas Golden Knights

LAS VEGAS MOTOR SPEEDWAY

THOMAS & MACK CENTER
UNLV Runnin' Rebels

MGM GRAND ARENA
Boxing/MMA

ℹ INSIDER INFO In 2017, the Oakland Raiders received approval from the NFL to move to Las Vegas. The team will relocate once a stadium is built for them, perhaps as soon as 2019. The Raiders will be the first pro football team in town since the Outlaws of the XFL, which played its only season in 2001.

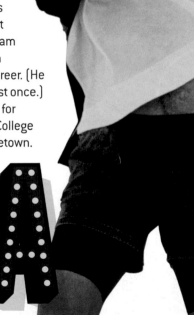

★ NEVADA STAR ★

Andre Agassi

In Las Vegas in the 1970s, Agassi's father made an offer to a manager at the Tropicana casino: *I'll fix up your run-down tennis courts and give lessons if my kids can play there.* And with that a great tennis career was jump-started. As a four-year-old, Andre hit balls with Jimmy Connors, a winner of eight Grand Slam tournaments. That's the same number of Grand Slam tournaments that Agassi would go on to win in his career. (He won each of the four Grand Slam tournaments at least once.) Agassi has used his success to create opportunities for disadvantaged children, founding the Andre Agassi College Preparatory Academy in a poorer section of his hometown.

NEVADA

HOMEGROWN HEROES

BRYCE HARPER

Harper took the GED exam after his sophomore year at Las Vegas High, and at age 17 he played baseball at the College of Southern Nevada. As a 19-year-old he was the National League Rookie of the Year for the Washington Nationals, and in 2015, the outfielder was the league's MVP.

KRIS BRYANT

Bryant's dad was a former Red Sox minor league prospect who became a hitting instructor in Las Vegas. His son is his greatest student, winning Rookie of the Year with the Chicago Cubs in 2015 and the NL MVP award in 2016 when his team won the World Series.

KURT & KYLE BUSCH

The sons of a NASCAR driver, these brothers from Las Vegas have each made a mark in racing. Kyle has 43 wins in NASCAR's top-level series and was the 2015 season champion, while Kurt was the 2004 season champion and has 29 career wins.

GREG MADDUX

Maddux's 355 wins are the most by any pitcher in the last half century. Raised in Las Vegas, the four-time Cy Young winner was a master tactician. He played most of his 23 seasons with the Chicago Cubs and the Atlanta Braves.

GREATEST MOMENT

APRIL 2, 1990
UNLV vs. Duke

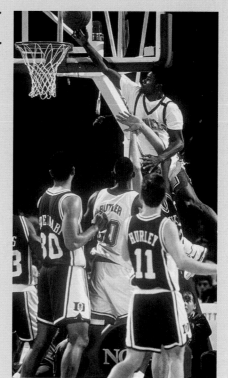

The basketball teams of towel-chewing coach Jerry Tarkanian were the most exciting in UNLV history. Tark's 20-season run reached its apex at the 1990 NCAA championship game, in which the high-octane Runnin' Rebels faced a straightlaced (and very talented) Duke squad. Led by stars such as Larry Johnson, Greg Anthony, Stacey Augmon, and Anderson Hunt, UNLV dominated the Blue Devils, winning 103–73 and giving the school its only national hoops title.

ℹ INSIDER INFO NFL All-Pro quarterback Randall Cunningham received an All-America honorable mention as a QB at UNLV. But the Rebels' greatest player ever was a first-team All-America—as a punter.

THE NUMBERS

1/2
LENGTH, IN MILES, of the Truckee River Whitewater Park, which is open to kayakers in downtown Reno.

1
HIGH SCHOOL STATE TITLE won by future mixed martial arts star Frank Mir.

4
GUESTS on hand when Michael Jordan got married at A Little White Wedding Chapel in Las Vegas in 1989.

HOMEGROWN HEROES

BODE MILLER

Miller, from Franconia, is a five-time Olympian and has won more medals than any other male American skier (six). In 2014, he won a bronze medal in the Super-G in Sochi. That made Miller, then 36, the oldest skier to win an Olympic medal. His 33 World Cup victories are the eighth most in history.

JENNY THOMPSON

Between 1992 and 2004, the swimmer won 12 Olympic medals (eight gold), the most of any U.S. woman. She also earned a medical degree from Columbia University and became an anesthesiologist. She now practices in Portland, Maine.

JERRY AZUMAH

The Division I-AA player of the year in 1998, Azumah rushed for more than 1,000 yards in each of his four seasons at the University of New Hampshire. In the NFL, he switched to cornerback and played seven seasons with the Chicago Bears, making one Pro Bowl.

CHRIS CARPENTER

All-state for three years in both baseball and hockey, the Exeter native stuck with pitching. After going 21–5, Carpenter won the 2005 Cy Young Award for the St. Louis Cardinals. He was a starter on two World Series winners.

Carlton Fisk

After the Boston Red Sox catcher famously homered in the 12th inning of Game 6 of the 1975 World Series, celebratory church bells started ringing in Charlestown, the small town where Fisk grew up. New Hampshire isn't the easiest place to be a baseball player: Fisk and his teammates sometimes had to shovel snow off the field before practice. He went to the University of New Hampshire on a basketball scholarship and played as a 6' 2" power forward but committed to baseball after being drafted by the Sox.

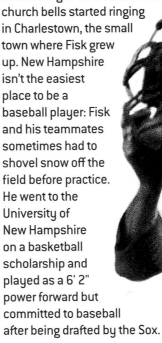

ENEMY OF THE STATE

NEW YORK YANKEES

Fenway Park, home of the Boston Red Sox, is just an hour from the New Hampshire border. So pinstripes are definitely not welcome in the Granite State.

SPORTY SITES

New Hampshire Motor Speedway New England's only NASCAR track opened in Loudon in 1990. It hosts two races in stock car racing's top division each year.

Northeast Delta Dental Stadium Located on the Merrimack River in Manchester, the minor league park drew its biggest crowd (8,903) in 2009, when Hall of Famer John Smoltz made a rehab start for the visiting Portland Sea Dogs.

Memorial Field Built in 1893, Dartmouth's football stadium holds 11,000.

Whittemore Center Go to a hockey game at this University of New Hampshire arena and you'll see a fan throw a fish on the ice after the first Wildcats goal.

THE NUMBERS

7
FROZEN FOUR BERTHS for UNH hockey. The most recent was in 2003.

14
AP RANK of the 1970 Dartmouth football team, the last Ivy League squad to end the season ranked.

4
SECONDS between goals scored by Deron Quint of Durham in 1995 for the Winnipeg Jets, tying an NHL record.

STATE-MENT

"Last time I checked, there is no Hall of Average."

CHIP KELLY, UCLA football coach, New Hampshire native, and former UNH offensive coordinator

PRO TEAMS

Double A **New Hampshire Fisher Cats**

The Manchester-based **Fisher Cats**, an affiliate of the Toronto Blue Jays, arrived in the Granite State in 2003.

HANOVER

NEW HAMPSHIRE MOTOR SPEEDWAY

WHITTEMORE CENTER
UNH Wildcats

MEMORIAL FIELD
Dartmouth Big Green

NORTHEAST DELTA DENTAL STADIUM
New Hampshire Fisher Cats

LOUDON

MANCHESTER

NEW HAMPSHIRE

METLIFE STADIUM
New York Jets
New York Giants

YOGI BERRA MUSEUM

BALTUSROL GOLF CLUB

NEWARK

PRUDENTIAL CENTER
New Jersey Devils

RED BULL ARENA
New York Red Bulls

PISCATAWAY

HIGHPOINT.COM STADIUM
Rutgers Scarlet Knights

ⓘ INSIDER INFO Elysian Fields in Hoboken claims to be the site of the first organized baseball game, in 1846. The last game was played there in 1873, before the property was developed. For years the location was home to a famed rock-and-roll club called Maxwell's.

★NEW JERSEY STAR★

Carli Lloyd

Lloyd, the top-scoring midfielder in U.S. women's national team history, was at her most spectacular in the 2015 World Cup. She scored three goals in the first 16 minutes of the final against Japan, putting the match out of reach early. That made her the first woman ever to score a hat trick in a World Cup final. Lloyd has also dazzled in the Olympics. She netted the game-winning goal in the gold medal match against Brazil in the 2008 Olympics, and she scored both goals as the U.S. beat Japan for the gold in 2012. Lloyd grew up in Delran, a block from a soccer field, and went to Rutgers. In January 2018 she was traded, by request, from the Houston Dash of the National Women's Soccer League to the New Jersey–based Sky Blue FC so she could finish her career at home.

SPORTY SITES

MetLife Stadium Though the Giants and the Jets have *New York* in their names, the teams play their home games in East Rutherford.

Baltusrol Golf Club The Springfield Township course has been the site of seven U.S. Opens and the 2005 and 2016 PGA Championships.

HighPoint.com Stadium The Rutgers football stadium is the 11th largest in the 14-team Big Ten, with a capacity of 52,454.

Prudential Center The arena that hosts Devils hockey games was also home to the NBA's New Jersey Nets before they moved to Brooklyn.

Red Bull Arena The Red Bulls are another New York team, but they play their MLS games across the state line, in Harrison.

Yogi Berra Museum & Learning Center The museum in Little Falls documents the life of the beloved Yankees catcher on and off the field.

GREATEST MOMENT

NOVEMBER 6, 1869
First College Football Game

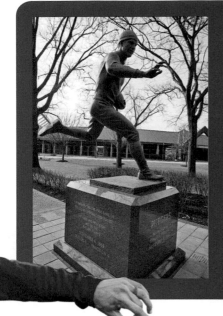

When Princeton (then known as the College of New Jersey) visited New Brunswick to take on Rutgers in what is recognized as the first football game, the rules were very different from what fans see today. Players couldn't carry the ball or throw passes. Teams scored when the ball was kicked or batted into the goal. The game consisted of 10 "mini-games," which ended with each score. Rutgers won 6–4. About 100 spectators were on hand; most folks understandably elected to wait until the forward pass was invented.

PRO TEAMS

NHL   New Jersey Devils

The Devils had company in the Garden State—until the **Nets** moved to Brooklyn in 2012.

STATE-MENT

"It's AWESOME, baby."

Energetic basketball announcer and former coach **DICK VITALE**

NEW JERSEY

NEW JERSEY

COOL SCHOOLS

Rutgers

The most significant fan of Rutgers football might be Bill Belichick. Among the many Scarlet Knights to play for the Patriots' coach are Kenny Britt, Logan Ryan, Duron Harmon, Jonathan Freeny, and Devin McCourty. Despite its long athletic history, Rutgers can claim only one national title in any sport: fencing (in 1949). The school has influenced soccer, however. Alexi Lalas took the Knights to the NCAA title game before starring for the U.S. national team.

Princeton

For a school primarily known for its academics, Princeton has an impressive sports tradition. Basketball star Bill Bradley had the epitome of a well-rounded résumé (NCAA Player of the Year, Olympic gold medalist, Rhodes Scholar, NBA champion, U.S. Senator). In the 1990s, the Princeton Offense designed by Tigers coach Pete Carril changed the basketball landscape. And in January 2018 the school named the alumni most influencing today's world: three Supreme Court justices were joined on the list by Jason Garrett, a former Tigers quarterback and coach of the Dallas Cowboys.

Seton Hall

If not for two free throws by Michigan's Rumeal Robinson in 1989, Seton Hall's trophy case would have some extra sparkle. That year the Pirates made a spirited run in the NCAA tournament, knocking off Indiana, UNLV, and Duke. In the final they held the lead in overtime, but Robinson's free throws with three seconds left gave the Wolverines a one-point win. Overall, Seton Hall has made 11 NCAA tournament appearances, including in 2016 and 2017. The Pirates were coached for 11 seasons by Bill Raftery, a Garden State native whose calls on CBS broadcasts have made a mark on tournament history.

HOMEGROWN HEROES

MIKE TROUT

In his first five MLB seasons, the pride of Millville won two American League MVP awards and finished second in the other three years. In the offseason the Los Angeles Angels centerfielder can often be seen in the front row at Philadelphia Eagles games.

RICK PORCELLO

The hard-throwing pitcher won the 2016 Cy Young Award with the Boston Red Sox, going 22–4 and striking out 189 batters. At Seton Hall Prep in West Orange he was a member of the Spanish National Honor Society.

TOBIN HEATH

The two-time gold medal winner in women's soccer hails from Basking Ridge. In 2016, she was voted Female Player of the Year by U.S. Soccer.

TIM HOWARD

From North Brunswick, Howard overcame Tourette syndrome to set the record for appearances by a goalkeeper for the U.S. men's national soccer team. He has been the top goalkeeper for the U.S. since 2007, and he had a record 16 saves against Belgium in the 2014 World Cup.

NEW JERSEY'S TROPHY SHELF

3 Stanley Cup Wins

The Devils won it all in 1995, 2000, and 2003. It's no coincidence that their goalie in each of those seasons was Martin Brodeur. In his 20 seasons in New Jersey (ending in 2014), Brodeur led the Devils to the playoffs 17 times.

ⓘ **INSIDER INFO** Chris Hogan played lacrosse at Penn State, but an injury left him with a year of eligibility left. So he tried football at Monmouth. It worked out well. The native of Wyckoff is now a New England Patriots receiver.

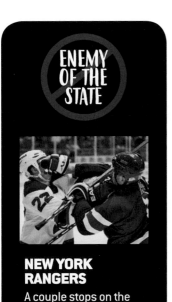

ENEMY OF THE STATE

NEW YORK RANGERS

A couple stops on the New Jersey Transit train system are all that separate these rivals. The Devils aren't so friendly with the New York Islanders, either.

THE NUMBERS

59

SCORELESS INNINGS pitched consecutively for the L.A. Dodgers by Orel Hershiser of Cherry Hill, a record.

9

GOLD MEDALS in track won by Carl Lewis of Willingboro in four Olympics, from 1984 to 1996.

2

ALL-STAR TEAMS made by Todd Frazier of Toms River and Rutgers. He now plays for the New York Mets.

FAN FAVORITES

C. VIVIAN STRINGER
Rutgers women's basketball coach

Stringer is responsible for leading the most successful athletic program at Rutgers. Under her guidance the Scarlet Knights had a run of 10 consecutive tournament berths, from 2003 to 2012. Stringer has led Rutgers to two Final Four appearances. That makes her the first coach in women's or men's basketball to lead three schools (the others are Cheyney and Iowa) to the Final Four.

TAYLOR HALL
Devils forward

After losing in the 2012 Stanley Cup finals, the Devils went through a down stretch. But Hall gives fans a reason to look forward. The first overall pick of the 2010 draft, Hall was traded to New Jersey by the Edmonton Oilers in 2016, and since then he has emerged as a leader for the young Devils club. A left wing who can deliver big scores in tight games, Hall has been named to the All-Star team in each of his two seasons in New Jersey.

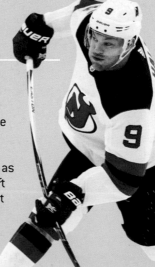

SPORTY SITES

Dreamstyle Stadium New Mexico students cheer on the Lobos football team from the Howl Raisers section. **New Mexico Tech Golf Course** The course, in Socorro, is where the annual Elfego Baca Shootout ends. The event begins on a mountain three miles away. Golfers tee off and hack their way across wild terrain to the shootout's lone hole.

Pan American Center The New Mexico State Aggies basketball team, which plays here, has made the NCAA tournament 24 times. **Taos Ski Valley** The largest resort in the state includes Kachina Peak, with an elevation of 12,481 feet. **The Pit** The University of New Mexico basketball arena, which is largely below ground level, is one of the country's loudest.

TAOS SKI VALLEY

ISOTOPES PARK
Albuquerque Isotopes

ALBUQUERC

THE PIT
University of New Mexico Lobos

DREAMSTYLE STADIUM
University of New Mexico Lobos

NEW MEXICO TECH GOLF COURSE

PAN AMERICAN CENTER
New Mexico State Aggie

PRO TEAMS

Triple A
Albuquerque Isotopes

Attention! Fans of *The Simpsons*! The Colorado Rockies' affiliate's name was inspired by the Springfield Isotopes.

NEW MEXICO

Nancy Lopez

As a little girl Nancy Lopez would go out with her father, an auto mechanic, to play a public course in Roswell. From those beginnings came historic success. At age 12, Lopez won the New Mexico Women's Amateur, and in college at Tulsa she won a national title.

Then it was on to the LPGA, where she came out blazing. Lopez won nine tournaments in her first year and was named 1978 rookie of the year as well as golfer of the year. With charm to match her game, she became as big a star as women's golf has ever seen, winning 48 tournaments—even though she scaled back her schedule in the 1980s to raise three daughters.

ℹ INSIDER INFO In 2003, New Mexico's Katie Hnida kicked two extra points in a win over Texas State to become the first woman to score in a Division I-A football game.

BIG EVENT

Albuquerque International Balloon Fiesta

One of the more picturesque annual events in the country, the Balloon Fiesta, which happens each October, fills the sky with orbs of color. A small group of balloons goes up before sunrise in the Dawn Patrol, and then more than 500 rise over the course of two hours during the Mass Ascension. About 80,000 spectators converge on the 78-acre launch area to ooh and aah.

BRIAN URLACHER
Linebacker

The 6' 4" 258-pounder was a hybrid linebacker-safety at New Mexico. With the Chicago Bears his ability to deliver big hits and cover receivers made him the 2005 NFL Defensive Player of the Year.

MASCOT FACE-OFF

PISTOL PETE *New Mexico State*	VS.	LOBO LOUIE AND LOBO LUCY *New Mexico*
1950s	**BORN**	1960s (Louie), 1980s (Lucy)
Local lawman	**INSPIRATION**	Local wildlife
Pistols	**STRENGTH**	Numbers
A Pete with a big fake head	**THEY TRIED . . .**	Having a real live wolf
Because the head was too hot	**IT FAILED . . .**	When the wolf bit a child

GREATEST MOMENT

APRIL 4, 1983
NCAA Title Game

Perhaps the best ending to an NCAA final occurred at the Pit, when North Carolina State's Lorenzo Charles grabbed a missed shot and dunked it home as time expired. That gave the underdog Wolfpack a win over Houston—and memorably sent coach Jim Valvano running around in search of someone to hug.

★NEW YORK STAR★

Aaron Judge

The Yankees have long been known as the Bronx Bombers, but in 2016, the franchise renowned for its supersluggers finished a sad 11th in the league in home runs. In 2017, though, they were back on top of the AL, hitting a whopping 241. What was the difference? Aaron Judge. The 6' 7", 282-pound rookie sensation took New York by storm, hitting 52 homers as his team returned to the AL Championship Series for the first time since 2012. Fans quickly christened a section of Yankee Stadium the Judge's Chambers; those who sit there wear black robes and swing foam gavels. As impressive as the new face of the Yankees was in the regular season, his most amazing display came during an exhibition. Judge won the 2017 Home Run Derby, knocking the ball out of the park on 47 of his 76 swings. Thanks to four homers that went more than 500 feet, Judge's dingers in the contest traveled a total of 3.9 miles.

BUFFA

KEYBANK
CENTER
*Buffalo
Sabres*

ⓘ **INSIDER INFO**
The headquarters of Major League Baseball and the NFL, NBA, NHL, and MLS are all located within walking distance of one another in midtown Manhattan.

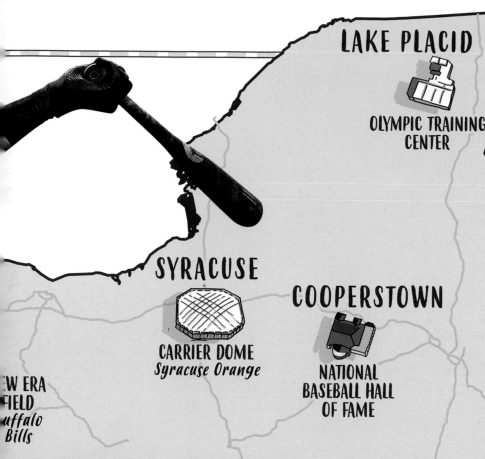

LAKE PLACID
OLYMPIC TRAINING CENTER

SYRACUSE
CARRIER DOME
Syracuse Orange

COOPERSTOWN
NATIONAL BASEBALL HALL OF FAME

NEW ERA FIELD
Buffalo Bills

NEW YORK CITY
YANKEE STADIUM — *New York Yankees*
CITI FIELD — *New York Mets*
MADISON SQUARE GARDEN — *New York Knicks / New York Rangers*
BARCLAYS CENTER — *Brooklyn Nets / New York Islanders*
NATIONAL TENNIS CENTER
BETHPAGE BLACK COURSE
BELMONT RACE TRACK

PRO TEAMS

NFL	**Buffalo Bills** **New York Giants** **New York Jets**
MLB	**New York Mets** **New York Yankees**
NBA	**Brooklyn Nets** **New York Knicks**
WNBA	**New York Liberty**
NHL	**Buffalo Sabres** **New York Islanders** **New York Rangers**
MLS	**New York City FC** **New York Red Bulls**

The Jets played at the Mets' old Shea Stadium and the **Giants** at Yankee Stadium before their home games moved to New Jersey.

SPORTY SITES

Belmont Race Track The Belmont Stakes, the final leg of horse racing's Triple Crown, had its 150th running in June 2018.

Bethpage Black Course In 2002, the most difficult of the five courses at Bethpage State Park in Farmingdale became the first publicly owned and operated golf course to host the U.S. Open.

Madison Square Garden The world's most famous arena is home to the Knicks and the Rangers (and occasionally the Liberty).

National Baseball Hall of Fame and Museum Displays in Cooperstown range from artifacts to the recent history of each MLB team.

New Era Field The Bills' football stadium also hosted the NHL's first outdoor Winter Classic, in 2008.

STATE-MENT

"We're going to win Sunday, I'll guarantee you."

JOE NAMATH, making the most famous sports prediction ever. The Jets quarterback was speaking before Super Bowl III, in which his team was an 18-point underdog against the Baltimore Colts. Namath proved to be a man of his word. New York won 16–7.

147

NEW YORK

THE NUMBERS

42 — **UNIFORM NUMBER** of Jackie Robinson with the Brooklyn Dodgers. It is now retired across baseball in honor of the majors' first African-American player.

8 — **GOLF COURSES** in New York that have hosted the U.S. Open, including Shinnecock Hills in 2018.

4 — **CONSECUTIVE SUPER BOWL LOSSES** by the Buffalo Bills between 1991 and 1994, the most by an NFL team.

127 — **RUNNERS** in the first New York City Marathon, in 1970. In 2017, there were 51,307 participants, making it America's largest marathon.

FAN FAVORITES

KRISTAPS PORZINGIS
Knicks forward

In the basketball realm, a unicorn is a player whose skill set is so amazing it's almost impossible to believe it exists. Porzingis is one of the reasons the term was coined. At 7' 3", he constantly has fans saying, "How can a guy that big do *that*?" He's a vicious dunker and a three-point threat. He's sleek but scrappy. He's a great passer and an imposing shot blocker. Add it up and you have the most compelling Knick in years. Growing up in Latvia, Porzingis was enrolled in English classes at age 11 by a coach who could see that the NBA was in his future. Good move.

ODELL BECKHAM JR.
Giants wide receiver

Great receivers are usually described as having "great hands," but Beckham has made plenty of jaw-dropping catches using only one. With 38 touchdowns in 44 career games and more than 1,300 receiving yards in each of his three full seasons, Beckham is as steady as he is spectacular.

NOAH SYNDERGAARD
Mets pitcher

If you think Thor is mighty, check out his namesake. Syndergaard, who picked up the nickname Thor after posting a picture of himself dressed as the superhero, has a 102-mph fastball. Through his first three seasons, the 6' 6" Syndergaard struck out 418 batters in 364 innings.

HENRIK LUNDQVIST
Rangers goalie

Lundqvist comes from Sweden, where he grew up in a town of 1,000 people. But since 2005, King Henrik has ruled in the NHL's biggest market. The four-time All-Star reached 400 wins faster than any other goalie in history. He won the Vezina Trophy as the top netminder in the NHL in 2011–2012.

GREATEST MOMENT

FEBRUARY 22, 1980
Miracle on Ice

This was an upset that all of America could enjoy. At the Winter Olympics in Lake Placid, during the height of the Cold War, a meeting between the Soviet Union and the U.S. felt as if it was about more than hockey. The Soviet team, which had won five of the last six gold medals, was stocked with pro-quality players and was heavily favored against a U.S. team made up of college players. In fact, the Soviets had beaten the U.S. team 10–3 in an exhibition game a few weeks earlier. But the underdogs delivered the magic when the teams met in the medal round. The U.S. trailed 3–2 after two periods but tied the game on a power-play goal by Mark Johnson. The captain, Mike Eruzione, scored the go-ahead goal with 10 minutes left. As the clock approached zero, announcer Al Michaels delivered the call: "Do you believe in miracles? Yes!" The U.S. still had to win one more game for the gold (which it did, against Finland), but this stunner was the Games' most memorable moment.

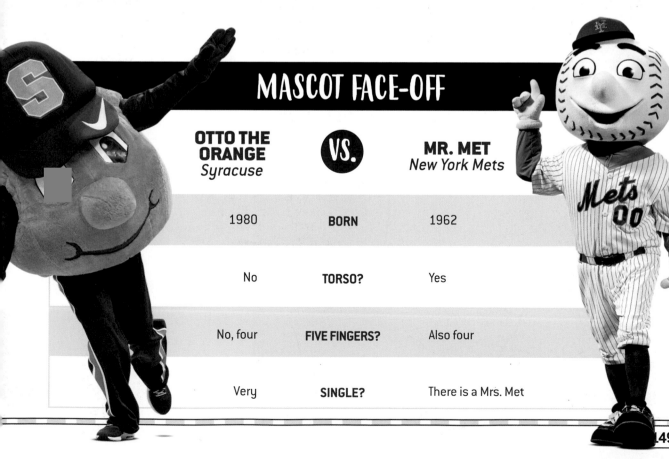

MASCOT FACE-OFF

OTTO THE ORANGE *Syracuse*	VS.	MR. MET *New York Mets*
1980	**BORN**	1962
No	**TORSO?**	Yes
No, four	**FIVE FINGERS?**	Also four
Very	**SINGLE?**	There is a Mrs. Met

149

COOL SCHOOLS

Syracuse

At Syracuse, 44 is a big number. It was worn by several legendary running backs: Hall of Famer Jim Brown, 1961 Heisman Trophy winner Ernie Davis, and three-time All-America Floyd Little. Brown also wore the number in basketball, as did Derrick Coleman, the No. 1 pick in the 1990 draft. Brown's best sport was lacrosse. The NCAA didn't begin crowning a national lacrosse champion until well after Brown left Syracuse, but the Orange have since won the tournament 11 times, most recently in 2009. So who's the greatest Orange athlete who didn't wear 44? That would be NBA star Carmelo Anthony *(above)*.

St. John's

The New York City school has accomplished plenty on the hardwood, but a national championship has eluded the Red Storm. The team, which plays several dates a year in Madison Square Garden, is in the top 10 all time in wins, many of which came under coach Lou Carnesecca, who was famous for his colorful sweaters. St. John's has produced two college players of the year, Chris Mullin and Walter Berry, along with NBA stars such as Mark Jackson (fourth all time in assists) and Ron Artest (the defensive maven now known as Metta World Peace). While basketball is king, the school did take a soccer title in 1996.

Cornell

If the sport involves nets and sticks, the Big Red have something to say about it. The Ithaca school won the NCAA's first-ever lacrosse championship in 1971, and two more later that decade. The hockey team enjoyed its greatest success between 1967 and 1972, when it went to four NCAA finals, winning twice. Cornell's most famous sports alum is Ken Dryden, one of the best goalies in NHL history. And in 1971, running back Ed Marinaro was a runner-up for the Heisman Trophy. He later found greater fame as an actor.

HOMEGROWN HEROES

JOHN MCENROE

The feisty tennis player, who grew up in the New York City borough of Queens, won four U.S. Opens and three Wimbledon championships.

JIM BROWN

Brown, raised in Manhasset, was an All-America in both football and lacrosse at Syracuse. For the Cleveland Browns he became the only NFL running back to average more than 100 yards a game for his career.

KAREEM ABDUL-JABBAR

The NBA's all-time leading scorer, who grew up in Manhattan, won three NCAA championships at UCLA and six pro titles for the Milwaukee Bucks and Los Angeles Lakers.

SANDY KOUFAX

From 1962 to 1966, the Brooklyn-born Koufax won five National League ERA titles and had a record of 111–34. He had an 0.95 ERA in four World Series.

LOU GEHRIG

The New York City native and Columbia alum won the 1934 Triple Crown. He hit a record 23 grand slams while playing in 2,130 consecutive games for the Yankees.

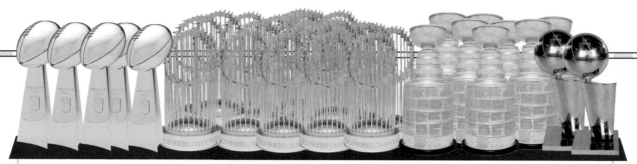

NEW YORK'S TROPHY SHELF

5 Super Bowl Wins The Jets' lone title came on a massive upset of the Colts in 1969. The Giants have won four times, including in 1991, when Buffalo's last-second field goal sailed wide, and 2008, when they beat the 18–0 Patriots.

29 World Series Championships The Yankees have the most World Series wins of any team, with 27. The Mets, who began play in 1962, won the World Series in 1969 and 1986. The Giants won five World Series in New York, and the Dodgers one in Brooklyn, but those trophies went west when the teams moved to California in 1957.

8 Stanley Cup Wins The Rangers lifted the Stanley Cup in 1928, 1933, 1940, and (after a really, really long wait) 1994. The Islanders won their four championships in consecutive years, from 1980 to 1983, behind stars such as Denis Potvin, Mike Bossy, and Bryan Trottier.

2 NBA Championships The Knicks won titles in 1970 and 1973 with teams featuring Walt Frazier, Bill Bradley, and Willis Reed. A hobbled Reed sinking two baskets and sparking his team to victory in 1970 is one of the NBA's mythic moments.

ⓘ INSIDER INFO Two of sports' greatest coaches were raised in Brooklyn: Red Auerbach (nine NBA titles with the Boston Celtics) and Vince Lombardi (five championship seasons with the Green Bay Packers). Lombardi played on the offensive line at Fordham, where he was one of the famed Seven Blocks of Granite.

BIG EVENT

The U.S. Open

Of the four Grand Slam events in tennis, only one takes place in the United States. Since 1915, the Open has been held in Queens—first at the West Side Tennis Club in Forest Hills, and since 1978 at the USTA National Tennis Center in Flushing Meadows. Attendance for the two-week event approaches 700,000 spectators. The main stadium of the complex is named for Arthur Ashe, who won the Open in 1968. In 1973, the Open became the first major tournament to award equal prize money to the men's and women's champions.

ENEMY OF THE STATE

BOSTON RED SOX

The Yankees' rivalry with their AL East foes is baseball's fiercest, and the Mets won one of their two World Series at the expense of the boys from Beantown.

ⓘ INSIDER INFO
Babe Ruth most likely hit his first professional home run as a 19-year-old playing minor league ball at the Cape Fear Fair Ground.

DURHAM

CHARLOTTE MOTOR SPEEDWAY

CHAPEL HILL

CAMER INDOC STADIC Duke b Devi

CHARLOTTE

BANK OF AMERICA STADIUM
Carolina Panthers

DEAN SMITH CENTER
North Carolina Tar Heels

SPECTRUM CENTER
Charlotte Hornets

PNC ARENA
Carolina Hurricanes

NASCAR HALL OF FAME

PINEHURST RESORT

RALEIGH

SPORTY SITES

Bank of America Stadium The home of the Carolina Panthers also hosts college football's annual Belk Bowl. In the 2017 edition, Wake Forest topped Texas A&M in a shootout 55–52.

Cameron Indoor Stadium With a seating capacity of 9,314, tickets to Blue Devils basketball can be hard to come by.

Charlotte Motor Speedway In a state rich with racetracks, this is the biggest, with a seating capacity of 89,000.

Dean Smith Center Also known as the Dean Dome, the 21,750-seat basketball arena is named for North Carolina's late coach, winner of 879 games.

◀ **NASCAR Hall of Fame** Attractions at the Charlotte shrine, which opened in 2010, include Glory Road, a banked section of track with classic race cars.

Pinehurst Resort There are nine golf courses here, and the most famous is No. 2, which in 2014 hosted both the men's and women's U.S. Opens.

PNC Arena See the Hurricanes on ice and N.C. State basketball at this Raleigh arena.

Spectrum Center The home of the Hornets opened in 2005, when the team was known as the Charlotte Bobcats.

NORTH CAROLINA'S TROPHY SHELF

1 Stanley Cup Win

In the relatively brief history of pro sports in North Carolina, the Hurricanes have brought home the only title, topping the Edmonton Oilers in 2006 behind playoff MVP goaltender Cam Ward.

ⓘ INSIDER INFO In the most talked-about high school roster decision ever, in 1978, Michael Jordan didn't make the varsity basketball team as a sophomore at Emsley A. Laney High.

NORTH CAROLINA

Richard Petty

Here's a story from when Richard Petty was a 21-year-old NASCAR rookie. In his second race he was competing in a field that included his father, three-time NASCAR champion Lee Petty. His dad was gunning for the lead and coming up from behind when, as Richard said, "Daddy thought I was in the way, so he hit me. I ran into the wall, tore it all up." How did he feel about his dad's rough tactics? "Man, to a 21-year-old kid who had never done anything, all of it felt good." Petty did plenty after that. He won a record 200 races and seven NASCAR championships, and became CEO of Richard Petty Motorsports. Also, he has a pretty cool nickname: the King. He and his family are celebrated in the Richard Petty Museum in his hometown of Level Cross.

PRO TEAMS

NFL	Carolina Panthers
NBA	Charlotte Hornets
NHL	Carolina Hurricanes

The **Hurricanes** arrived in 1997 from Hartford, where the team was known as the Whalers.

153

COOL SCHOOLS

Duke

Around the country Duke basketball can arouse great passion—and not all of it is positive. That's what happens when a small private school reels in so many top recruits. But even the haters have to agree that the Blue Devils have one of the finest home arenas in the sport (cozy Cameron Indoor Stadium), a passionate set of fans (the Cameron Crazies), and a coach who knows what to do with all that talent. Mike Krzyzewski has won the most games in the history of college basketball, and in his 37 years in Durham, he has led the program to five NCAA titles and reached 16 Final Fours. The list of great players goes on and on: Bobby Hurley, Grant Hill, Elton Brand, Shane Battier, Luol Deng, Brandon Ingram, Jayson Tatum. . . . Beyond basketball, Duke's second-strongest sport is lacrosse: The team won national championships in 2010, 2013, and 2014.

FAMOUS BLUE DEVILS

J.J. REDICK
One of the NBA's top three-point shooters

KYRIE IRVING
Won an NBA title in Cleveland

North Carolina

Ever notice how a basketball player who scores a basket points to the player who passed him the ball to thank him? That gentlemanly tradition was started by North Carolina coach Dean Smith, who coached the Tar Heels from 1961 through 1997. He defined a program that has won six NCAA titles, gone to a record 20 Finals Fours, and produced hoops luminaries such as Michael Jordan, James Worthy, Vince Carter, and Kenny Smith. The football team featured two alltime NFL sack masters in Lawrence Taylor and Julius Peppers, as well as current Chicago Bears quarterback Mitchell Trubisky. As impressive as those two programs are, they can't compare with the accomplishments of the school's women's soccer team. Led by coach Anson Dorrance, it has won 21 national titles and turned out U.S. national team stars such as Mia Hamm, Kristine Lilly, and Tobin Heath.

FAMOUS TAR HEELS

LAWRENCE TAYLOR
NFL's most feared pass rusher ever

MIA HAMM
Two-time World Cup winner

North Carolina State

The Wolfpack's NCAA basketball titles both involved major upsets. The 1974 team, led by David Thompson, knocked off UCLA, which had won seven championships in a row. Nine years later, coach Jim Valvano's group beat a Houston team with two future NBA Hall of Famers, Hakeem Olajuwon and Clyde Drexler. Los Angeles Chargers QB Philip Rivers is the pride of Wolfpack football.

Wake Forest

The athletic legacy of the Demon Deacons is defined by two of the best players in recent pro basketball history. Tim Duncan spent four years on the Winston-Salem campus before becoming a five-time NBA champion with the San Antonio Spurs. And point guard Chris Paul played two seasons at the school before heading to the NBA, where he has led the league in assists four times while making nine All-Star teams.

BIG EVENT

Duke vs. North Carolina

The schools are 10 miles apart. Duke is a private school that draws many students from out of state, while Carolina is a state school with more local students. One, if not both, is usually a top contender for the national championship. These are the essential ingredients for one of the tastiest rivalries in sports, which is rekindled (at least) twice a year. The Tar Heels have the alltime edge, having won 137 of the 248 matchups.

ⓘ INSIDER INFO
Tim Duncan was the 1997 national player of the year at Wake Forest. But in his first game as a Demon Deacon he scored zero points.

MASCOT FACE-OFF

	DEMON DEACON *Wake Forest*	VS.	BLUE DEVIL *Duke*	VS.	THE PIRATE *East Carolina*
BORN	1941		1930s		1983
BASED ON	Baptist deacon		Satan		Blackbeard
ACCESSORY	Motorcycle		Basketball uniform		Sword
DEMONIC?	Not at all, which is strange given his name		Yes—demonically peppy		Wouldn't want to meet him in a dark alley

NORTH CAROLINA

158

RECEPTIONS by Zay Jones for East Carolina in 2016, an NCAA record for a single season. Jones now plays for the Buffalo Bills.

5

RANK of the Michigan team that was upset by Appalachian State in football in 2007. It's still the only time an FCS school has beaten a ranked FBS team.

7

NASCAR CHAMPIONSHIPS won by Dale Earnhardt Sr. of Kannapolis, tied with Richard Petty for the most ever.

5' 3"

HEIGHT of Muggsy Bogues, who was all-ACC at Wake Forest and played 10 of his 14 NBA seasons in Charlotte.

FAN FAVORITES

KEMBA WALKER
Hornets point guard

He hasn't gotten much national attention, because his team has yet to make a serious postseason run, but the 6' 1" Walker has developed into one of the NBA's elite point guards. He was drafted out of Connecticut in 2011 after leading the Huskies to an NCAA title and being named the tournament's Most Outstanding Player. As a pro, Walker has proved to be equally clutch, hitting many buzzer beaters. In 2016–2017, he averaged a career-best 23.2 points along with 5.5 assists and 3.9 rebounds. That was good enough to land him a spot on his first All-Star team.

CAM NEWTON
Panthers quarterback

The 6' 6", 260-pound Newton threatened defenses more with his legs than his arm as a rookie in 2011, when he rushed for 706 yards. By 2015, he had matured as a passer and become one of the NFL's most complete QBs. He won the league's MVP award and led the Panthers to a 15–1 record and a Super Bowl berth.

JEFF SKINNER
Hurricanes forward

Skinner became the youngest player to appear in an All-Star Game—not just in the NHL but in any sport—when he represented the Hurricanes in 2011 at the tender age of 18. He was also honored as rookie of the year that season. Since then the sniper has been a steady scoring threat for the Hurricanes.

GREATEST MOMENT

MARCH 28, 1992
Christian Laettner's Buzzer Beater

Of all the crazy endings in March Madness, this was the maddest. In the East Regional final, Duke was trailing Kentucky 103–102 with 2.1 seconds left in overtime. Grant Hill's inbounds pass traveled nearly the length of the court into the hands of Christian Laettner. The big man caught the ball at the free throw line, dribbled once, turned, and hit the jump shot as the buzzer sounded. Duke went on to win the NCAA title, and Laettner's shot remains the most memorable buzzer beater in history.

HOMEGROWN HEROES

MICHAEL JORDAN
His game-winning jump shot gave North Carolina an NCAA title in 1982. After a legendary NBA career, Jordan, from Wilmington, returned to his home state and became the owner of the Charlotte Hornets.

STEPHEN CURRY
The son of former Hornets marksman Dell Curry, Steph led Davidson to the Elite Eight in 2008 before becoming a two-time NBA MVP with the Golden State Warriors.

ROY WILLIAMS
The native of Marion coached North Carolina to three NCAA basketball titles, most recently in 2017. He was an assistant to Dean Smith on the Tar Heels' 1982 championship team, and he twice coached Kansas in NCAA title games.

ENEMY OF THE STATE

ATLANTA FALCONS
Either the Panthers or the Dirty Birds has won the NFC South in six of the past eight seasons. Their matchups usually have playoff implications.

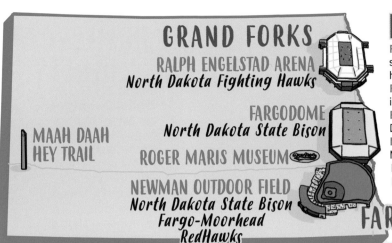

GRAND FORKS

RALPH ENGELSTAD ARENA
North Dakota Fighting Hawks

MAAH DAAH HEY TRAIL

FARGODOME
North Dakota State Bison

ROGER MARIS MUSEUM

NEWMAN OUTDOOR FIELD
*North Dakota State Bison
Fargo-Moorhead
RedHawks*

FARGO

SPORTY SITES

FargoDome The home of North Dakota State football seats 19,000. The NBA's Minnesota Timberwolves have played preseason games there.

Roger Maris Museum A shrine to the Yankees great is located in a shopping mall in Fargo.

Ralph Engelstad Arena The 11,640-seat North Dakota hockey arena is also known as the Ralph.

Newman Outdoor Field The field is shared by North Dakota State baseball and the independent Fargo-Moorhead RedHawks.

Maah Daah Hey Trail The scenic course hosts road races ranging from 3.1 to 106 miles.

★NORTH DAKOTA STAR★

Carson Wentz

It's about 1,400 miles from Fargo to Philadelphia, but at Eagles home games you can usually find fans waving the flag of the North Dakota State Bison. They've made the journey to cheer on Carson Wentz. From Bismarck, Wentz led the Bison to FCS national titles in 2014 and 2015 before ascending to the big time. The No. 2 overall pick in the 2016 draft, Wentz was a starter—and a winner—from Week 1. In his second season he was a top MVP contender before tearing his ACL in a Week 14 loss. Despite missing three games he still finished second in the NFL in touchdown passes, with 33 (against only seven interceptions). Wentz made the leap from North Dakota State to the NFL seem not so big at all.

NORTH DAKOTA

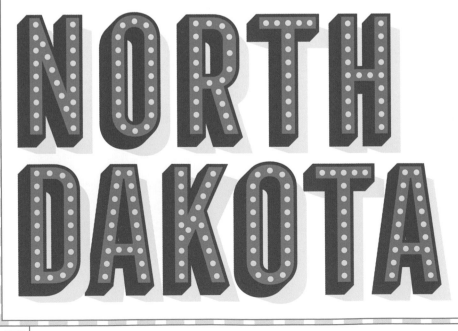

HOMEGROWN HEROES

ROGER MARIS

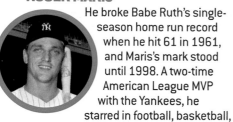

He broke Babe Ruth's single-season home run record when he hit 61 in 1961, and Maris's mark stood until 1998. A two-time American League MVP with the Yankees, he starred in football, basketball, and track as a high schooler in Fargo, playing baseball only with the American Legion during the summer.

PHIL JACKSON

Raised in Williston, the Zen Master won two NBA titles as a New York Knicks player and 11 more rings as a coach. (He won six with the Chicago Bulls and five with the Los Angeles Lakers.) Jackson was known for his unconventional approach and would assign his players books to read on topics unrelated to basketball.

STATE-MENT

"If you meet the Buddha in the lane, feed him the ball."

PHIL JACKSON

🛈 **INSIDER INFO** The first North Dakotan to play in the NHL was Cliff (Fido) Purpur. When the U.S. Hockey Hall of Fame inductee died in 2008, his funeral procession on the streets of Grand Forks was led by a Zamboni.

North Dakota

One of America's least populous states is home to the school that leads the NCAA in hockey attendance. That's because if you come to their spacious arena you're going to see top-level talent. The Fighting Hawks have had 22 finalists for the Hobey Baker Award, which is given to the top college player, including future NHL stars Zach Parise and T.J. Oshie. Those two also played against another former North Dakota star, Jonathan Toews, at the 2014 Olympics. Before they were in Sochi, they were all in Grand Forks.

North Dakota State

It's appropriate that North Dakota State wears green and yellow, because the Bison have racked up titles like the Green Bay Packers have. In addition to Carson Wentz, players in the NFL include Indianapolis Colts tackle Joe Haeg and Denver Broncos tackle Billy Turner. In basketball, the men's team has made it to three NCAA tournaments, while the women have won five Division II titles, between 1991 and 1996.

NORTH DAKOTA'S TROPHY SHELF

14 NCAA Football Championships Before 2004, North Dakota State played in Division II, winning eight championships. After moving up to Division I FCS, the Bison have won six titles in seven years, starting in 2011.

8 NCAA Hockey Championships Following titles in 1959 and 1963, North Dakota went through a dry spell. But the Fighting Hawks resumed their winning ways in 1980 and have added six more championships, most recently in 2016.

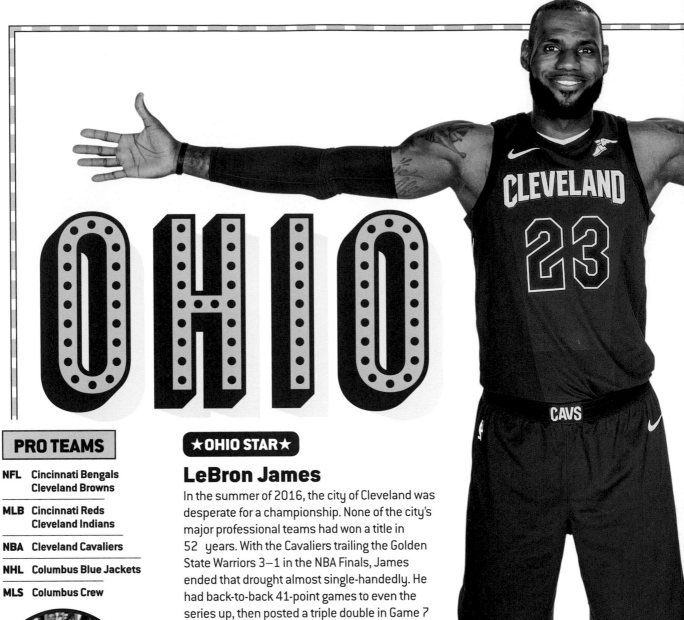

OHIO

PRO TEAMS

NFL	Cincinnati Bengals Cleveland Browns
MLB	Cincinnati Reds Cleveland Indians
NBA	Cleveland Cavaliers
NHL	Columbus Blue Jackets
MLS	Columbus Crew

The **Blue Jackets'** name has Civil War roots. Ohioans fought for the Union, whose blue jackets were made in Columbus.

★OHIO STAR★

LeBron James

In the summer of 2016, the city of Cleveland was desperate for a championship. None of the city's major professional teams had won a title in 52 years. With the Cavaliers trailing the Golden State Warriors 3–1 in the NBA Finals, James ended that drought almost single-handedly. He had back-to-back 41-point games to even the series up, then posted a triple double in Game 7 as Cleveland completed its remarkable comeback. James, who won three state championships at St. Vincent–St. Mary High in Akron, controversially left the Cavaliers twice in free agency. But in his 11 seasons with the team he took them to five Finals, including four in a row.

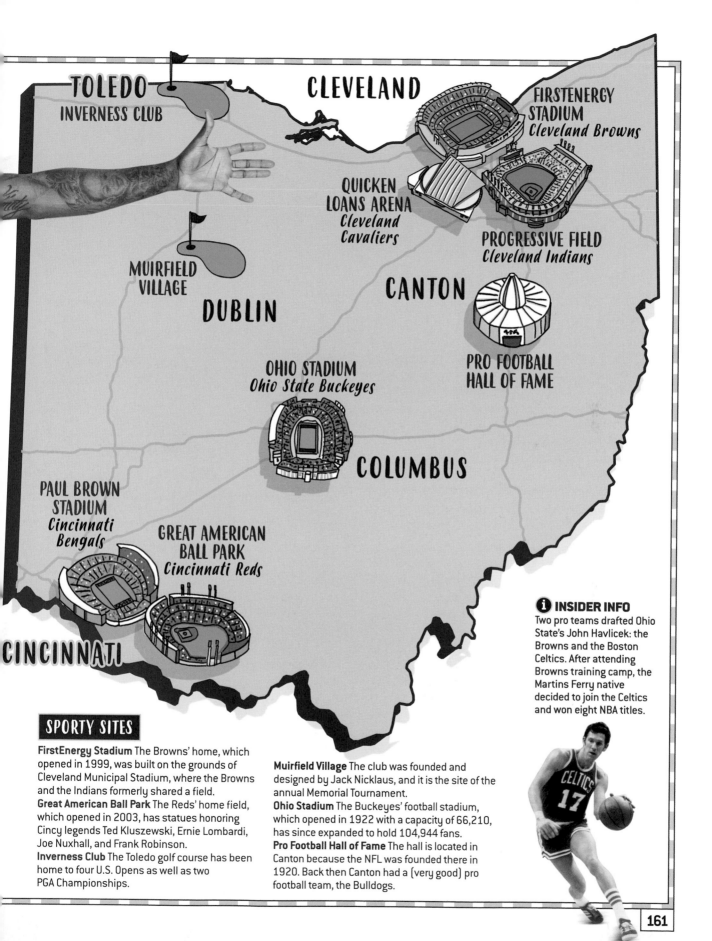

TOLEDO
INVERNESS CLUB

CLEVELAND

FIRSTENERGY STADIUM
Cleveland Browns

QUICKEN LOANS ARENA
Cleveland Cavaliers

PROGRESSIVE FIELD
Cleveland Indians

MUIRFIELD VILLAGE

DUBLIN

CANTON

OHIO STADIUM
Ohio State Buckeyes

PRO FOOTBALL HALL OF FAME

COLUMBUS

PAUL BROWN STADIUM
Cincinnati Bengals

GREAT AMERICAN BALL PARK
Cincinnati Reds

CINCINNATI

🛈 INSIDER INFO

Two pro teams drafted Ohio State's John Havlicek: the Browns and the Boston Celtics. After attending Browns training camp, the Martins Ferry native decided to join the Celtics and won eight NBA titles.

SPORTY SITES

FirstEnergy Stadium The Browns' home, which opened in 1999, was built on the grounds of Cleveland Municipal Stadium, where the Browns and the Indians formerly shared a field.
Great American Ball Park The Reds' home field, which opened in 2003, has statues honoring Cincy legends Ted Kluszewski, Ernie Lombardi, Joe Nuxhall, and Frank Robinson.
Inverness Club The Toledo golf course has been home to four U.S. Opens as well as two PGA Championships.

Muirfield Village The club was founded and designed by Jack Nicklaus, and it is the site of the annual Memorial Tournament.
Ohio Stadium The Buckeyes' football stadium, which opened in 1922 with a capacity of 66,210, has since expanded to hold 104,944 fans.
Pro Football Hall of Fame The hall is located in Canton because the NFL was founded there in 1920. Back then Canton had a (very good) pro football team, the Bulldogs.

OHIO

COOL SCHOOLS

Ohio State

We could fill this entire space listing the Buckeyes' accomplishments (eight national titles in football, for starters, and 26 more in synchronized swimming). Or we could talk about the scores of players who have gone on to the pros, or the legendary coaches, such as Woody Hayes (football) and Fred Taylor (basketball). But let's talk instead about the coolest aspect of Ohio State athletics: the marching band. At football games, the performance of "Script Ohio" with the sousaphone dotting the *i*, has long been one of the grand traditions of college sport. But the band also shows inventiveness as it develops new routines. Witness the show at halftime of a 2017 game in which the 195 members of the band aligned to form the image of a stick figure with boxing gloves hitting a punching bag with the logo of archrival Michigan draped across it.

Cincinnati

The bearcat is a small mammal native to East Asia, but it became the Cincinnati mascot in 1914, after a fullback whose last name was Baehr (nickname: Teddy) had a good game against Kentucky. The crowd chanted, "They may be Wildcats, but we have a Baehr-cat." The Cincinnati basketball team won two NCAA titles, in 1961 and 1962. It has sent several players to the pros, including alltime great Oscar Robertson, 2000 No. 1 overall pick Kenyon Martin, and current Lakers guard Lance Stephenson. NFL Pro Bowlers from the Bearcats' program include Kansas City Chiefs tight end Travis Kelce and New York Giants linebacker Connor Barwin. The program's best run was under coach Brian Kelly, who took the Bearcats to the 2009 Orange Bowl and the 2010 Sugar Bowl.

HOMEGROWN HEROES

URBAN MEYER

Meyer, who coached Ohio State to a football championship in 2014, has roots all over the state. He grew up in Ashtabula, where he was an outstanding football and baseball player. He was a defensive back at the University of Cincinnati, and his first head coaching job was at Bowling Green. He found success with Utah and Florida before returning home to the Buckeyes in 2012.

KAREEM HUNT

As a running back at Toledo, the Willoughby native led the nation in missed tackles as a senior. Drafted by the Kansas City Chiefs, he had 246 yards from scrimmage in his first NFL game, in 2017, a record for a debut. He finished the year with 1,327 yards rushing.

CRIS COLLINSWORTH

Collinsworth was born in Dayton, and though he moved to Florida as a child, he returned to star with the Cincinnati Bengals for eight seasons in the 1980s. As a wide receiver, he made three Pro Bowls. His first broadcasting job was on talk radio in Cincinnati, and the affable analyst has been in the booth for *Sunday Night Football* since 2009.

INSIDER INFO

Through 2017, Ohio State had 77 first-round NFL picks, second only to USC. Recent high picks include cornerback Marshon Lattimore by the New Orleans Saints in 2017 and running back Ezekiel Elliott *(above)* by the Dallas Cowboys in 2016.

GREATEST MOMENT

AUGUST 1936

Jesse Owens Wins Four Gold Medals

In 1936 the world was moving toward war. German dictator Adolf Hitler saw the Olympics, being held in his country's capital of Berlin, as an opportunity to assert the supremacy of the Aryan race. He expected his German athletes to dominate. That backdrop made Owens's performance in the Berlin Games one that is still talked about today. Owens, an African-American who grew up in Cleveland and competed for Ohio State, became the star of the Games. He won gold medals in the 100 meters, the 200 meters, the long jump, and the 4 × 100-meter relay. Owens's four-medal haul wouldn't be repeated by a U.S. athlete until 1984.

MASCOT FACE-OFF

SLIDER *Cleveland Indians*	VS.	MR. REDLEGS *Cincinnati Reds*
1990	**BORN**	2007
Some crazy fuschia	**THAT IS . . .**	One big mustache
A muppet	**LOOKS LIKE**	Mr. Met in disguise
Chief Wahoo	**PALS**	Gapper, Rosie Red, Mr. Red

OHIO

THE NUMBERS

22

CONSECUTIVE VICTORIES by the 2017 Cleveland Indians, the longest winning streak (without a tie) in major league history.

104.1

YARDS PER GAME that running back Jim Brown averaged for the Browns. He is the only NFL player to average more than 100 yards per game.

3

SEASONS in the 1990s that Cleveland had no pro football team. The Browns moved to Baltimore and became the Ravens. The new Browns began play in 1999.

2

HEISMAN TROPHIES won by Columbus native and Ohio State running back Archie Griffin. He is the only player ever to win two Heismans.

FAN FAVORITES

COREY KLUBER
Indians pitcher

Kluber won his first Cy Young Award in 2014, with an 18–9 record and a 2.44 earned run average. He bested those marks in 2017, as he went 18–4 with a 2.25 ERA and won his second Cy Young, the first Indian ever to do so. He roared through August and September, going 10–1 and leading Cleveland's push to the playoffs.

JOEY VOTTO
Reds first baseman

You have to love a guy with a good eye, and Joey Votto has led the majors in walks in 2013, 2015, and 2017. The 2010 NL MVP nearly won the award again in 2017, a season that he said was his best because he cut down on his strikeouts and showed improvement on defense.

MYLES GARRETT
Browns defensive end

The top overall pick in the 2017 draft had a sack in his first play from scrimmage, and seven in 11 games as a rookie. Garrett's rare strength and speed impressed Joe Thomas, the Browns' longtime All-Pro offensive lineman, who declared, "I've never seen a player that plays like he does."

A.J. GREEN
Bengals wide receiver

The lanky 6' 4" receiver has been a big-play target ever since he arrived in Cincinnati as the No. 4 pick out of Georgia in 2011. He made the Pro Bowl in each of his first seven seasons—the first Bengal ever to do that. If he's even a little bit open, please, just throw it to him. He'll get it.

BIG EVENT

Pro Football Hall of Fame Enshrinement Ceremony

Every NFL season begins with a look back, as the newest class of Hall of Famers receive their gold blazers and see their busts unveiled. The speeches in Canton can be funny, sentimental, and sometimes weighty. In 2017, running back LaDainian Tomlinson reflected on how his great-great-great-grandfather was a slave: "On America's team, let's not choose to be against one another. Let's choose to be for one another. My great-great-great grandfather had no choice. We have one."

OHIO'S TROPHY SHELF

7 World Series Championships The Reds have won five World Series trophies. The most recent was in 1990, but the most memorable were in 1975 and 1976, when the Big Red Machine teams were led by stars such as Johnny Bench, Joe Morgan, and Pete Rose. The Reds' other titles were in 1919 and 1940. The Indians have won two World Series, in 1920 and 1948.

1 NBA Championship The Cavaliers won the state's most recent championship in 2016.

1 MLS Cup Win In 2008, Columbus defeated the New York Red Bulls 3–1 in the MLS Cup.

ENEMY OF THE STATE

MICHIGAN FOOTBALL

One of the greatest rivalries in all of sports is Ohio State against Michigan. Whether the teams are great or merely good that year, The Game is a huge deal.

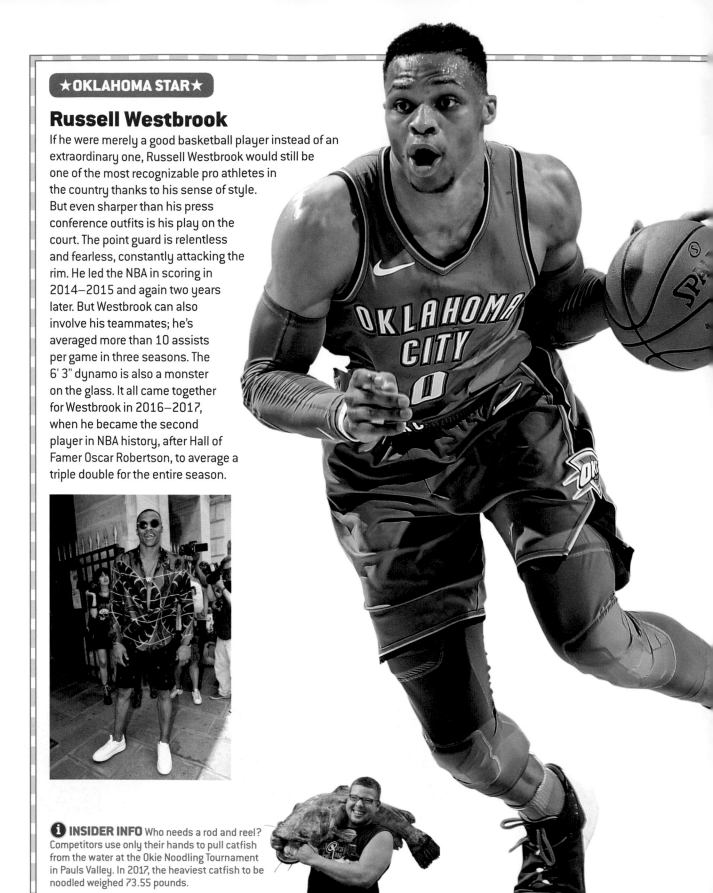

Russell Westbrook

If he were merely a good basketball player instead of an extraordinary one, Russell Westbrook would still be one of the most recognizable pro athletes in the country thanks to his sense of style. But even sharper than his press conference outfits is his play on the court. The point guard is relentless and fearless, constantly attacking the rim. He led the NBA in scoring in 2014–2015 and again two years later. But Westbrook can also involve his teammates; he's averaged more than 10 assists per game in three seasons. The 6' 3" dynamo is also a monster on the glass. It all came together for Westbrook in 2016–2017, when he became the second player in NBA history, after Hall of Famer Oscar Robertson, to average a triple double for the entire season.

ⓘ INSIDER INFO Who needs a rod and reel? Competitors use only their hands to pull catfish from the water at the Okie Noodling Tournament in Pauls Valley. In 2017, the heaviest catfish to be noodled weighed 73.55 pounds.

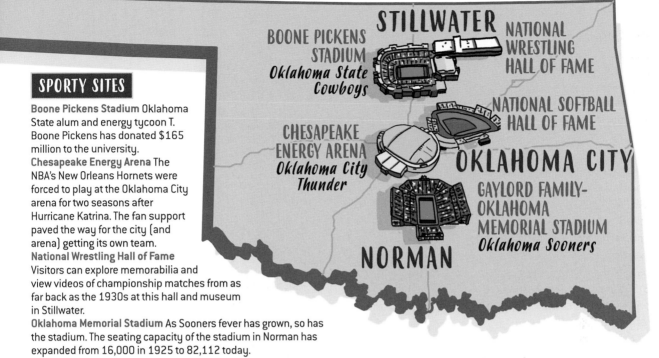

STILLWATER

BOONE PICKENS STADIUM
Oklahoma State Cowboys

NATIONAL WRESTLING HALL OF FAME

NATIONAL SOFTBALL HALL OF FAME

CHESAPEAKE ENERGY ARENA
Oklahoma City Thunder

OKLAHOMA CITY

GAYLORD FAMILY-OKLAHOMA MEMORIAL STADIUM
Oklahoma Sooners

NORMAN

SPORTY SITES

Boone Pickens Stadium Oklahoma State alum and energy tycoon T. Boone Pickens has donated $165 million to the university.

Chesapeake Energy Arena The NBA's New Orleans Hornets were forced to play at the Oklahoma City arena for two seasons after Hurricane Katrina. The fan support paved the way for the city (and arena) getting its own team.

National Wrestling Hall of Fame Visitors can explore memorabilia and view videos of championship matches from as far back as the 1930s at this hall and museum in Stillwater.

Oklahoma Memorial Stadium As Sooners fever has grown, so has the stadium. The seating capacity of the stadium in Norman has expanded from 16,000 in 1925 to 82,112 today.

OKLAHOMA

STATE-MENT

"**There are really only two plays: *Romeo and Juliet*, and put the darn ball in the basket.**"

ABE LEMONS, a native of Walters and a longtime Oklahoma City University basketball coach

PRO TEAMS

NBA Oklahoma City Thunder

Seattle's loss was OKC's gain when the SuperSonics moved to town and became the **Thunder** in 2008.

OKLAHOMA

Oklahoma

From the "Boomer Sooner" fight song to the Sooner Schooner wagon that is led across the football field by a pair of ponies (named Boomer and Sooner, of course), Oklahoma football is all about tradition. OU has won seven national titles and sent a who's who of stars to the NFL. Adrian Peterson, DeMarco Murray, Sam Bradford, and Trent Williams are just some of the former Sooners in the league now, and the program has produced two Hall of Famers: Lee Roy Selmon and Tommy McDonald. The Sooners' basketball team has reached the Final Four six times, including in 2016 (when the team was led by Buddy Hield) and 2009 (when Blake Griffin was the main weapon). OU has also won seven wrestling championships, but don't think that the Sooners are all about brute strength. Oklahoma's men's gymnastics team has won 11 national titles, and former Sooner Bart Conner won a pair of gold medals at the 1984 Olympics. The women's gymnastics team has three national titles of its own.

Oklahoma State

The teams in Stillwater were called the Tigers before changing to the Cowboys—which is how you end up with a cowboy mascot who wears orange and black. The two greatest players in the school's history were on the football team at the same time—and played the same position. For two years running back Barry Sanders *(right)* was a backup to Thurman Thomas. When Sanders finally took over as the featured back, he won the Heisman Trophy. Both players went on to make it to the Pro Football Hall of Fame. The most successful Cowboys program is wrestling, with 34 national titles. The golf team has won 10—and you can see PGA star Rickie Fowler wearing the OSU colors on the course every Sunday.

HOMEGROWN HEROES

MICKEY MANTLE
Nicknamed the Commerce Comet after his hometown, Mantle hit monster home runs that inspired people to start measuring their distances. His 565-foot shot in Washington's Griffith Stadium is the best remembered of the 536 homers he hit in his career.

DALLAS KEUCHEL
The 2015 Cy Young winner was undrafted when he graduated from Bishop Kelley High in Tulsa. In 2017, he went 14–5 for the world champion Houston Astros.

SHANNON MILLER
Raised in Edmond, Miller won seven Olympic medals in gymnastics, including golds in the 1996 Games for balance beam and team competition. That squad was the first U.S. gymnastics team to capture gold.

JOHNNY BENCH
Regarded by many as baseball's greatest catcher, the Binger native won the first of his two MVP awards at age 22 for the Cincinnati Reds. Bench regularly returns to his hometown, where there is a museum in his honor, to aid in fund-raising. He gave his first son the middle name Binger.

GREATEST MOMENT

1953 TO 1957
Oklahoma's 47-Game Winning Streak

Coach Bud Wilkinson's team started the 1953 season with a loss and a tie. The next time the Sooners knew anything but victory came on November 16, 1957, when they were beaten 7–0 by Notre Dame. Oklahoma's 47 wins in a row is still a college football record. Since then, the most consecutive wins by a team was Toledo's 35-game stretch from 1969 to 1971. That's a full season short of OU's achievement.

MASCOT FACE-OFF

PISTOL PETE *Oklahoma State*	VS.	CAPTAIN CANE *Tulsa*
1923	**BORN**	1977
Frank Eaton, a U.S. Marshal	**INSPIRATION**	Team is Golden Hurricane
Scofflaws	**CONTROLS**	The weather, allegedly
Just a man in cowboy gear (giant head added in 1958)	**OLD COSTUME**	Tried to look like weather itself (didn't work)

OKLAHOMA

5 CONSECUTIVE HALL OF FAMERS struck out by Carl Hubbell of Meeker in the 1934 All-Star Game: Babe Ruth, Lou Gehrig, Jimmie Foxx, Al Simmons, and Joe Cronin.

6 SOONERS to win the Heisman Trophy: Baker Mayfield, Sam Bradford, Jason White, Billy Sims, Steve Owens, and Billy Vessels.

3 NFL HALL OF FAMERS who went to the University of Tulsa: receiver Steve Largent, tackle Bob St. Clair, and general manager Jim Finks.

4 GAMES that Troy Aikman of Henryetta *(below)* started at Oklahoma before transferring to UCLA.

BIG EVENT

Women's College World Series

The NCAA began staging a world series for softball in 1982, and since 1990, Oklahoma City has been the tournament's home base. The tournament takes place at USA Softball Hall of Fame Stadium—which, as you may have guessed, is right by the Softball Hall of Fame. The Sooners have cashed in on the home state advantage to win four championships, including consecutive titles in 2016, when they beat Auburn, and 2017, over Florida.

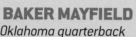

FAN FAVORITES

STEVEN ADAMS
Thunder center

The big man (7 feet) came to Oklahoma City by way of New Zealand. While he was considered a raw prospect after his one year of college in Pittsburgh, he has developed into one of the NBA's most reliable centers. Adams is the youngest of 18 siblings. His father was 6' 11", and many of his siblings are tall as well. Adams's sister Valerie is 6' 4" and won two Olympic medals in shot put for New Zealand.

ⓘ INSIDER INFO He has a town named after him in Pennsylvania, but Jim Thorpe, who played pro football and baseball and won the decathlon and pentathlon at the 1912 Olympics, was born in Prague, Oklahoma.

BAKER MAYFIELD
Oklahoma quarterback

The legend of Baker Mayfield is this: He walked on at Texas Tech and immediately became the starting quarterback. He then left the school, showed up at Oklahoma unannounced, and ultimately took over the starting job as a sophomore. He threw for at least 3,700 yards in each of his three seasons and won the Heisman Trophy as a senior after leading the Sooners to the College Football Playoff. Not a bad legend.

ⓘ INSIDER INFO The World Cow Chip Throwing Contest takes place annually in Beaver, with the winning throws approaching 190 feet. Experts advise throwing overhand rather than sidearm.

OKLAHOMA'S TROPHY SHELF

7 NCAA Football Championships Three coaches have led Oklahoma to national championships, and the school has won a title in four different decades. Bud Wilkinson's teams won three between 1950 and 1956. Barry Switzer also brought home three trophies, and Bob Stoops led the school to its most recent title, in 2000.

ENEMY OF THE STATE

TEXAS FOOTBALL
The Red River Showdown between Texas and Oklahoma is one of the top rivalries in football, and Oklahoma State has had several high-stakes battles with its Big 12 foe as well.

Clyde Drexler

The Trail Blazers have been to the NBA Finals three times, and twice they did it with Clyde (the Glide) Drexler leading the way. Few stars have played above the rim with Drexler's combination of power and grace. He could leap effortlessly and then throw down thunder. Drexler was an all-around performer, averaging 20.4 points, 6.1 rebounds, and 5.6 assists per game over his 15-year career. Teams led by other alltime greats (Magic Johnson's Lakers in the Western Conference playoffs, and Michael Jordan's Bulls and Isiah Thomas's Bad Boy Pistons in the Finals) kept Drexler from winning a ring in Portland. But the Glide showed he belonged with the game's best when he was named to the 1992 Olympic Dream Team, the first to feature professional players.

THE NUMBERS

2 NCAA HIGH JUMP TITLES won by Dick Fosbury of Oregon State. His "Fosbury flop" became the standard technique for high jumpers.

4 GOLD MEDALS won at the 1964 Olympics by swimmer Don Schollander of Lake Oswego, a record at the time.

2 WORLD RECORDS held by Ashton Eaton, in decathlon and heptathlon. The Portland native competed at the University of Oregon.

1 HEISMAN WINNER from Oregon State: quarterback Terry Baker, in 1962. He was the top pick in the 1963 NFL draft.

OREGON'S TROPHY SHELF

1 NBA Championship
In 1977, Bill Walton's Blazers topped the Philadelphia 76ers 4–2. A foot injury to Walton derailed a possible repeat.

1 MLS Cup Win The Timbers won the Cup in 2015, their fifth year of MLS play. They defeated the Columbus Crew 2–1 in the final game.

OREGON

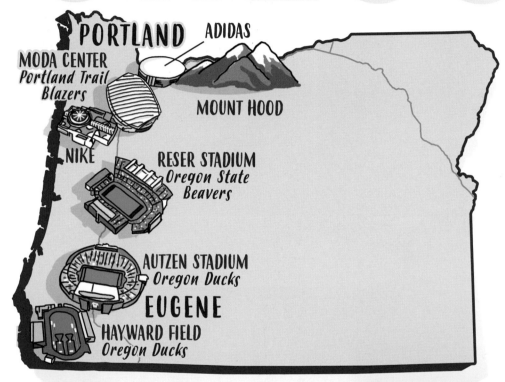

PORTLAND

ADIDAS

MODA CENTER
Portland Trail Blazers

MOUNT HOOD

NIKE

RESER STADIUM
Oregon State Beavers

AUTZEN STADIUM
Oregon Ducks

EUGENE

HAYWARD FIELD
Oregon Ducks

PRO TEAMS

NBA	Portland Trail Blazers
MLS	Portland Timbers

The **Timbers** were a team in the 1970s' North American Soccer League and two other leagues before being revived for MLS.

SPORTY SITES

Adidas This sportswear company is German, but its American headquarters are in Portland.

Autzen Stadium Ducks students cross the Willamette River by bridge to get from campus to football games.

Hayward Field The Eugene track stadium has been host to NCAA championships, Olympic trials, and U.S. championships.

Moda Center With a capacity of 19,980, the arena holds about 6,500 more fans than the previous home of the Trail Blazers, Memorial Coliseum.

Mount Hood The most climbed mountain in North America, located east of Portland, has an elevation of 11,250 feet.

Nike The sportswear behemoth, founded in 1964 and named after the Greek goddess of victory, is headquartered in Beaverton.

Reser Stadium The Beavers have played in this on-campus stadium for 65 years.

ⓘ INSIDER INFO The annual football game between Oregon and Oregon State is known as the Civil War. The Ducks won the 2017 game 69–10, the widest margin of victory in the 121 games of the series. The old mark had been set in their second meeting, in 1895, when Oregon won 44–0.

OREGON

COOL SCHOOLS

Oregon

The best word to characterize athletics at Oregon would be *speed*. The school has one of the top track programs—the men have won 17 NCAA titles in cross-country and indoor and outdoor track, while the women have 14 NCAA titles in those sports. On the football field the Ducks also go-go-go. Their success with an up-tempo style (they reached the 2015 national championship game) has influenced college and pro football. Quarterback Marcus Mariota of the Tennessee Titans is the biggest current NFL star from those recent teams. He followed in the footsteps of Ducks QBs Dan Fouts and Norm Van Brocklin, who are both in the Pro Football Hall of Fame.

Oregon State

Quite an amazing collection of talented (and often colorful) athletes has passed through Corvallis over the years. The Beavers had Chad Johnson, who as an NFL receiver with the Cincinnati Bengals changed his last name to Ochocinco to match his uniform number, 85. Their greatest basketball player was Gary Payton, an NBA Hall of Famer who earned the nickname the Glove because of his tight defense. Jacoby Ellsbury was the brightest star from the baseball team—which is OSU's most successful program. The school won NCAA baseball titles in 2006 and 2007. One of the stars from those teams, Darwin Barney, is now an infielder for the Texas Rangers.

ℹ INSIDER INFO
The largest relay race in the country is the Hood to Coast Relay. More than 1,000 teams of eight to 12 runners tackle the distance of 199 miles. All slots have been filled on the opening day of registration for the last 19 years.

MASCOT FACE-OFF

OREGON DUCK *University of Oregon*	VS.	TIMBER JOEY *Portland Timbers*
1947	**BORN**	1970s
FBS's only duck	**UNIQUE?**	Yes. That's a real chain saw.
Not so much	**RUGGED?**	So much
Dodged Disney legal action over resemblance to Donald	**BIG FEAT**	Saws off a log section when Timbers score

HOMEGROWN HEROES

KEVIN LOVE

The Cleveland Cavaliers forward grew up in Lake Oswego. In Little League he was teammates with another Oregon kid who went on to big things: Golden State Warriors guard Klay Thompson.

JACOBY ELLSBURY

The Yankees outfielder, who spent his early life on the Warm Springs Indian Reservation, is believed to be the first player of Navajo descent to make it to the majors.

STEVE PREFONTAINE

Prefontaine, born in Coos Bay, held U.S. records in multiple distances when he died in a car accident in 1975, at just 24 years old. His life has been the subject of two movies, and the annual Prefontaine Classic in Eugene is one of the top track meets in the U.S.

FAN FAVORITES

DAMIAN LILLARD AND C.J. MCCOLLUM
Trail Blazers guards

These teammates make up one of the most dangerous and fun-to-watch backcourts in the NBA. At 6' 3", they are both on the small side. And they each came to the league from colleges that aren't exactly hoops factories. Lillard *(far right)*, a three-time All-Star, attended Weber State. McCollum *(near right)* studied at Lehigh, where in addition to leading an upset of Duke in the 2012 NCAA tournament, he served as an assistant sports editor at the school newspaper.

DIEGO VALERI
Timbers midfielder

The high-scoring Valeri was named MLS MVP in 2017 after netting 21 goals and assisting on 11 others. The native of Argentina was the MLS Newcomer of the Year in 2013 and MLS Cup MVP in 2015. He's been named to the league's Best XI three times.

STATE-MENT

> "To give anything less than your best is to sacrifice the gift."

STEVE PREFONTAINE, who was revered for his all-out running style

ENEMY OF THE STATE

WASHINGTON FOOTBALL

Both Oregon and Oregon State vie for Pac-12 supremacy with the hated Huskies, their rival to the north.

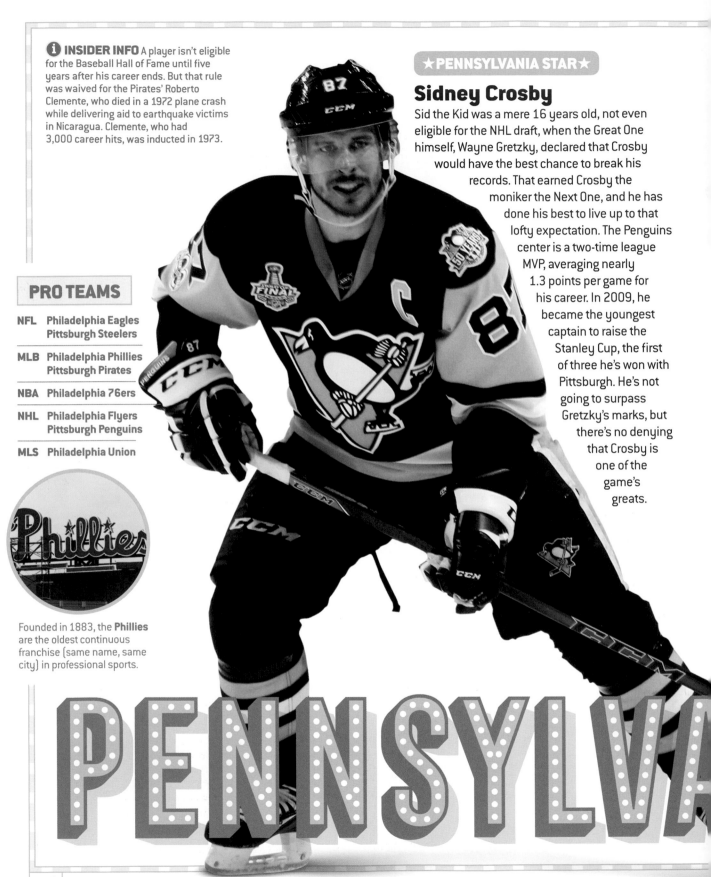

INSIDER INFO A player isn't eligible for the Baseball Hall of Fame until five years after his career ends. But that rule was waived for the Pirates' Roberto Clemente, who died in a 1972 plane crash while delivering aid to earthquake victims in Nicaragua. Clemente, who had 3,000 career hits, was inducted in 1973.

PRO TEAMS

NFL Philadelphia Eagles / Pittsburgh Steelers
MLB Philadelphia Phillies / Pittsburgh Pirates
NBA Philadelphia 76ers
NHL Philadelphia Flyers / Pittsburgh Penguins
MLS Philadelphia Union

Founded in 1883, the **Phillies** are the oldest continuous franchise (same name, same city) in professional sports.

★PENNSYLVANIA STAR★

Sidney Crosby

Sid the Kid was a mere 16 years old, not even eligible for the NHL draft, when the Great One himself, Wayne Gretzky, declared that Crosby would have the best chance to break his records. That earned Crosby the moniker the Next One, and he has done his best to live up to that lofty expectation. The Penguins center is a two-time league MVP, averaging nearly 1.3 points per game for his career. In 2009, he became the youngest captain to raise the Stanley Cup, the first of three he's won with Pittsburgh. He's not going to surpass Gretzky's marks, but there's no denying that Crosby is one of the game's greats.

PENNSYLVA

176

WILLIAMSPORT

LITTLE LEAGUE WORLD SERIES

POCONO RACEWAY

PITTSBURGH

OAKMONT COUNTRY CLUB

BEAVER STADIUM
Penn State Nittany Lions

JIM THORPE

THE PALESTRA
Penn Quakers

CITIZENS BANK PARK
Philadelphia Phillies

FRANKLIN FIELD
Penn Quakers

PNC PARK
Pittsburgh Pirates

HEINZ FIELD
Pittsburgh Steelers

PHILADELPHIA

WELLS FARGO CENTER
Philadelphia 76ers
Philadelphia Flyers

PPG PAINTS ARENA
Pittsburgh Penguins

LINCOLN FINANCIAL FIELD
Philadelphia Eagles

STATE-MENT

"[Teammate Chris Long and I] were talking at lunch. Thought it'd be a cool idea, really funny, so we went to Amazon and got it."

LANE JOHNSON, Eagles offensive lineman, on the idea to wear dog masks after the Eagles were made underdogs at home for a playoff game. The masks became a craze, and the Eagles went on to win the 2018 Super Bowl. They were underdogs in every postseason game.

SPORTY SIGHTS

Beaver Stadium Named for former governor James Beaver, Penn State's 106,572-seat stadium is the country's second largest.
Franklin Field The Eagles played for 13 seasons and won the 1960 NFL title at the current home of Penn football. The University of Pennsylvania stadium also hosts the Penn Relays track meet.
Jim Thorpe The town of Mauch Chunk changed its name to Jim Thorpe after Thorpe's family agreed that he would be buried there. The town hoped that the renowned athlete's grave site would attract tourists.
Oakmont Country Club Nine U.S. Opens have been held at the suburban Pittsburgh golf club.
PNC Park The Pirates' stadium, with its view of the Pittsburgh skyline beyond the outfield wall, is one of baseball's most picturesque.
Pocono Raceway With its three severe turns, the track—which has hosted IndyCar and NASCAR events—is known as the Tricky Triangle.
World of Little League Museum The museum is located in Williamsport, site of the Little League World Series.

ⓘ INSIDER INFO Even when they wear their throwback uniforms, the Steelers still take the field in black and yellow. Those are the same colors worn by Pittsburgh's other two major pro squads, the Penguins and the Pirates.

PENNSYLVANIA

3.1

WAGNER, PITTSBURG

MILLION DOLLARS paid at auction in 2016 for a 1911 baseball card of the Pirates' Honus Wagner, of Carnegie. That's a record for a piece of sports memorabilia.

153

MEETINGS between Lehigh and Lafayette as of 2017, making their rivalry the most played in college football. The eastern Pennsylvania schools first met in 1884.

11

DIVISION I WRESTLING PROGRAMS at Pennsylvania colleges, the most of any state.

17

AGE at which Christian Pulisic, of Hershey, scored against Bolivia in 2016, making him the youngest U.S. player with a goal in international competition.

FAN FAVORITES

EVGENI MALKIN
Penguins center

It's nice to have more than one elite-level center, a situation the Penguins are blessed with. Malkin has twice led the NHL in scoring, in 2008–2009 and again in 2011–2012. Fellow center Sidney Crosby missed much of the latter season because of concussions, and Malkin was named the NHL MVP. He was also the playoff MVP after the Penguins won the Stanley Cup in 2009.

JOEL EMBIID
76ers center

Because of injuries, the gregarious big man from Cameroon missed two years after he was drafted in 2014. That may explain why he seems to take so much joy in simply playing the game. The All-Star is the face of the 76ers' rebuilding "Process," and he gives them reason to feel good about the future.

ANTONIO BROWN
Steelers wide receiver

A sixth-round pick out of Central Michigan in 2010, the 5' 10" speedster blossomed into a four-time All-Pro. Brown—whose father was an Arena Football League legend—has twice led the NFL in receiving yards, and in three seasons he's averaged more than 100 yards per game.

CARSON WENTZ
Eagles quarterback

The quarterback led the Eagles to an 11–2 record in 2017 before a season-ending ACL tear meant he had to watch from the sidelines as his team finally won its first Super Bowl. Wentz threw for 33 TDs and only seven interceptions and was regarded as an NFL MVP favorite before the injury.

INSIDER INFO
Western Pennsylvania is regarded as the cradle of quarterbacks. Hall of Famers from there include Joe Montana, Johnny Unitas, Joe Namath, Dan Marino, Jim Kelly, and George Blanda.

BIG EVENT

Little League Baseball World Series

The only thing little about this Williamsport event is the name. In its 71 years, the competition between U.S. and international teams has grown into a phenomenon, with games now broadcast on ESPN. The highest attendance was in 2015, when nearly half a million people watched 32 games. That's what you get when you have a great event—and free admission.

MASCOT FACE-OFF

NITTANY LION *Penn State*	VS.	HAWK *St. Joe's*
1907	BORN	1956
Scarf	ACCESSORY	None whatsoever
One-armed push-ups	FEAT	Nonstop wing flapping
Crowd surfing has its hazards, but . . .	HARDER JOB?	. . . flapping your arms for three hours is pretty tough.

PENNSYLVANIA

Penn State

The team with the plainest uniforms in college football—no logos on the helmets, no names on the jerseys—has won two national championships and produced six Pro Football Hall of Famers. (Among the players enshrined are former Steelers greats Franco Harris and Jack Ham.) But it's about more than football in State College. The wrestling team won seven national titles between 2011 and 2018, and the volleyball programs have 12 championships (seven for the women and five for the men).

Pitt

Only three colleges have produced more Pro Football Hall of Famers than Pittsburgh. The former Panthers in the hall are quarterback Dan Marino, running backs Tony Dorsett and Curtis Martin, tight end Mike Ditka, offensive lineman Russ Grimm, defensive lineman Chris Doleman, and linebackers Rickey Jackson and Joe Schmidt. The list of Panthers active in the NFL is impressive, too, including Arizona Cardinals receiver Larry Fitzgerald, Buffalo Bills running back LeSean McCoy, and Los Angeles Rams defensive tackle Aaron Donald. It's not too hard to imagine Pitt's Hall contingent getting even bigger.

Temple

Temple, which began playing basketball in 1894, ranks fifth all time in wins, behind only Kentucky, Kansas, North Carolina, and Duke. In 1938, the Owls won an NIT title. (That was the year before the NCAA began staging its tournament.) Overall, Temple has made 32 tournament appearances, although the Owls haven't made it to the Final Four in 60 years. Football has been a secondary sport at the Philadelphia school, but in 2016, Temple won its second American Conference championship. The previous season, linebacker Tyler Matakevich was named the country's best defensive player.

HOMEGROWN HEROES

WILT CHAMBERLAIN
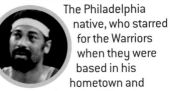
The Philadelphia native, who starred for the Warriors when they were based in his hometown and later the 76ers, has perhaps the most amazing statistics of any NBA player. He once scored 100 points in a game, and in 1961–1962, the four-time MVP averaged a record 50.4 points (and 25.7 rebounds) for the season.

ARNOLD PALMER
The Latrobe golfer, whose dad was a club pro, won seven major titles as his charm elevated golf's popularity. His adventurous shotmaking thrilled his legions of fans, known as Arnie's Army.

MO'NE DAVIS
At age 13, going up against boys, Davis showed what it really means to "throw like a girl." In 2014, the star pitcher of Philadelphia's Taney Dragons, with her 70-mph fastball, became the first girl to pitch a shutout at the Little League World Series.

LESEAN MCCOY
From Harrisburg, McCoy starred at the University of Pittsburgh before being drafted by the Eagles in 2009. He led the NFL in touchdowns in 2011 and rushing yards in 2013.

PENNSYLVANIA'S TROPHY SHELF

7 Super Bowl Wins Pittsburgh won four titles with its Steel Curtain teams from 1975 to 1980, and added two more in 2006 and 2009. The Eagles upset the New England Patriots to win their first Super Bowl in 2018.

2 NBA Championships The 76ers have won a pair, in 1967 and 1983. (The Warriors were the 1956 champions, while the franchise was still in Philadelphia.)

7 World Series Championships The Pirates have won the Fall Classic five times, but not since 1979.

The Phillies ended a 77-year drought with their first title in 1980. They added a second in 2008. (The Philadelphia Athletics won five World Series between 1910 and 1930 before leaving town in 1954.)

7 Stanley Cup Wins The Penguins have won three Stanley Cups during the Sidney Crosby years (2009, 2016, and 2017) and two with Mario Lemieux as star (1991 and 1992). The Philadelphia Flyers' physical Broad Street Bullies teams won back-to-back titles in 1974 and 1975.

GREATEST MOMENT

APRIL 1, 1985
Villanova's near-perfect game

Playing in the NCAA finals against a top-seeded team led by a future Hall of Famer, eighth-seed Villanova had no room for error. The Wildcats' plan for dealing with imposing Georgetown center Patrick Ewing was to be exceedingly patient, pass the ball, and create good shot opportunities. Villanova executed its plan brilliantly, making 22 of 28 shot attempts for a field goal percentage (78.6%) that remains a Final Four record. The Hoyas, who were the defending champs, kept the game tight until the end, but Villanova won 66–64.

ⓘ INSIDER INFO
Bethlehem's Chuck Bednarik was the last of the NFL's Sixty-Minute Men, who played both offense and defense. An All-America at Penn, Bednarik made a game-saving tackle in the Eagles' 1960 NFL title game win over Green Bay.

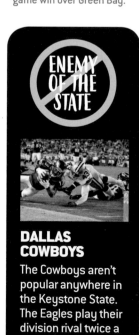

ENEMY OF THE STATE

DALLAS COWBOYS

The Cowboys aren't popular anywhere in the Keystone State. The Eagles play their division rival twice a year, and the Steelers have met Dallas in the Super Bowl three times.

RHODE ISLAND

MCCOY STADIUM
Pawtucket Red Sox

DUNKIN' DONUTS CENTER
Providence Friars

PROVIDENCE

INTERNATIONAL TENN
HALL OF FAME

RYAN CENTER
University of Rhode Island Rams

PRO TEAMS

Triple A Pawtucket Red Sox

Many future Red Sox stars have passed through **Pawtucket** on the way to Boston, which is only about 45 miles away.

ℹ️ **INSIDER INFO** The first-ever X Games were held in Newport in 1995. Competitions included skateboard, street luge, and bicycle stunts. Rhode Island hosted the event in 1996 as well.

SPORTY SITES

International Tennis Hall of Fame The hall is the site of an annual tournament that coincides with the enshrinement ceremony.
Dunkin' Donuts Center The 12,400-seat arena is the home court of the Providence Friars.
McCoy Stadium The dugouts are under the front row of seats, so Pawtucket Red Sox fans get autographs by "fishing" for them: They attach a ball to a string and drop it down to a player, then reel it in.
Ryan Center NBA stars such as Lamar Odom and Cuttino Mobley played their college ball at this University of Rhode Island 8,000-seat arena.

★RHODE ISLAND STAR★

Nap Lajoie

When Lajoie first started playing baseball in the 1890s, he still had a day job working as a driver for the Consolidated Livery Stable. He played semipro ball for different teams at the rate of two dollars a game, plus transportation. If it was a big game, maybe he'd get five bucks. LaJoie, from Woonsocket, wisely decided to make baseball his full-time job. He played 21 major league seasons with three teams. Very little got by this Hall of Famer, in the field at second base, or at the plate. The Slugging Cabby as he was known, led the majors in batting four times, including in 1901, when he won the American League Triple Crown.

HOMEGROWN HEROES

DAVEY LOPES

From East Providence, the second baseman was a four-time All-Star and an accomplished base stealer. He had 557 swipes in his career and led the league twice. He starred on Los Angeles Dodgers teams that reached four World Series, and he became a manager and coach after he retired.

BRAD FAXON

Raised in Barrington, Faxon won eight PGA Tour events and is now a successful broadcaster. He and another Rhode Island golfer, Billy Andrade, started a charity that has donated more than $19 million to children's organizations in the state and in southeastern Massachusetts.

BIG EVENT

Newport International Polo Series

Newport is home to America's first polo club, which was founded in 1876. Since 1992, the club has hosted this series featuring teams from around the world. Over the years, 33 countries have sent teams. Fun fact: The six periods in a polo match are called chukkers.

FAN FAVORITE

ED COOLEY
Providence Friars coach

Cooley grew up in Providence, where he twice was the state basketball player of the year. In 2011, he returned to coach his hometown school. His Friars have reached the NCAA tournament every year since 2014, with an opening-round win over USC in 2016. He coached NBA players Kris Dunn and Ricky Ledo.

THE NUMBERS

.302
BATTING AVERAGE in 2006 of Rocco Baldelli from Woonsocket, whose MLB career was cut short by a rare muscle disorder.

1
SUPER BOWL RING won by cornerback Will Blackmon, from Providence, when he was with the New York Giants.

33
INNINGS played in baseball's longest game, between the Pawtucket Red Sox and the Rochester Red Wings in 1981. Pawtucket eventually won 3–2.

CLEMSON MEMO
STAD
Clemson Ti

★SOUTH CAROLINA STAR★

A'ja Wilson

At Heathwood Hall Episcopal School in Columbia, Wilson was the nation's top girls' basketball player. She was recruited by every traditional power, including Connecticut and Tennessee. But the 6' 5" forward shocked them all when she held a press conference that was televised live to announce that she was staying at home to play for coach Dawn Staley at South Carolina. The Gamecocks had never been to the Women's Final Four, but Wilson led them there in 2015, her first season. In 2017, South Carolina went even further, winning its first national title. Wilson had 23 points, 10 rebounds, and four blocks in the title game against Mississippi. After shooting 59.4% for the tournament, she was named the Final Four's Most Outstanding Player.

GREATEST MOMENT

JANUARY 9, 2017
A Title for the Tigers

In the 2016 College Football Playoff National Championship, Alabama snatched the title away from Clemson with a 24-point fourth quarter. But in the rematch, the Tigers got their revenge. The lead changed hands three times in the fourth quarter, but Clemson went up for good when Deshaun Watson threw a two-yard touchdown pass to Hunter Renfrow with one second left. The Tigers won 35–31 to hand Bama coach Nick Saban his only title game defeat.

LITTLEJOHN
COLISEUM
*Clemson
Tigers*

LEMSON

GIBBS STADIUM
*Wofford College
Terriers*

COLUMBIA

COLONIAL
LIFE ARENA
*South Carolina
Gamecocks*

DARLINGTON
RACEWAY

WILLIAMS-BRICE
STADIUM
*South Carolina
Gamecocks*

CHARLESTON

JOHNSON
HAGOOD STADIUM
*The Citadel
Bulldogs*

HARBOUR TOWN
GOLF LINKS

PRO TEAMS

Class A
Charleston RiverDogs
Columbia Fireflies
Greenville Drive
Myrtle Beach Pelicans

The **RiverDogs**, now a New York Yankees affiliate, have also been tied to the Kansas City Royals and San Diego Padres.

SPORTY SITES

Darlington Raceway The "track too tough to tame" has an unusual oval shape because during construction in 1949, the landowner asked that a minnow pond not be disturbed.
Gibbs Stadium The home of the Wofford Terriers has hosted Carolina Panthers training camps.
Harbour Town Golf Links The course, with its signature red-and-white lighthouse, hosts an annual PGA tournament.
Johnson Hagood Stadium The Citadel plays home football games in a stadium named for a 19th-century South Carolina governor and Citadel alumnus.
Williams-Brice Stadium With a seating capacity of more than 80,000, University of South Carolina football is usually in the top 20 in the nation in attendance.

ⓘ **INSIDER INFO** You could play golf every day for months at Myrtle Beach without visiting the same course twice. The resort town has more than 100 courses.

SOUTH CAROLINA

Clemson

One of college football's most distinctive traditions is when Clemson players rub Howard's Rock (named for former coach Frank Howard) and then race downhill into Memorial Stadium. The intimidating stadium is nicknamed Death Valley, and it has claimed many victims in recent years. The Tigers have made the College Football Playoff in each of the past three seasons. In 2018, the school saw its first alum inducted into the Pro Football Hall of Fame when safety Brian Dawkins was enshrined. There are plenty of former Tigers in the NFL, most notably in Houston, where quarterback Deshaun Watson throws passes to receiver DeAndre Hopkins. Clemson is also strong in men's soccer (they won the title in 1987) and golf (2003).

South Carolina

The 2016–2017 season was a big one for Gamecocks hoops fans. The women's team won its first national title, and the men made a surprising run to the Final Four behind Sindarius Thornwell, who is now with the Los Angeles Clippers. But the football program is more star-studded. Running back George Rogers won the 1980 Heisman Trophy and was the top pick in the next year's NFL draft. Linebacker Jadeveon Clowney also went first overall, in the 2014 draft. And at Super Bowl LII, Eagles receiver Alshon Jeffery was covered by his former South Carolina roommate, Patriots cornerback Stephon Gilmore.

SOUTH CAROLINA'S TROPHY SHELF

2 NCAA Football Championships

Clemson won titles in 1981 and 2016. The 1981 team, coached by Danny Ford, went undefeated, including a win over Nebraska in the Orange Bowl.

1 NCAA Women's Basketball Championship
No. 1 seed South Carolina triumphed in 2017.

2 NCAA Baseball Championships

Under coach Ray Tanner, South Carolina won in 2010 and 2011 behind Most Outstanding Players Jackie Bradley Jr. and Scott Wingo.

FAN FAVORITES

DABO SWINNEY
Clemson football coach

He was born William Christopher Swinney, but he got his nickname when his brother tried to call him "that boy." As a player, Swinney was a walk-on receiver at Alabama. As a coach, the charismatic, enthusiastic Swinney took over Clemson during the 2008 season and elevated the Tigers program to the greatest heights in school history.

DUSTIN JOHNSON
PGA golfer

The long-driving, 6' 4" Columbia native, who played at Coastal Carolina University, has won 17 times on the PGA Tour, including the U.S. Open in 2016. He is one of only three players, along with Jack Nicklaus and Tiger Woods, with a win in each of their first 10 seasons.

HOMEGROWN HEROES

KEVIN GARNETT

From Mauldin, the Kid jumped directly from high school to the NBA in 1995. (He was the first player to have done that since the 1970s.) Garnett led the NBA in rebounding four times, made 12 all-defensive teams, and won an NBA title with the Boston Celtics in 2008.

MATT WIETERS

The catcher and four-time All-Star, now with the Washington Nationals, played at Stratford High in Goose Creek. His father, a former minor league pitcher, began teaching him to switch-hit at age five.

JUSTIN SMOAK

Another Goose Creek native, the former Gamecock is now a Blue Jays first baseman. Smoak made his first All-Star team in 2017, his eighth season in the majors, when he walloped a career-best 38 home runs.

JOE FRAZIER

Born in Laurel Bay, Smokin' Joe was a heavyweight boxing champion and the first fighter to beat the Greatest, Muhammad Ali. (Ali, however, won both of their rematches.) Frazier also won gold in the 1964 Olympics.

BIG EVENT

South Carolina–Clemson Football Game

At Clemson, the student body gets excited for this intrastate rivalry by holding a mock funeral for Cocky, the Gamecocks' mascot. Over in Columbia, South Carolina fans stage the Tiger Burn. Students from the school's chapter of the American Society of Mechanical Engineers build a tiger as big as 30 feet tall—and then set it on fire. On the field, Clemson holds a 69-42-4 lead in a series that dates back to 1896.

STATE-MENT

"When I was little, I was big."

WILLIAM (THE REFRIGERATOR) PERRY, an Aiken native and Clemson star who won a Super Bowl as a 335-pound defensive tackle with the 1985 Chicago Bears

ENEMY OF THE STATE

GEORGIA FOOTBALL

Georgia often has the edge in this SEC East border war, but South Carolina landed a blow when it clobbered the No. 5 Bulldogs in 2012.

STURGIS MOTORCYCLE MUSEUM & HALL OF FAME

MITCHELL

RAPID CITY

BROOKINGS

DANA J. DYKHOUSE STADIUM
South Dakota State Jackrabbits

CORN PALACE

DAKTRONICS

DAKOTADOME
South Dakota Coyotes

SPORTY SITES

Corn Palace The Dakota Wesleyan Tigers play in an arena that also hosts rodeos.

DakotaDome In Vermillion, the 10,000-seat dome is the home of South Dakota football. Offensive lineman Tom Compton of the Chicago Bears starred there.

Daktronics The maker of stadium video boards is based in Brookings. The company was started by South Dakota State engineering professors.

Dana J. Dykhouse Stadium Named for a former Jackrabbits player, South Dakota State's home field seats 19,340 fans.

Rapid City The town hosts the annual Lakota Nation Invitational. Schools from Native American reservations compete in basketball, cheerleading, archery, wrestling, and more.

Sturgis Motorcycle Museum & Hall of Fame Unusual and historic cycles have been on display here since 2001.

★SOUTH DAKOTA STAR★

Brock Lesnar

Growing up on a dairy farm in Webster, young Brock performed chores so taxing that he had two hernias before he was five years old. These days his heavy lifting involves opponents like Roman Reigns and Braun Strowman in the choreographed fights of the WWE. But he's also fought in contests where the outcomes weren't predetermined. At Minnesota he was the NCAA heavyweight wrestling champion, and he once interrupted his WWE career to try out for the Minnesota Vikings as a defensive tackle. (He made it to the final cut.) Lesnar also won a mixed martial arts title in the UFC.

SOUTH DAKOTA

THE NUMBERS

2 NBA TITLES won by Mitchell native Mike Miller. The sharpshooting guard was also the 2001 Rookie of the Year.

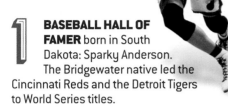

1 BASEBALL HALL OF FAMER born in South Dakota: Sparky Anderson. The Bridgewater native led the Cincinnati Reds and the Detroit Tigers to World Series titles.

1 PLAYER to ever pinch-hit for legendary slugger Ted Williams: Carroll Hardy of Sturgis. After Williams hit a foul off his foot, Hardy hit into a double play.

GREATEST MOMENT

OCTOBER 14, 1964
Mills's Medal

When he was asked after the 1964 Olympic 10,000-meter final if he had been worried about Billy Mills, prerace favorite Ron Clarke of Australia said, "Worried about him? I never heard of him." Mills, a Marine raised on the Pine Ridge Indian Reservation, raced past Clarke in the final stretch in Tokyo to become the only American ever to win gold in the 10,000. Mills's story was made into the 1983 movie *Running Brave*.

ⓘ INSIDER INFO Josh Heupel, who was the QB for Oklahoma when the Sooners won the national championship in 2000, grew up in Aberdeen. Heupel, who is now the coach at Central Florida, learned the game from his dad, who coached at Northern State.

HOMEGROWN HEROES

ADAM VINATIERI

The Yankton native and South Dakota State alum is the most clutch kicker in NFL history. Nicknamed Iceman, he's made two last-second Super Bowl–winning kicks. Vinatieri has played on four Super Bowl champion teams and ended the 2017 season as the NFL's second-highest scorer of all time.

STATE-MENT

"I'm grateful they value my experience as a basketball player and threw gender out the window."

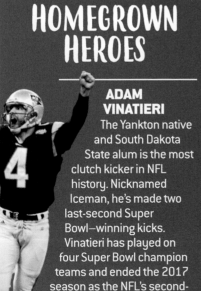

BECKY HAMMON, from Rapid City, on being hired by the San Antonio Spurs as the NBA's first full-time female assistant coach in 2014. Hammon had been a six-time All-Star in the WNBA.

TENNESSEE

PRO TEAMS

NFL Tennessee Titans

NBA Memphis Grizzlies

NHL Nashville Predators

After moving from Houston, the **Titans** played in Memphis for one season before settling in Nashville in 1998.

STATE-MENT

"For when the One Great Scorer comes to write against your name, He marks—not that you won or lost—but how you played the game."

GRANTLAND RICE, legendary sportswriter, who was born in Murfreesboro and graduated from Vanderbilt

ⓘ INSIDER INFO

Before Memphis had an NBA team called the Grizzlies, it had a football team of that name that played in the now-defunct World Football League in 1975. Believe it or not, the NBA team that arrived in 2001 was already named the Grizzlies when it came into the league in Vancouver.

NASHVILL[E]

BRIDGESTONE ARENA
Nashville Predators

MEMPHIS

AUTOZONE PARK
Memphis Redbirds

MEMORIAL GYMNASIUM
Vanderbilt Commodores

GRAND JUNCTION

FEDEX FORUM
Memphis Grizzlies

NATIONAL BIRD DOG MUSEUM

Pat Summitt

When young Pat was growing up on a farm in Montgomery County, her main form of recreation, after completing her many chores, was playing two-on-two basketball with her brothers in the hayloft.

At age 22, in 1974, the earliest days of intercollegiate women's basketball, she became Tennessee's head coach—and once again she had many chores. These included not only coaching but also taping ankles, driving the team van, and washing uniforms. But she pushed her players as her father had pushed her, and before long Summitt had built the first dynasty in women's college basketball. Her teams won eight national titles. When she left the program in 2012, she had 1,098 victories, the most for a Division I basketball coach, men's or women's.

SPORTY SITES

AutoZone Park The downtown stadium of the Memphis Redbirds, the Triple A affiliate of the St. Louis Cardinals, has a capacity of 10,000.
Bridgestone Arena The home of the Predators is also the primary venue for the SEC men's basketball tournament.
FedExForum The Grizzlies' home arena is nicknamed the Grindhouse because of the team's gritty, tough style of play. The name was given by guard Tony Allen, who made six All-Defensive Teams.
National Bird Dog Museum Celebrate the hunting companions at this museum in Grand Junction.

KNOXVILLE
NEYLAND STADIUM
Tennessee Volunteers

SAN
DIUM
nessee
ans
nessee
ate
ers

Neyland Stadium The visual signature of the Vols' home field is the orange-and-white checkerboard pattern in the end zones. That effect gets magnified when fans at the 102,455-seat stadium mirror the pattern by wearing orange and white in alternate sections.
Nissan Stadium The home of the Titans and Tennessee State football has also became a regular home field for the U.S. soccer team in international matches.
Memorial Gymnasium For the first football game at the 40,555-seat stadium, in 1922, the game ball was dropped from an airplane. The Commodores and the Michigan Wolverines played to a scoreless tie.

TENNESSEE

9
LENGTH, IN INCHES, of the saber-toothed tiger tooth found in Nashville in 1971, which inspired the Predators' nickname.

68
BABIES NAMED PEYTON born at the University of Tennessee Medical Center between 1996 and 1998, when Peyton Manning starred for UT. Only 10 had been given that name in the previous decade.

1
YARD by which Titans receiver Kevin Dyson missed scoring a potential game-tying touchdown when he was in the last play of the 2000 Super Bowl against the St. Louis Rams.

4
TOUCHDOWNS thrown by Todd Helton for Tennessee before he switched sports and became a five-time major league All-Star for the Colorado Rockies.

FAN FAVORITES

MARCUS MARIOTA
Titans quarterback

Many quarterbacks who ran frequently in college struggle with their transition to the NFL. But Mariota, the 2014 Heisman Trophy winner at Oregon, has demonstrated the throwing ability of a man who can lead the Tennessee offense for many years to come. In 2017, he threw for 3,232 yards and ran for 312 more as he led the Titans to their first playoff appearance since 2008.

P.K. SUBBAN
Predators defenseman

Born in Canada to parents from Jamaica and Montserrat, Subban brought a spark to Nashville when he was acquired from the Montreal Canadiens in 2016. The deft-passing, big-hitting defenseman with an outsized personality led the Predators to their first Stanley Cup appearance, in 2017.

MARC GASOL
Grizzlies center

In 2008, the Grizzlies acquired Gasol in a trade for another Gasol. Memphis sent Marc's brother Pau to the Los Angeles Lakers for a package that included Marc, who at the time was still playing in Europe. When Marc, a native of Spain, came to the U.S., the versatile scorer and passer developed into an All-Star for Memphis, just as Pau had before him.

GREATEST MOMENT

JANUARY 8, 2000
Music City Miracle

One of the all-time craziest endings to an NFL playoff game came in this wild-card matchup between Buffalo and Tennessee. The Bills had taken a 16–15 lead on a field goal with 16 seconds remaining. Buffalo's short kickoff was fielded by Titans fullback Lorenzo Neal, who handed it to tight end Frank Wycheck. Wycheck threw a pass across the field to wide receiver Kevin Dyson, who sprinted down the sideline for a 75-yard game-winning score.

MASCOT FACE-OFF

SMOKEY *Tennessee*	VS.	MR. COMMODORE *Vanderbilt*
1953	ESTABLISHED	1873
Bluetick coonhound	BREED	Naval
Yes	NATIVE TO TENNESSEE?	No. State is landlocked.
Checkerboard on cowl	BOARD GAME REFERENCE	Looks like he escaped from a Stratego box

TENNESSEE

COOL SCHOOLS

Tennessee

In Knoxville the big letter is *T*, the big song is "Rocky Top," and the biggest name to ever don the orange and white is Peyton Manning *(right)*. The quarterback endeared himself forever to fans in Knoxville when he passed up the chance to be the top pick in the NFL draft after his junior season to come back for one more year as a Volunteer. Manning came up short in his quest to bring Tennessee a national championship, but the Vols did win one in 1998, the

year after Peyton. (Tee Martin was the quarterback of that squad.) It was the school's first title since 1967. The Vols also won four championships between 1938 and 1951 under coach Robert Neyland, for whom the football stadium is named. That's an impressive haul, but it's nothing compared to what the Lady Vols have done on the basketball court. Coach Pat Summitt's teams won eight national titles and turned out such legendary players as Chamique Holdsclaw, Tamika Catchings, and Candace Parker, a two-time WNBA Most Valuable Player.

Vanderbilt

At Commodores football games, festivities begin when students drop an anchor at midfield. That's in honor of the school's seafaring nickname, which traces back to the university's founder, shipping magnate Cornelius Vanderbilt. The football program competes in the tough SEC East and has produced NFL talents such as quarterback Jay Cutler. He's not the only former Commodores athlete to make a living with his arm. The baseball program—which won the 2014 College World Series and was runner-up the next year—has sent numerous players to the majors, including Cy Young winner David Price (now of the Boston Red Sox) and All-Star Sonny Gray (New York Yankees).

Memphis

Here's a fun fact: Both kickers from Super Bowl LII (Philadelphia's Jake Elliott and New England's Stephen Gostkowski) were former Memphis Tigers. The school also produced Denver Broncos quarterback Paxton Lynch, a first-round pick in 2016. But Memphis is known more for its long basketball tradition. The program is led by coach Anfernee (Penny) Hardaway, who was the No. 4 pick of the 1993 draft and starred in a series of classic shoe commercials in which he interacted with his alter ego, a sassy doll named Lil Penny. The Tigers made it to the NCAA title game in 2008, when the team was led by future NBA Most Valuable Player Derrick Rose.

BIG EVENT

Under the Lights at Bristol

Twice a year NASCAR nation descends on the tiny town of Bristol. More than 150,000 people pack the stands at Bristol Motor Speedway, which is just over half a mile long, making it one of the circuit's most exciting tracks. The ultimate spectacle is the summer race, which is held on a Saturday night late in August. The race has been dominated by legends of racing: Darrell Waltrip has seven wins, Cale Yarborough won five, and Dale Earnhardt Sr. took the checkered flag four times.

ⓘ INSIDER INFO Pro Bowl linebacker Dont'a Hightower, who has won two championships each in the NFL (New England Patriots) and in college (Alabama), went to Marshall County High in Lewisburg.

ENEMY OF THE STATE

ALABAMA FOOTBALL

The Vols meet Bama on the third Saturday in October. The winner has been known to pass out cigars—and then self-report the NCAA violation for extra benefits.

HOMEGROWN HEROES

WILMA RUDOLPH

The Clarksville native had polio and pneumonia as a child and wore a brace on her left leg. But she overcame all that to star in track at Tennessee State and become the first U.S. woman to win three gold medals, at the 1960 Olympics.

REGGIE WHITE

From Chattanooga, White was an All-America at Tennessee. Before accumulating 198 career sacks in the NFL, he played two seasons for the Memphis Showboats of the short-lived United States Football League.

MICHAEL OHER

When he was at Memphis's Briarcrest Christian School, the future All-America offensive tackle was adopted by the Tuohy family. His story became the basis of the book and movie *The Blind Side*.

MOOKIE BETTS

The Red Sox outfielder was a high school star in Nashville—and he was also named boys bowler of the year in Tennessee in 2010. He's rolled three perfect games.

PRO TEAMS

NFL	**Dallas Cowboys** **Houston Texans**
MLB	**Houston Astros** **Texas Rangers**
NBA	**Dallas Mavericks** **Houston Rockets** **San Antonio Spurs**
WNBA	**Dallas Wings**
NHL	**Dallas Stars**
MLS	**FC Dallas** **Houston Dynamo**

The **Cowboys**, who began play in 1960 (going 0-11-1), are the oldest pro sports franchise in the state.

★TEXAS STAR★

José Altuve

In 2017, the shortest (5' 6") player in the majors came up big. Very big. Altuve, the American League MVP, led the Astros to their first World Series win. In the postseason he hit seven home runs, including three in Game 1 of the AL Division Series. His batting average in front of the home fans in the playoffs was a stellar .472. After that performance, it's hard to believe that when Altuve was 16, the Astros cut him from a tryout camp in Venezuela. He came back the next day anyway and eventually won over the scouts. He made his major league debut in 2011 and was an All-Star the next season. Altuve has had at least 200 hits in each of the last four seasons, and he's a three-time AL batting champ.

TEXAS

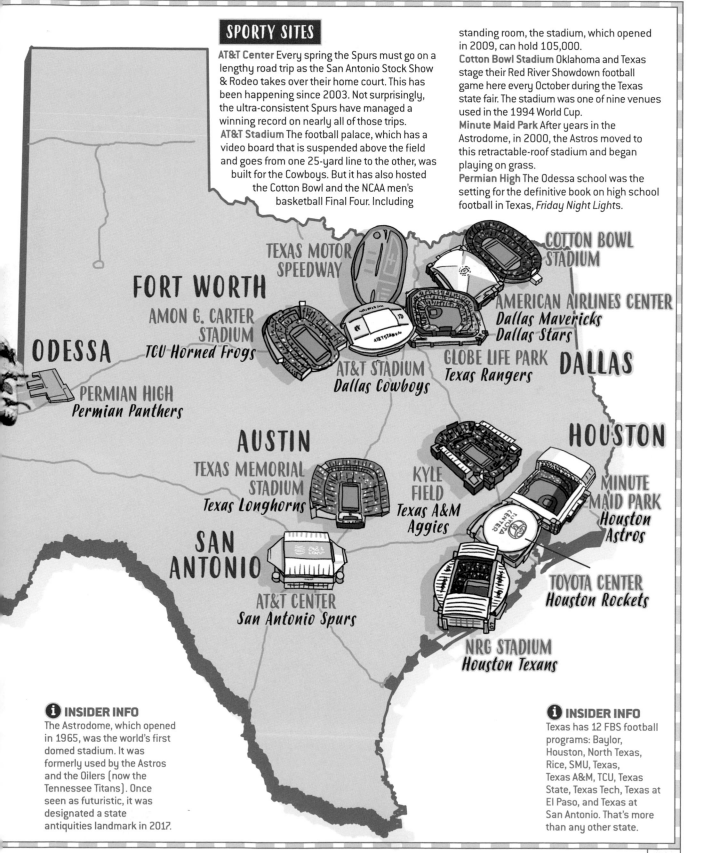

SPORTY SITES

AT&T Center Every spring the Spurs must go on a lengthy road trip as the San Antonio Stock Show & Rodeo takes over their home court. This has been happening since 2003. Not surprisingly, the ultra-consistent Spurs have managed a winning record on nearly all of those trips.

AT&T Stadium The football palace, which has a video board that is suspended above the field and goes from one 25-yard line to the other, was built for the Cowboys. But it has also hosted the Cotton Bowl and the NCAA men's basketball Final Four. Including standing room, the stadium, which opened in 2009, can hold 105,000.

Cotton Bowl Stadium Oklahoma and Texas stage their Red River Showdown football game here every October during the Texas state fair. The stadium was one of nine venues used in the 1994 World Cup.

Minute Maid Park After years in the Astrodome, in 2000, the Astros moved to this retractable-roof stadium and began playing on grass.

Permian High The Odessa school was the setting for the definitive book on high school football in Texas, *Friday Night Lights*.

TEXAS MOTOR SPEEDWAY

COTTON BOWL STADIUM

FORT WORTH

AMON G. CARTER STADIUM
TCU Horned Frogs

AMERICAN AIRLINES CENTER
Dallas Mavericks
Dallas Stars

ODESSA

PERMIAN HIGH
Permian Panthers

AT&T STADIUM
Dallas Cowboys

GLOBE LIFE PARK
Texas Rangers

DALLAS

HOUSTON

AUSTIN

TEXAS MEMORIAL STADIUM
Texas Longhorns

KYLE FIELD
Texas A&M Aggies

MINUTE MAID PARK
Houston Astros

SAN ANTONIO

AT&T CENTER
San Antonio Spurs

TOYOTA CENTER
Houston Rockets

NRG STADIUM
Houston Texans

ℹ INSIDER INFO
The Astrodome, which opened in 1965, was the world's first domed stadium. It was formerly used by the Astros and the Oilers (now the Tennessee Titans). Once seen as futuristic, it was designated a state antiquities landmark in 2017.

ℹ INSIDER INFO
Texas has 12 FBS football programs: Baylor, Houston, North Texas, Rice, SMU, Texas, Texas A&M, TCU, Texas State, Texas Tech, Texas at El Paso, and Texas at San Antonio. That's more than any other state.

TEXAS

THE NUMBERS

5 **AFRICAN-AMERICAN** starters on the Texas Western (now UTEP) basketball team when it won an NCAA title in 1966, which was a first for the sport.

7 **NO-HITTERS** thrown by Nolan Ryan, of Alvin, a major league record. He also had a record 5,714 strikeouts in his 27-year career, which included stints with the Astros and the Rangers.

2 **HIGH SCHOOL QUARTERBACKS** from Texas who have gone on to start and win a Super Bowl: Nick Foles and Drew Brees, who both played at Westlake High in Austin.

5 **SONS** of former heavyweight champion George Foreman, of Marshall, who are also named George.

FAN FAVORITES

DAK PRESCOTT
Cowboys quarterback

He reportedly wasn't the Cowboys' preference at quarterback in the 2016 draft. But after Dallas failed to trade up, they took Mississippi State's Prescott in the fourth round. When starter Tony Romo was lost to an injury in the preseason, Prescott was pressed into service—and the Cowboys thanked their lucky stars they had "settled" for him. Prescott threw for 23 touchdowns and just four interceptions and led the Cowboys to the playoffs. He was named Offensive Rookie of the Year, displaying a poise and decision-making ability that marked him as a player with a long future.

JAMES HARDEN
Rockets guard

The Beard is one of basketball's most effective offensive threats. He led the NBA in assists in 2016–2017, and the next year he won the scoring crown as Houston set a franchise record for wins.

KAWHI LEONARD
Spurs forward

The low-key Leonard's value became clear when he clamped down on LeBron James as the Spurs won the 2014 NBA Finals. The two-time Defensive Player of the Year has also developed into a top scorer.

DIRK NOWITZKI
Mavericks forward

During 20 seasons in Dallas, the German star's step-back jumper has become one of the NBA's most recognizable (and imitated) shots. Nowitzki was the Finals MVP in 2011, Dallas's only championship season.

J.J. WATT
Texans defensive end

The three-time NFL Defensive Player of the Year became as well known for his philanthropy as his football in 2017. Watt's charity for Houston hurricane relief raised a whopping $37 million.

TEXAS'S TROPHY SHELF

5 Super Bowl Wins The Cowboys won three of their five titles in the 1990s behind Hall of Famers Troy Aikman, Emmitt Smith, and Michael Irvin. Hall of Fame coach Tom Landry's teams won two Super Bowl championships in the 1970s.

8 NBA Championships The Spurs won five titles with coach Gregg Popovich and star Tim Duncan between 1999 and 2014. The Mavericks won their title in 2011, while the Rockets won in 1994 and 1995 behind center Hakeem Olajuwon.

1 World Series Championship The Astros won the first title for the state in 2017.

1 Stanley Cup Win In 1999, the Stars won their lone Cup after a three-overtime thriller in the clinching Game 6. Brett Hull put the Cup-winning goal past Buffalo Sabres goaltender Dominik Hasek.

GREATEST MOMENT

NOVEMBER 1, 2017
The Astros Are Finally Champs

The Astros' victory in the 2017 World Series was all the more remarkable because of the depths from which they rose. From 2011 to 2013 the team had lost more than 100 games each season. Those were the three worst seasons since the franchise's founding in 1962. But then the rebound began behind young stars such as José Altuve, Carlos Correa, George Springer, and Alex Bregman. The World Series drama escalated in Game 5, when the Astros won a wild five-hour, 10-inning, 13–12 slugfest. After dropping Game 6, the Astros came through with a 5–1 win over the Los Angeles Dodgers in Game 7 to complete the journey from the bottom of the standings to the top of the world.

STATE-MENT

"When you get to the end zone, act like you've been there before."

DARRELL ROYAL, former University of Texas coach

COOL SCHOOLS

University of Texas

Why use all five fingers to wave to someone when you can say everything you need to say with just two fingers? Longhorns greet each other with the Hook 'em Horns hand sign—pinkie and index finger extended. It is a signal of loyalty for Texas fans on campus in Austin and all around the world. (And there are plenty of fans: The school's enrollment is more than 50,000.) Over the years those fans have had an awful lot to cheer about. The football team won three national championships in the 1960s under coach Darrell Royal and a fourth in 2005 under Mack Brown. Running backs Ricky Williams and Earl Campbell won Heisman Trophies for the Longhorns. Football might be king in Texas, but baseball isn't far behind. No school has been to the College World Series more than Texas, which has 35 appearances. The Longhorns have won it all six times, including in 1983 when Roger Clemens was the staff ace. Texas has a strong presence in the NBA, led by Kevin Durant (Golden State Warriors) and LaMarcus Aldridge (San Antonio Spurs). And the women's hoops team, which won the NCAA title in 1986, has made the Sweet 16 in each of the past four years.

Texas A&M

The most famous person associated with the Aggies is the "12th Man." The legend goes like this: At a 1922 game, with injuries mounting, a student was waved onto the field and told to suit up in case he was needed. He changed into a uniform and stood on the sideline for the rest of the game. Now at football and basketball games the entire student section stands for the duration of the action, symbolizing their readiness to play for their teams. When it comes to people who actually play, the most famous Aggie might be quarterback Johnny Manziel, who in 2012 became the first freshman to win the Heisman Trophy.

Texas Christian University

When TCU joined the Big 12 in 2012, it was a return to the big time for a team that had played a major role in the early days of college football. The Horned Frogs won national titles in 1935 and 1938. The 1935 team was led by Sammy Baugh, a two-way player who went on to lead the NFL in passer rating as a quarterback and interceptions as a defensive back. The 1938 squad was led by Davey O'Brien. He must have done something right, because the trophy given to the best college QB is named for him. And coach Jim Schlossnagle has turned the Horned Frogs into a baseball power, leading the team to the College World Series every year from 2014 to 2017.

HOMEGROWN HEROES

SIMONE BILES

Biles, who was raised in the Houston suburbs, won gold medals in vault, floor routine, and individual all-around at the 2016 Olympics. She was also part of the U.S. squad that won a team gold. The golden girl also won 10 titles at the world championships in 2013 and 2015.

BEN HOGAN

The Fort Worth native is one of five golfers to win a career Grand Slam. He almost pulled it off in a single season: In 1953 he won three majors but didn't compete in the PGA Championship.

BABE DIDRIKSON ZAHARIAS

The Beaumont native excelled in virtually every sport imaginable. She was the 1932 Olympic champ in the javelin and 80-meter hurdles and won 41 pro golf tournaments.

MIA HAMM

An icon who helped elevate the sport of women's soccer, Hamm, who grew up in Wichita Falls, led the United States to a pair of World Cups and finished her career with 158 international goals.

BIG EVENT

Houston Livestock Show & Rodeo

More than 2.5 million people attended the event in 2017, so you know it's big. This 19-day competition, which dates back to 1932, features bullriding, steer wrestling, tie-down roping, and more. There's music and—of course—barbecue, so saddle up!

MASCOT FACE-OFF

BEVO *University of Texas*	VS.	REVEILLE *Texas A&M*
1916	ESTABLISHED	1931
Longhorn	BREED	Rough collie
Yes, if worked up	FEARSOME?	Not so much
Absolutely not	SLEEP ON YOUR BED?	Sure!

ENEMY OF THE STATE

WASHINGTON REDSKINS

Games between the Cowboys and the Redskins usually have high stakes: The two teams have combined to win 32 division titles since the rivalry was inaugurated in 1960.

UTAH

PRO TEAMS

NBA Utah Jazz

MLS Real Salt Lake

The **Jazz** franchise originated in New Orleans—hence the musical name—before moving to Utah in 1979.

SPORTY SITES

Bonneville Speedway Come to the wide-open expanses to set a land speed record.

LaVell Edwards Stadium The BYU football stadium in Provo is named for the man who coached at the school from 1972 to 2000.

Rice-Eccles Stadium The home of Utah Utes football was also the site of the opening and closing ceremonies of the 2002 Olympic Games.

Slickrock Trail If you're into mountain biking, this Moab trail is a mecca.

Snowbasin The Wasatch Range resort has 3,000 skiable acres and 3,000 feet of vertical drop.

Vivint Smart Home Arena The Jazz arena also hosts an NBA summer league.

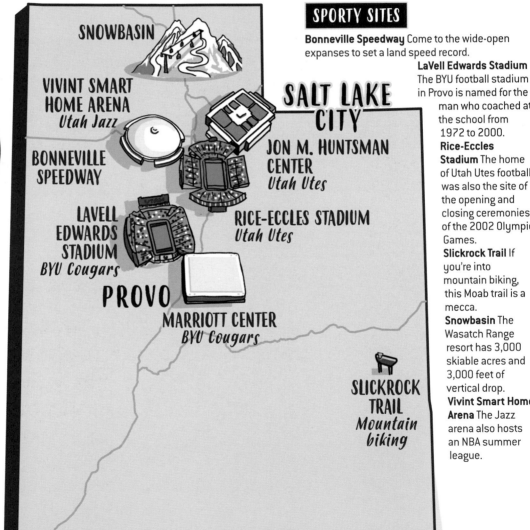

SNOWBASIN

VIVINT SMART HOME ARENA
Utah Jazz

BONNEVILLE SPEEDWAY

SALT LAKE CITY

JON M. HUNTSMAN CENTER
Utah Utes

LAVELL EDWARDS STADIUM
BYU Cougars

RICE-ECCLES STADIUM
Utah Utes

PROVO

MARRIOTT CENTER
BYU Cougars

SLICKROCK TRAIL
Mountain biking

John Stockton and Karl Malone

It's no coincidence that the NBA's second-leading career scorer played alongside its all-time assists leader. Businesslike and efficient point guard John Stockton arrived first, in 1984, from Gonzaga. The next season the Jazz drafted Karl (the Mailman) Malone at power forward, and the pick-and-rolls immediately began to flow. For 18 remarkable seasons the pair defined Jazz basketball. The two stars went to the playoffs every season they were on the court together, and they led the Jazz to the NBA Finals in 1997 and 1998. Between them they were named to 24 All-Star teams. Never has one team been defined for so long by such a dynamic duo.

STATE-MENT

"When I die, they might as well bury me at the finish line at Churchill Downs so they can run over me one more time."

RICK MAJERUS, longtime University of Utah basketball coach whose teams lost to Kentucky—the home state of Churchill Downs—six times in the NCAA tournament

GREATEST MOMENT

FEBRUARY 8–24, 2002
XIX Olympic Winter Games

In February 2002, nearly 2,400 athletes from 78 countries skied, skated, and soared in Utah during the greatest spectacle in winter sports. Norway tied the Olympic record by winning 13 gold medals, while figure skater Sarah Hughes of the United States turned in a masterly performance to win a surprise gold. The Games went so well that Utah is seeking to host another Winter Olympics.

HOMEGROWN HEROES

MERLIN OLSEN

The Hall of Fame defensive tackle and member of the Los Angeles Rams' Fearsome Foursome won the Outland Trophy while playing at Utah State, in his hometown of Logan. After the NFL he starred in the TV series *Little House on the Prairie* and *Father Murphy*.

JIM MCMAHON

At BYU, the audacious quarterback set 70 NCAA records from 1978 to 1981. In 1985, he led the Chicago Bears to a 15–1 record and a win in Super Bowl XX. That squad is widely considered to be the greatest team in NFL history.

COOL SCHOOLS

Brigham Young University

The most significant era of sports at BYU was during the reign of coach LaVell Edwards. That's true not just because the school won a national title in football (1984) or because of quarterbacks such as Jim McMahon, Steve Young, Marc Wilson, and Ty Detmer. The success of BYU's passing offense under Edwards helped reshape the way football is played. In basketball, BYU has produced a pair of guards who were national players of the year: Danny Ainge in 1981 and Jimmer Fredette in 2011.

Utah

Despite not playing in one of the major conferences aligned with the bowl system, the 2004 Utah football team was invited to one of the biggest postseason games. The Utes promptly pummeled Pittsburgh 35–7 in the Fiesta Bowl to finish the season 12–0. The team, which finished the campaign ranked No. 4, was coached by Urban Meyer, who went on to win national titles at Florida and Ohio State. The quarterback was Alex Smith, the top overall pick in the 2005 draft. Utah moved from the Mountain West Conference to the bigger Pac-12 in 2011.

FAN FAVORITES

RUDY GOBERT
Jazz center

When you are from France and a 7' 1" shot-blocking specialist, perhaps it is inevitable that you'll end up with the nickname the Stifle Tower. Gobert, who led the NBA in rejections in 2016–2017, was born to a 7-foot father who had played college ball in the U.S. at Marist before returning to France. Gobert brings not just height but also a tenacity that those who attack the rim find truly, well, stifling.

KYLE BECKERMAN
Real Salt Lake midfielder

Beckerman made headlines in 2017 when he cut off his dreadlocks, a drastic change for one of the most recognizable players in MLS. The tough-tackling midfielder and outstanding passer has been Real Salt Lake's captain since 2008. He has also earned more than 50 caps for the U.S. men's national team.

THE NUMBERS

14 **SEED** of Weber State when the Wildcats upset Michigan State (1995) and North Carolina (1999) in March Madness.

935 **NBA GAMES** won as a head coach by Sandy native Dick Motta. In 25 seasons he lost 1,017 games.

74 *JEOPARDY!* **GAMES** won in a row by former BYU quiz bowl team member Ken Jennings.

76 **UNIFORM NUMBER** of 7' 6" Shawn Bradley, of Castle Dale and BYU, when he first played in the NBA.

BIG EVENT

Speed Week
Located west of Salt Lake City, the Bonneville Salt Flats are wide open areas of densely packed salt that make for a perfect speedway. Every August drivers meet there to test the limits of their cars, trucks, motorcycles, and jet-propelled vehicles. Vehicles on the Flats have surpassed 600 mph.

ENEMY OF THE STATE

CHICAGO BULLS
Each time the Utah Jazz made it to the NBA Finals, Michael Jordan's Bulls halted their run. Viewed from Utah, Jordan's series-clinching shot in 1998 looks less like clutch heroics and more like a push-off that should have been called.

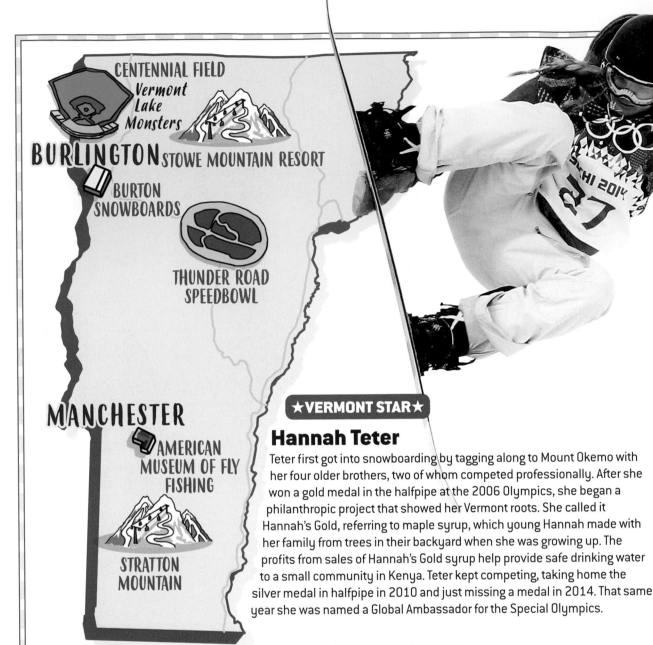

CENTENNIAL FIELD
Vermont Lake Monsters

BURLINGTON STOWE MOUNTAIN RESORT

BURTON SNOWBOARDS

THUNDER ROAD SPEEDBOWL

MANCHESTER

AMERICAN MUSEUM OF FLY FISHING

STRATTON MOUNTAIN

★VERMONT STAR★

Hannah Teter

Teter first got into snowboarding by tagging along to Mount Okemo with her four older brothers, two of whom competed professionally. After she won a gold medal in the halfpipe at the 2006 Olympics, she began a philanthropic project that showed her Vermont roots. She called it Hannah's Gold, referring to maple syrup, which young Hannah made with her family from trees in their backyard when she was growing up. The profits from sales of Hannah's Gold syrup help provide safe drinking water to a small community in Kenya. Teter kept competing, taking home the silver medal in halfpipe in 2010 and just missing a medal in 2014. That same year she was named a Global Ambassador for the Special Olympics.

SPORTY SITES

American Museum of Fly Fishing More than 40,000 flies are on display at an 1800s-era farmhouse in Manchester.
Burton Snowboards The famed board-making company is based in Burlington. Founder Jake Burton Carpenter began making snowboards in his garage in Londonderry in the 1970s.
Stowe Mountain Resort The area known as the Ski Capital of the East was originally a lumber camp.
Stratton Mountain The resort hosted the U.S. Open Snowboarding Championships for nearly 30 years.
Thunder Road Speedbowl Thousands attend weekly car races during warm-weather months at this quarter-mile, high-banked asphalt oval in Barre. The season-ending event is called the Milk Bowl.

THE NUMBERS

6
NCAA SKIING TITLES
won by the University of Vermont, most recently in 2012.

11
WINTER OLYMPIANS
who have come from Norwich, a town of about 3,000 people.

2
VEZINA TROPHIES won by Vermont alum Tim Thomas as a goalie for the Boston Bruins, in 2009 and 2011.

VERMONT

GREATEST MOMENT

MARCH 18, 2005

UVM's Upset

This was the day much of America learned what a catamount is. In the opening round of the 2005 NCAA tournament 13th-seeded Vermont (whose mascot is a mountain cat known as a catamount) stunned third-seeded Syracuse 60–57 in overtime. Behind the outside shooting of Germain Mopa Njila and T.J. Sorrentine *(right)*, Vermont scored its first-ever tournament win.

PRO TEAM

Class A
Vermont Lake Monsters

The **Monsters**, an affiliate of the Oakland A's, play at Centennial Field on the UVM campus in Burlington.

ℹ INSIDER INFO

Ross Powers, from South Londonderry, won the 2002 Olympic gold medal in halfpipe. In 2010, he began running the snowboarding program at Stratton Mountain School.

HOMEGROWN HEROES

ANDREA MEAD LAWRENCE

The Rutland native won two gold medals in Alpine skiing at the 1952 Olympics. She grew up skiing at the resort her family owned at Pico Peak and qualified for the 1948 Olympics at age 15.

KEEGAN BRADLEY

The Woodstock native was an all-state skier but chose to focus on golf. His three Tour victories include one major, the 2011 PGA Championship.

BILL KOCH

Koch was the first American to medal in cross-country skiing, a sport usually dominated by Scandinavian teams. The native of Brattleboro won a silver in the 30-kilometers in 1976.

VIRGINIA

PRO TEAMS

Rookie	Bristol Pirates
	Danville Braves
	Pulaski Yankees
Class A	Lynchburg Hillcats
	Salem Red Sox
	Potomac Nationals
Double A	Richmond Flying Squirrels
Triple A	Norfolk Tides

The **Tides**, after a 38-season affiliation with the New York Mets, became part of the Baltimore Orioles organization in 2007.

SPORTY SITES

Fork Union Military Academy The school has sent countless graduates to the NFL, including former Heisman winners Eddie George and Vinny Testaverde.

Lane Stadium In the first varsity game here, in 1965, host Virginia Tech defeated visiting William & Mary 9–7.

Martinsville Speedway At .526 miles, this paperclip-shaped track, which was built in 1947, is the shortest on the NASCAR circuit.

Oak Hill Academy The prep school in Mouth of Wilson has turned out more than two dozen players who were selected in the NBA draft, including Carmelo Anthony, Rajon Rondo, Jerry Stackhouse, and Josh Smith.

Richmond Raceway The .75-mile track is the site of two NASCAR races—both of which are held at night.

Scott Stadium Football games at the Charlottesville stadium begin with a costumed Cavalier riding across the turf on horseback.

Wood Brothers Racing Museum Legends who have driven for the Wood Brothers include A.J. Foyt, Junior Johnson, and Cale Yarborough.

SCOTT STADIUM
Virginia Cavaliers

BLACKSBURG

OAK HILL ACADEMY

WOOD BROTHERS RACING MUSEUM

LANE STADIUM
Virginia Tech Hokies

MARTINSVILLE SPEEDWAY

ⓘ INSIDER INFO

Virginia Tech helped set a record for the largest college football crowd. In 2016, the Hokies played Tennessee just across the state line at the Bristol Motor Speedway in front of 156,590 fans.

BIG EVENT

Blue Ridge Marathon

The Roanoke race calls itself the toughest road marathon in the country—and for good reason. Runners must cover 26.2 miles while also coping with brutal climbs and descents. The total elevation change is 7,430 feet. The amazing views make all the work worthwhile.

Arthur Ashe

When Ashe died in 1993, he lay in state at the executive mansion of Virginia, a recognition of his accomplishments both in and beyond tennis. In 1968, he won the U.S. Open, becoming the first African-American man to win a tennis Grand Slam event. Ashe later added titles at Wimbledon and the Australian Open. He wrote a history of the black athlete in America and was arrested for protesting apartheid (the former system of legal racial discrimination in South Africa). He created tennis programs for inner-city kids. After contracting AIDS as a result of a blood transfusion during surgery, he spent the last years of his life campaigning for awareness of the disease. His was a full life, and one worth celebrating.

HARLOTTESVILLE

JOHN PAUL
JONES ARENA
*Virginia
Cavaliers*

RICHMOND

FORK UNION
LITARY ACADEMY
'MA Blue Devils

RICHMOND
RACEWAY

ℹ️ INSIDER INFO

Wendell Scott, from Danville, became the first African-American to compete in a NASCAR race, in 1961. Two years later he became the first (and still the only) African-American to win a top-level NASCAR race.

COOL SCHOOLS

Virginia

Virginia touts itself as a school that offers both intellectual and athletic excellence, and no recent grad personifies that high-minded ideal more than Chris Long. A defensive end for the Philadelphia Eagles, Long donated his entire 2017 salary to charities, including educational programs in Charlottesville. On the field, Virginia is strong in many sports. In 2015, UVA men won the Capital One Cup for general excellence, thanks to national titles in baseball, soccer, and tennis.

Virginia Tech

Virginia Tech athletes are called Hokies, from a chant dating back to the 1890s when the school was called by its formal name, Virginia Polytechnic Institute. The cheer went "Hoki, Hoki, Hoki, Hy. Techs, Techs, V.P.I." During coach Frank Beamer's tenure, from 1987 to 2015, Hokies football was defined by special teams excellence, especially blocked kicks. His teams made it to 23 bowl games and one national title game.

MASCOT FACE-OFF

WEBSTUR *Richmond*	**VS.**	**CAVMAN** *Virginia*
2011	**BORN**	1984
Division I's only spider	**UNIQUE?**	Division I's only Cavalier
Couldn't be called Spidey because Marvel Comics had that trademarked	**FUN FACT**	UVA also has an unmasked Cavalier, who rides on horseback

THE NUMBERS

3 **COLLEGE PLAYER OF THE YEAR AWARDS** in basketball won by Ralph Sampson of Harrisonburg at the University of Virginia from 1981 to 1983.

122 **FOOTBALL GAMES** played between North Carolina and UVA in the South's Oldest Rivalry.

5 **FUTURE MLB STARS** on the same youth travel team: David Wright, Ryan Zimmerman, Mark Reynolds, and Justin and Melvin Upton.

82 **PGA EVENTS** won by Sam Snead, who caddied at age seven at the Homestead in Hot Springs.

GREATEST MOMENT

MARCH 26, 2006
George Mason's Cinderella Run

Before 2006, George Mason had never won an NCAA tournament basketball game, but that changed in a hurry. The Patriots barely qualified for the field as a No. 11 seed, and opened against a tournament stalwart, Michigan State. But down went the Spartans, 75–65. Next the Patriots took down defending champion North Carolina. After knocking off another upstart, Wichita State, the Patriots met No. 1 seed Connecticut, a team with five future NBA draft picks. George Mason had no NBA talent, but coach Jim Larranaga rallied his players for an 86–84 overtime stunner to reach the Final Four.

HOMEGROWN HEROES

BRUCE SMITH

The NFL's alltime sacks leader, with 200, and a two-time Defensive Player of the Year, Smith was born in Norfolk and played for Virginia Tech.

RUSSELL WILSON
The Seahawks QB, who led the team to victory in Super Bowl XLVIII, is from Richmond. His grandfather was president of Norfolk State University.

JUSTIN VERLANDER

The 2011 Cy Young winner fired his first fastballs in Goochland County before pitching at Old Dominion. In 2017, he helped the Astros to a World Series victory.

SECRETARIAT
Born at Meadow Stud in Caroline County, Secretariat is regarded as the greatest racehorse ever. He wrapped up the 1973 Triple Crown with a 31-length win in the Belmont Stakes.

Russell Wilson

Few third-round draft picks start at quarterback in their first NFL games, but that's what happened to Wilson, the son of a lawyer who woke up at 5:30 in the morning to run football drills with his son before going off to work. In fact, he's started every game in his first six seasons with the Seahawks. Considered too short by many to thrive in the NFL, the 5' 11" Wilson made four Pro Bowls and played in two Super Bowls, winning one. In 2017, he led the NFL in passing touchdowns with 34. By the way, Wilson had options beyond football. Drafted by the Colorado Rockies, he had the talent to become a major league baseball player, too.

PRO TEAMS

NFL	Seattle Seahawks
MLB	Seattle Mariners
WNBA	Seattle Storm
MLS	Seattle Sounders FC

When it rains, it pours. **Seattle** received the expansion Seahawks in 1976, and the Mariners began play in 1977.

WASHINGT

SEATTLE

HUSKY STADIUM
University of Washington Huskies

KEYARENA
*Seattle Storm
Seattle University
Redhawks*

CENTURYLINK FIELD
*Seattle Seahawks
Seattle Sounders*

SAFECO FIELD
Seattle Mariners

MOUNT RAINIER

SPOKANE

**MCCARTHEY
ATHLETIC CENTER**
Gonzaga Bulldogs

PULLMAN

MARTIN STADIUM
*Washington State
Cougars*

STATE-MENT

"Russell Wilson got pulled over, and the cop got a ticket."

MICHAEL BENNETT, former Seahawks defensive end, joking about his old teammate's popularity in Seattle

WASHINGTON

THE NUMBERS

3 **SKIING WORLD CUP OVERALL TITLES** won by Phil Mahre of White Pass from 1981 to 1983. He was the first American ever to win the overall title.

3 **LEGION OF BOOM MEMBERS** who made first- or second-team All-Pro for the Seahawks in 2013: Earl Thomas, Richard Sherman, and Kam Chancellor.

116 **WINS** by the 2001 Mariners, which tied the major league single-season record. The Mariners lost to the New York Yankees in the AL Championship Series.

1 **SEASON** that the Pilots played in Seattle (1969) before stadium issues forced them to move to Milwaukee, where they became the Brewers.

FAN FAVORITES

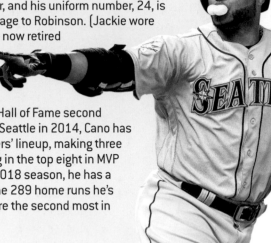

ROBINSON CANO
Mariners second baseman

He was named after Jackie Robinson by a baseball-loving—and playing—father, and his uniform number, 24, is an homage to Robinson. (Jackie wore 42, which is now retired throughout baseball.) Now in his 14th major league season, Cano could be on the road to joining his namesake as a Hall of Fame second baseman. Since arriving in Seattle in 2014, Cano has been the rock of the Mariners' lineup, making three All-Star teams and finishing in the top eight in MVP voting twice. Entering the 2018 season, he has a career .305 average, and the 289 home runs he's hit as a second baseman are the second most in major league history.

SUE BIRD
Storm point guard

The Storm have been in existence for 18 years, and for 16 of them Bird has been running the show. The top pick in the 2002 WNBA draft has led the team to a pair of league titles. She's a 10-time All-Star, and she ranks first in WNBA history in career assists.

JORDAN MORRIS
Sounders forward

When the Stanford star announced in 2015 that he was turning pro, fans in Seattle rejoiced. Since Morris is from Seattle, the Sounders held his rights as a homegrown player. It was quite a homecoming: Morris was the 2016 Rookie of the Year, and the Sounders won their first MLS Cup.

MARK FEW
Gonzaga basketball coach

Since taking over the Bulldogs in 1999, Few has built the program into a power. His teams have made the NCAA tournament 20 years in a row, and in 2017, he took the Bulldogs to the Final Four. Entering the 2017–2018 season, Few had the best winning percentage (.817) of any active coach.

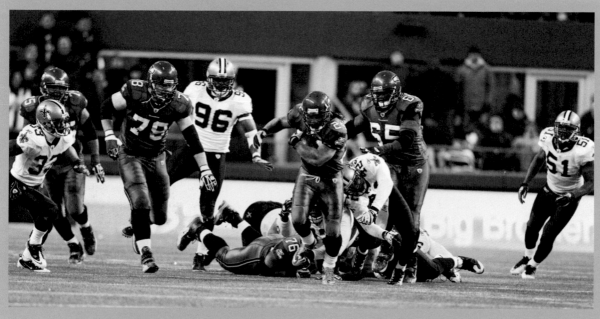

GREATEST MOMENT

JANUARY 8, 2011

The Beast Quake

Marshawn Lynch's 67-yard touchdown run through the Saints' defense—bouncing off some tacklers, pushing his way through others—was literally a seismic event. The fans' reaction registered on nearby earthquake monitors. Lynch's nickname, Beast Mode, never seemed more appropriate. The fourth-quarter run gave Seattle an 11-point lead in the NFC wild-card game, and the Seahawks held on to win 41–36.

ⓘ INSIDER INFO Gene Conley, from Richland, had quite the personal trophy shelf. He won championships in basketball (as a Celtics forward in 1959, 1960, and 1961) and in baseball (as a Braves pitcher in 1957).

WASHINGTON'S TROPHY SHELF

1 Super Bowl Win The Seahawks notched a safety on Denver's first snap and kept on rolling, dominating all over the field in a 43–8 win in 2014.

1 MLS Cup Win It came down to a shootout after 120 scoreless minutes, and the Sounders beat Toronto for the 2016 Cup.

2 WNBA Championships Betty Lennox was Finals MVP in 2004 against the Connecticut Sun, and Lauren Jackson took top honors in 2010 against the Atlanta Dream.

WASHINGTON

COOL SCHOOLS

Washington

The Huskies have had great success on the gridiron, especially in the 1991 season, when Washington went undefeated and won the national title. But the most storied athletes from the school might be the 1936 crew team. A boat of eight rowers was the U.S. entry at the Olympics in Berlin—and they won a gold medal. Their triumph in Berlin on the eve of World War II was chronicled in the book *The Boys in the Boat* and in a PBS documentary.

Washington State

It's not quite a pipeline, but the Cougars have sent a steady stream of quarterbacks to the NFL. Drew Bledsoe is 14th on the career passing yards list. Mark Rypien was the Super Bowl MVP for a Washington Redskins team that went 14–2 in the 1991 season. Jack Thompson, who played for the Cincinnati Bengals, had the nickname the Throwin' Samoan. And then there's Ryan Leaf, who was the No. 2 overall pick behind Peyton Manning in 1998. He lasted just three seasons and is routinely brought up at draft time to remind fans that when it comes to the draft, no one truly knows anything.

Gonzaga

Gonzaga is a small college in Spokane that has no football team and doesn't play in a major conference. But it has an outsized influence on college basketball. After making only one tournament appearance before 1999, the Bulldogs have become Big Dance regulars under coach Mark Few. They've spearheaded the mid-major revolution, showing that schools that aren't in the power conferences can compete year in and year out. The godfather of Zags basketball is alltime NBA assists leader John Stockton, a local kid who became a Bulldog before Bulldogs were cool.

HOMEGROWN HEROES

APOLO ANTON OHNO

The winner of eight Olympic medals in speedskating—including gold medals in 2002 and 2006—hails from Seattle. He was also a champ on *Dancing with the Stars*.

ISAIAH THOMAS

The 5' 9" guard from Tacoma was the last pick of the 2011 NBA draft, out of Washington. But in 2016–2017 he averaged 28.9 points for the Boston Celtics and finished fifth in MVP voting.

DREW BLEDSOE

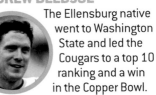

The Ellensburg native went to Washington State and led the Cougars to a top 10 ranking and a win in the Copper Bowl. Bledsoe was the top pick in the 1993 NFL draft and made four Pro Bowls.

TIM LINCECUM

Lincecum grew up in Bellevue, where his dad, a Boeing parts inventory employee, taught him to pitch. Using a distinctive motion, the 5' 11", 170-pound righty could bring the heat, with a fastball reaching 98 miles per hour. Lincecum won Cy Young Awards in 2008 and 2009 and pitched for three World Series winners with the San Francisco Giants.

MASCOT FACE-OFF

BLITZ
Seattle Seahawks

VS.

DOPPLER
Seattle Storm

BLITZ		DOPPLER
Bold defensive attack	**NAME MEANS . . .**	Weather forecast system
Fierce	**VIBE**	Goofy
Sacks	**LIVES FOR . . .**	Storm warnings
His mascot cohort Boom	**BIRD PAL**	Sue

BIG EVENT

Spokane Hoopfest

Every June the streets of downtown Spokane are taken over by a different type of driver, as basketball players take the ball to the hoop in this huge three-on-three extravaganza. What started in 1990 with a couple thousand players has grown into the world's largest outdoor basketball tournament, with divisions organized by age, gender, and height. In 2017, more than 25,000 players from 42 states played on 450 courts over 45 city blocks.

ⓘ INSIDER INFO The first American ever to reach the summit of Mount Everest was Seattle's Jim Whittaker, in 1963.

OREGON FOOTBALL

Both Washington and Washington State butt heads annually with their longtime Pac-12 foe to the south.

THE NUMBERS

2
SEASONS that Nick Saban, who is from Fairmont, coached defensive backs at West Virginia.

19
NCAA TITLES won by West Virginia in rifle, the most of any school.

6' 7"
HEIGHT of Georgeann Wells, who in 1984 became the first woman to dunk in an NCAA basketball game, for West Virginia.

PRO TEAMS

Rookie	**Bluefield Blue Jays**
	Princeton Rays
Class A	**West Virginia Black Bears**
	West Virginia Power

The **Black Bears** and the Power are both part of the Pittsburgh Pirates' farm system.

★WEST VIRGINIA STAR★

Jerry West

The son of a coal mine electrician, "Zeke from Cabin Creek" found his calling in a basketball hoop that was nailed to a neighbor's storage shed. He practiced tirelessly and became an All-America at West Virginia, taking the Mountaineers to an NCAA final. With the Los Angeles Lakers he made the NBA Finals nine times, winning once, in 1972. In 1969, West became the only player from a losing team ever to be named Finals MVP. West received the rarest of honors when a silhouetted likeness of him dribbling the ball was used for the NBA logo.

WEST VIRGINIA

MORGANTOWN

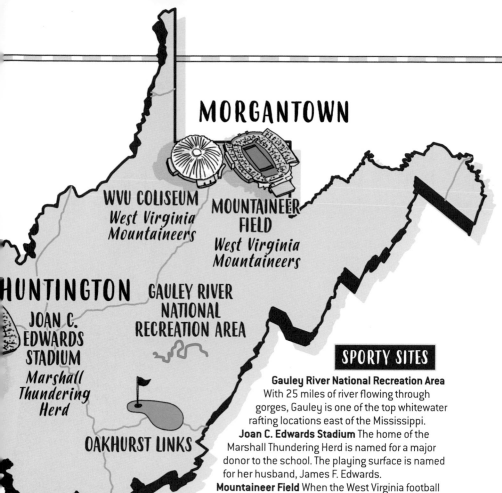

WVU COLISEUM
West Virginia Mountaineers

MOUNTAINEER FIELD
West Virginia Mountaineers

HUNTINGTON

GAULEY RIVER NATIONAL RECREATION AREA

JOAN C. EDWARDS STADIUM
Marshall Thundering Herd

OAKHURST LINKS

HOMEGROWN HEROES

MARY LOU RETTON
At the 1984 Olympics, the 16-year-old from Fairmont became the first American woman to win the gymnastics all-around gold. Her father, Ron, was a co-captain of the West Virginia basketball team with Jerry West.

RANDY MOSS
The receiver from Rand, who played college ball at Marshall, was as good as there's ever been at coming down with a deep ball. He is second all time in NFL receiving touchdowns, with 156. In 2007, with the New England Patriots, he caught 23 touchdowns, the record for a single season.

SPORTY SITES

Gauley River National Recreation Area With 25 miles of river flowing through gorges, Gauley is one of the top whitewater rafting locations east of the Mississippi.

Joan C. Edwards Stadium The home of the Marshall Thundering Herd is named for a major donor to the school. The playing surface is named for her husband, James F. Edwards.

Mountaineer Field When the West Virginia football stadium opened in 1980, singer John Denver was on hand to perform "Take Me Home, Country Roads."

Oakhurst Links Guests are given vintage equipment and advised to wear knickers and other old-fashioned golf gear when playing at this course, which was built in 1884.

STATE-MENT

"I'm not an athlete. I'm a professional baseball player."

JOHN KRUK,
Charleston native and three-time MLB All-Star who was never known for having a muscular physique

GREATEST MOMENT

JANUARY 2, 2006
Sugar Bowl

West Virginia was facing Georgia in the Georgia Dome—that hardly seems fair, right?—but that didn't matter. The underdog Mountaineers raced out to a 28–0 lead and then held off the Bulldogs for a thrilling 38–35 win, marking the beginning of strong run that saw West Virginia finish the season in the top 10 three years in a row.

WISCONSIN

PRO TEAMS

NFL Green Bay Packers

MLB Milwaukee Brewers

NBA Milwaukee Bucks

The Braves played in Milwaukee from 1953 to 1965 before they left for Atlanta. The **Brewers** arrived from Seattle (where they were the Pilots) in 1970.

★WISCONSIN STAR★

Aaron Rodgers

A Packers offensive lineman once commented that his team's quarterback was "smart to the point where he's kind of annoying." It's true. While Rodgers has a lightning-quick release on his passes and running ability that vexes defensive linemen, his mind may be his greatest weapon. He learned his college playbook in two days. Rodgers is a perfectionist who once taped potato chips to the bottoms of his heels to learn to stay up on his toes during a drill. Remarkably, he had no Division I scholarship offers coming out of high school, but now he has two MVP trophies and a Super Bowl ring.

ⓘ INSIDER INFO Can you surf in Wisconsin? You betcha. At the Lake Michigan shore town of Sheboygan, wind-whipped waves can get as big as six feet.

HAYWARD

LUMBERJACK WORLD CHAMPIONSHIPS SITE

SPORTY SITES

Camp Randall Stadium Originally part of the Wisconsin state fairgrounds, the site was used as a training ground for soldiers during the Civil War. A stadium was built in 1917. On game days, 80,321 fans turn it into a sea of red.

Lambeau Field The home of the Packers—the only NFL team owned by the city it plays in—opened in 1957. Named for Curly Lambeau, who was the team's cofounder, tailback, and coach, the stadium is also home to the Packers Hall of Fame. Current Packers celebrate scores with a Lambeau Leap into the crowd.

Miller Park The Brewers' stadium, with a retractable roof, opened in 2001.

Whistling Straits The picturesque golf course, situated on Lake Michigan, has hosted three PGA Championships and will be the site of the 2020 Ryder Cup.

Fiserv Forum The state-of-the-art home of the Bucks is the NBA's newest arena.

GREEN BAY

LAMBEAU FIELD
Green Bay Packers

WHISTLING STRAITS

CAMP RANDALL STADIUM
Wisconsin Badgers

KOHL CENTER
Wisconsin Badgers

FISERV FORUM
Milwaukee Bucks

MILLER PARK
Milwaukee Brewers

MADISON

MILWAUKEE

ⓘ INSIDER INFO
The first Harley-Davidson motorcycle was built in Milwaukee in 1903. Today the company sells a quarter million bikes a year.

WISCONSIN

THE NUMBERS

FAN FAVORITES

3.4 CAREER BLOCKS PER GAME, one of many Bucks team records still held by Kareem Abdul-Jabbar, who played in Milwaukee from 1969 to 1975.

13 NFL TITLES (including pre–Super Bowl era championships) won by the Packers, the most of any NFL franchise.

0 FOOTBALL GAMES that Kansas City Chiefs tight end Demetrius Harris played at the University of Wisconsin–Milwaukee, which has no team. He played basketball instead.

20 PEOPLE who can fit in the mouth of the giant fish sculpture outside the Fresh Water Fishing Hall of Fame & Museum in Hayward.

GIANNIS ANTETOKOUNMPO
Bucks guard-forward

In 2018, the Greek Freak had the most votes from his fellow players in the All-Star balloting, and he nearly edged out LeBron James in fan voting. That shows just how good, and popular, Antetokounmpo has become. One of four children of parents who emigrated from Nigeria to Greece in 1991, the 6' 11" Antetokounmpo had such a raw game that despite his athleticism he wasn't selected until the 15th pick of the 2013 draft. He's become Milwaukee's best scorer, rebounder, passer (he often plays point guard), and shot blocker. He's a magnetic star whose streaks toward the basket seem impossible to stop—and impossible for fans to take their eyes off of.

CLAY MATTHEWS III
Packers linebacker

With his flowing blond locks and his relentless activity, Matthews has stood out on the Green Bay defense ever since he was drafted in the first round out of USC in 2009. He is especially visible in the playoffs. In his 15 postseason games, the linebacker has 11 sacks and five forced fumbles. None of those turnovers was bigger than the fumble he forced in the 2011 Super Bowl. With Pittsburgh driving down the field and Green Bay clinging to a four-point lead, Matthews knocked the ball from Pittsburgh running back Rashard Mendenhall. It's no secret where Matthews gets his talent. His father, Clay Jr., was a Pro Bowl linebacker for the Cleveland Browns, and his uncle Bruce made the Pro Football Hall of Fame as an offensive lineman.

GREATEST MOMENT

DECEMBER 31, 1967

Ice Bowl

The temperature was 13° below zero, and the windchill made it feel like −48°. The turf in Green Bay was literally frozen. The Packers were losing to the Dallas Cowboys in the NFL title game, down three, but instead of kicking a field goal to tie in the final seconds, Bart Starr scored on a quarterback sneak. With the victory, the Packers advanced to Super Bowl I, which they won.

WISCONSIN'S TROPHY SHELF

4 Super Bowl Wins The Packers won the first two Super Bowls, in 1967 and 1968. They added wins in 1997 and 2011. Green Bay has lost the big game only once, in 1998.

1 NBA Championship The Bucks, led by league MVP Kareem Abdul-Jabbar, went 66–16 and swept the Baltimore Bullets in the 1971 Finals. Milwaukee lost the 1974 Finals to the Boston Celtics, and the Bucks haven't played for a title since.

ⓘ **INSIDER INFO** When talking about big winners from Wisconsin, don't forget about horse trainer D. Wayne Lukas. Born in Antigo, the former high school assistant basketball coach has seen his horses win a record 14 Triple Crown races.

STATE-MENT

"The way to catch a knuckleball is to wait until it stops rolling and then pick it up."

BOB UECKER, Brewers announcer and former Milwaukee Braves catcher who, was charged with several passed balls trying to catch the knuckler of Phil Niekro

COOL SCHOOLS

Wisconsin

If you want to feel the excitement of being a Badgers fan in Madison, show up to a football game at Camp Randall Stadium between the third and fourth quarters. That's when "Jump Around" plays over the P.A. and the entire student section does what the song tells them to. The Badgers have given their fans plenty of reasons to dance. Jonathan Taylor rushed for 1,977 yards in 2017, his first year on campus. As impressive as that total is, it's not the NCAA record for a freshman. That mark belongs to another Badger, Ron Dayne, who ran for 2,109 yards in 1996. Three years later Dayne won the Heisman Trophy, making him the second Wisconsin running back to do so, after 1954 winner Alan Ameche. In basketball, center Frank (the Tank) Kaminsky led the charge to consecutive Final Fours in 2014 and 2015. And the men's hockey team has won six national championships.

Marquette

Located in a football-mad region, Marquette hasn't fielded a team since 1960. The basketball program gives fans of the Milwaukee school plenty to cheer about, though. The Golden Eagles have made the tournament 32 times and won it all in 1977, when coach Al McGuire and star Butch Lee beat North Carolina in the final. Marquette reached the title game in 1974 and again in 2003, when a hot shooting guard named Dwyane Wade led the way. Wade went on to win three titles in the NBA. Other Golden Eagles in the pros include Minnesota Timberwolves guard Jimmy Butler and Utah Jazz forward Jae Crowder. Tune in to basketball games at Marquette, and you'll also see Big Noggins, giant pictures of celebrities' heads that fans wave to distract opponents as they shoot free throws.

HOMEGROWN HEROES

J.J. WATT

J.J. and his brothers, Derek and T.J., followed the same route. From their home in Waukesha they went to the University of Wisconsin, then on to the NFL. J.J., a defensive end with the Houston Texans, is a three-time Defensive Player of the Year.

JOE THOMAS

Thomas was fishing on Lake Michigan when he was taken No. 3 by the Cleveland Browns in the 2007 draft. The Wisconsin alum and surefire Hall of Famer played 10,363 straight snaps at left tackle for Cleveland.

DANICA PATRICK

From Beloit, she became the first woman to win an IndyCar series race, at the 2008 Indy Japan 300. Patrick owns the best finish by a woman in the Indy 500 and Daytona 500.

ERIC HEIDEN

Heiden, from Madison, became the first person to win five individual gold medals at a single Games when he set five Olympic records in speedskating in 1980. He then switched to cycling and rode in the Tour de France before becoming an orthopedic surgeon.

MASCOT FACE-OFF

RACING SAUSAGES
Milwaukee Brewers

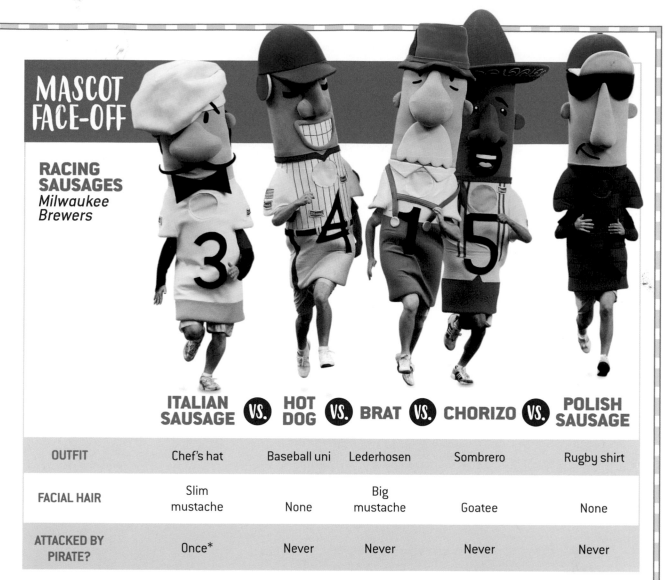

	ITALIAN SAUSAGE	**VS.** HOT DOG	**VS.** BRAT	**VS.** CHORIZO	**VS.** POLISH SAUSAGE
OUTFIT	Chef's hat	Baseball uni	Lederhosen	Sombrero	Rugby shirt
FACIAL HAIR	Slim mustache	None	Big mustache	Goatee	None
ATTACKED BY PIRATE?	Once*	Never	Never	Never	Never

*In 2003, Pittsburgh first baseman Randall Simon hit him with a bat during the sausage race.

BIG EVENT

Lumberjack World Championships

The events at this "Olympics of the Forest" include sawing, chopping, speed climbing, log rolling, ax throwing, and boom running. The three-day event for men and women (they're called Jills) takes place in Hayward over the last weekend of July.

ENEMY OF THE STATE

CHICAGO BEARS
The NFC North is filled with bitter rivalries, but the Packers and the Bears is the oldest. The bad blood between the teams has been brewing since 1921.

BIG EVENT

College National Finals Rodeo

For those of you who don't live in cowboy country: Yes, college rodeo is a thing, and it has been for more than half a century. Since 2001 the champions in individual and team events have been crowned in Casper. The disciplines include saddle bronc riding, bareback riding, bullriding, barrel racing, and goat tying. In 2017, 58 colleges sent teams. Panhandle State University (from Oklahoma) was the men's champ, while Sam Houston State (Texas) was the top women's team.

SPORTY SITES

Arena-Auditorium Nicknamed the Double A and the Dome of Doom, it is the home court of Wyoming basketball.
Devils Tower The Crook County geological protrusion, which attracted aliens in the classic science fiction movie *Close Encounters of the Third Kind*, is now a mecca for rock climbers.
Jackson Hole The area is home to the Jackson Hole Mountain, Grand Targhee, and Snow King ski resorts.
War Memorial Stadium Wyoming's stadium has the highest elevation of any Division I venue: 7,220 feet.

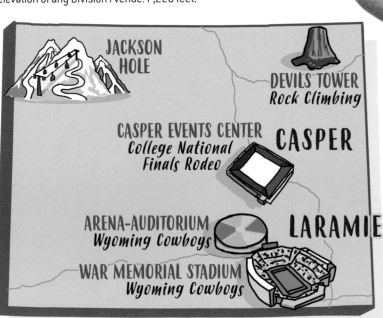

JACKSON HOLE

DEVILS TOWER
Rock Climbing

CASPER EVENTS CENTER
College National Finals Rodeo
CASPER

ARENA-AUDITORIUM
Wyoming Cowboys
LARAMIE

WAR MEMORIAL STADIUM
Wyoming Cowboys

GREATEST MOMENT

MARCH 30, 1943

Jump Shot

In 1943, Wyoming won the NCAA championship behind Kenny Sailors. The 5' 10" guard relied on a new invention called the jump shot. (Until then, most shots were taken flat-footed.) The jumper took off after Sailors used it to help beat Georgetown in the NCAA title game in New York City. Sailors and his teammates also beat NIT champion St. John's 52–47 in an exhibition game at Madison Square Garden.

★ WYOMING STAR ★

Rulon Gardner

It's not often that a Greco-Roman wrestler captures the nation's imagination, but that's what Gardner did in 2000. He became the breakout star of the Olympics with his stunning upset of Russian legend Aleksandr Karelin. Gardner grew up on a 250-acre dairy farm in Afton and woke up as early as 4 a.m. to complete his farm chores before going to school. When Gardner competed at the 2000 Olympics, the town of 1,200 held fund-raisers so his parents could afford to fly to Sydney to attend. Then they watched their boy shock the world.

THE NUMBERS

1 **FOUR-YEAR PUBLIC COLLEGE** in the state of Wyoming.

1 **COLLEGE** that offered Josh Allen a scholarship. Only Wyoming welcomed the QB, who was a first-round pick in 2018.

HOMEGROWN HEROES

CURT GOWDY

The famed announcer from Green River called major sports for NBC, including seven Super Bowls and 13 World Series. He also hosted the outdoors series *The American Sportsman* on ABC. A state park in the foothills of the Laramie Mountains is named after him.

FENNIS DEMBO

The ebullient 6' 6" forward led No. 12 seed Wyoming to the 1987 NCAA Sweet 16 and had the nation talking Cowboys basketball when he scored 41 points in an upset of Reggie Miller's UCLA team. He was on the cover of the SPORTS ILLUSTRATED college basketball preview the following season.

ⓘ INSIDER INFO When Wyoming made the Sugar Bowl in 1968, 10,000 fans made the trip to New Orleans for the game, which the Cowboys lost to LSU 20–13.

WYOMING

WASHINGTON

The Nationals played from 1969 to 2004 as the Montreal **Expos** before moving to Washington in 2005.

★ D.C. STAR ★

Katie Ledecky

Ledecky is a contradiction. Mild-mannered and unassuming out of the pool, she could look like a teenager walking into the locker room. But when she hits the water she becomes a beast. At the 2016 Olympics, Ledecky took four gold medals and one silver.

Her margin of victory in the 800-meter freestyle was an astonishing 11 seconds. Ledecky began swim lessons when she was six because her older brother was taking them. After joining a team she became obsessed. By the time she was 13 she was beating college-age swimmers, and she won her first Olympic gold in 2012 when she was 15.

ⓘ INSIDER INFO

The Washington Wizards were known as the Bullets until 1995, when owner Abe Pollin decided to change the name of his team due to sensitivity over gun violence in the nation's capital.

230

D.C.

ⓘ **INSIDER INFO** The Mystics have been part of the WNBA since 1998, the league's second season. But the team has never reached the league Finals. They hope that will change with the 2017 acquisition of Elena Delle Donne, the WNBA's MVP and scoring champ in 2015.

MARYLAND

GEORGE WASHINGTON UNIVERSITY

CAPITAL ONE ARENA
Washington Wizards
Washington Capitals
Washington Mystics
Georgetown Hoyas

RFK STADIUM

VIRGINIA

NATIONALS PARK
Washington Nationals

STATE-MENT

"Set goals that, when you set them, you think they're impossible."
KATIE LEDECKY

SPORTY SITES

Capital One Arena The Wizards and the Capitals played for a combined 47 seasons in nearby Landover, Maryland, before moving to this arena within the city limits in 1997.

George Washington University The Foggy Bottom school has made 11 NCAA basketball tournament appearances. Red Auerbach, coach of the great Celtics teams of the 1950s and 1960s, is an alumnus.

◀ **Nationals Park** The look of the 41,313-seat baseball stadium's exterior was inspired by the East Building of the National Gallery of Art, which was designed by noted architect I.M. Pei. The park opened in 2008.

RFK Stadium The stadium, built in 1960, has hosted games for the Nationals, the Redskins, D.C. United, and baseball's Washington Senators (who are now the Texas Rangers).

WASHINGTON, D.C.

THE NUMBERS

4
POSTSEASON APPEARANCES for the Nationals between 2012 and 2017. They failed to advance past the Division Series each time.

2
MAJOR LEAGUE TEAMS called the Senators that played in Washington. In 71 seasons, they won just one World Series.

0
AFRICAN-AMERICAN GOLFERS who had competed in the Masters before D.C.'s Lee Elder qualified for the tournament in 1975.

104
STOLEN BASES in 1962 for the Los Angeles Dodgers by Maury Wills, who had been a star pitcher and quarterback at Washington's Cardozo High.

FAN FAVORITES

ALEX OVECHKIN
Capitals left wing

One of the elite goal scorers in NHL history, Ovechkin led the league for the seventh time in 2017–2018. A three-time NHL MVP, Ovechkin has been incredibly consistent, scoring more than 30 goals in each of his 13 seasons. The Moscow native has spent all those years with Washington, which drafted him with the top pick in 2004. That means the forward has also played the most games in Capitals history. He is truly the face of the franchise.

MAX SCHERZER
Nationals pitcher

A pitcher with an analytical mind, a competitive spirit, and a blazing fastball is really tough to beat. That explains Scherzer's success. He entered the 2018 season having won two consecutive Cy Young Awards—and three for his career, after winning one in Detroit in 2013.

JOHN WALL
Wizards guard

The first overall pick, out of Kentucky, in the 2010 draft, Wall is one of the fastest point guards in the NBA. He has been a five-time All-Star. Also a fierce defender, Wall and deadeye shooting guard Bradley Beal form one of the league's most talented backcourts.

LUCIANO ACOSTA
D.C. United midfielder

Born in Argentina, Acosta joined the Black-and-Red in 2016. He led the team in assists that year with 11. In his second season—despite battling an ankle injury for much of the year—he led the team in scoring, with five goals. The 24-year-old began his career in his native country with famed club Boca Juniors.

GREATEST MOMENT

1991
Redskins' Dominant Season

In 2017, the website Football Outsiders ran a statistical analysis of every team in NFL history. The best ever? The 1991 Redskins. The squad, coached by Hall of Famer Joe Gibbs, had the league's best offense and second-best D. Washington went 14–2, and the losses were by a combined five points. The Skins beat the Buffalo Bills 37–24 in the Super Bowl.

WASHINGTON, D.C.'S TROPHY SHELF

3 Super Bowl Wins
Coach Joe Gibbs won Super Bowls with three quarterbacks: Joe Theismann (1983), Doug Williams (1988), and Mark Rypien (1992).

1 NBA Championship
The Washington Bullets, as the team was then known, won the 1978 title with a frontcourt that featured Hall of Famers Elvin Hayes and Wes Unseld.

1 Stanley Cup Win
After only one conference finals berth in their first 42 seasons, the Capitals finally broke through in 2018. They beat the Vegas Golden Knights to win their first Stanley Cup.

4 MLS Cup Wins
D.C. United was one of the top teams of the early days of MLS. United won Cups in 1996 and 1997 under future national team coach Bruce Arena. D.C. won again in 1999 and in 2004.

WASHINGTON, D.C.

Georgetown

This small, academically selective Catholic school in the nation's capital has produced some of the most physically imposing teams in college basketball history. Beginning with Patrick Ewing in 1982, the Hoyas featured a succession of dominant big men, including future NBA All-Stars Alonzo Mourning and Dikembe Mutombo. Ewing's teams went to three NCAA title games, winning one. They were coached by John Thompson. His son John Thompson III later ran the program. The Hoyas are now coached by Ewing *(above)*. About that nickname: A Georgetown team used to be known as the Stonewalls. It is believed that a student started the cheer *"Hoya saxa!"* which translates to "What rocks!" (*Hoya* is Greek for "what," and *saxa* is Latin for "rocks." Students back then were required to study the classical languages.) Eventually Hoyas was adopted as the nickname.

FAMOUS HOYAS

PATRICK EWING
1985 No. 1 pick,
11-time NBA All-Star

DIKEMBE MUTOMBO
No. 2 in career NBA
blocks

ALLEN IVERSON
1996 No. 1 pick,
2001 NBA MVP

HOMEGROWN HEROES

ELGIN BAYLOR

Had Baylor played in the modern age, video clips of his acrobatic moves would have been viral sensations. The Lakers forward, an 11-time NBA All-Star, averaged 27.4 points and 13.5 rebounds in his career, which ended in 1972. The D.C. native was a three-time all-city player in high school.

JOHN THOMPSON

Born and raised in Washington, Thompson starred at Archbishop Carroll High. He was the backup to Hall of Fame center Bill Russell on two Boston Celtics NBA championship teams. He then returned home and got into coaching. Thompson led Georgetown to 14 straight NCAA tournament berths and the 1984 national title.

VERNON DAVIS

The athletic tight end grew up in D.C. and played college ball at nearby Maryland before being drafted No. 6 overall by the San Francisco 49ers in 2006. He made two Pro Bowls in San Francisco before winning a Super Bowl with Denver in 2015. He returned to D.C. the following season to play for the Redskins.

MASCOT FACE-OFF

GEORGE 1 *George Washington*	VS.	JACK *Georgetown*
1948	**ESTABLISHED**	1962
President	**BREED**	English bulldog
Colonials	**REPRESENTS**	Hoyas
See university name	**WHY?**	Because *hoya* is Greek for "what," and it's hard to dress as a what

BIG EVENT

Army Ten-Miler

The race, held every October, is one of the largest in the country, with 35,000 runners. Once registration opens, the field fills up in less than a week. The course takes runners on a sweaty tour of the capital. It begins and ends at the Pentagon and takes participants past landmarks such as the Kennedy Center, the Washington Monument, the Lincoln Memorial, the Jefferson Memorial, and the National Air and Space Museum.

ENEMY OF THE STATE

PENGUINS HOCKEY

Pittsburgh's rivalry with the Capitals features competition between two of the league's top stars: the Penguins' Sidney Crosby and the Caps' Alex Ovechkin.

INDEX

Gordon, Alex, 130
Gordon, Jeff, 75
Gowdy, Curt, 229
Grange, Red, 68
Green, A.J., 56, 164
Gressel, Julian, 58
Gretzky, Wayne, 19, 176
Gronkowski, Rob, 22, 109

H

Hall, Taylor, 143
Hamilton, Bethany, 61
Hamm, Mia, 154, 203
Hammon, Becky, 42, 191
Harbaugh, Jim, 112
Harden, James, 200
Harper, Bryce, 137
Haslem, Udonis, 52
Heath, Tobin, 142, 154
Heiden, Eric, 226
Helena Brewers, 132
Henderson, Rickey, 37
Hershiser, Orel, 143
Hightower, Dont'a, 197
Hill, Grant, 154, 157
Hogan, Ben, 203
Hogan, Chris, 143
Hoiberg, Fred, 82–83
Holyfield, Evander, 56, 136
Horford, Al, 50
Horry, Robert, 14
Howard, Jordan, 66
Howard, Tim, 40, 142
Howe, Gordie, 114–115
Hubbell, Carl, 170
Hunt, Kareem, 162

I

Inciarte, Ender, 58
Irvin, Michael, 51, 201
Irving, Kyrie, 109, 154
Iverson, Allen, 234
Izzo, Tom, 112

J

Jackson, Bo, 14, 83
Jackson, Phil, 159

James, LeBron, 17, 53, 64,
   160, 200, 224
Jeter, Derek, 6, 112
Johnson, David, 20
Johnson, Dustin, 188
Johnson, Dwayne "The Rock,"
   61
Johnson, Joe, 27
Johnson, Lane, 177
Johnson, Magic, 31, 37, 72,
   110, 112, 115, 172
Johnson, Zach, 83
Jokić, Nikola, 40
Jones, Adam, 100
Jones, Bobby, 56–57
Jones, Jerry, 27
Jones, Julio, 55, 58
Jordan, Michael, 8, 25,
   64–65, 69, 137, 152, 154,
   157, 172, 207
Joyner-Kersee, Jackie, 68
Judge, Aaron, 109, 146

K

Kariya, Paul, 97
Kelce, Travis and Jason, 130,
   162
Kelly, Chip, 139
Kershaw, Clayton, 30
Keuchel, Dallas, 168
Killebrew, Harmon, 63
Kim, Chloe, 30
King, Stacey, 65
Kinnick, Nile, 80
Kluber, Corey, 164
Knievel, Evel, 133
Koch, Bill, 209
Korver, Kyle, 83
Koufax, Sandy, 30, 150
Kramer, Jerry, 63
Kruk, John, 221

L

Laettner, Christian, 91, 157
Lajoie, Nap, 184
Lange, Patrick, 60
Larkin, Barry, 112

Larkin, Dylan, 114
Lawrence, Andrea Mead, 209
Ledecky, Katie, 230–231
Lee, Cliff, 26
Lemons, Abe, 167
Leonard, Kawhi, 200
Lesnar, Brock, 190
Lillard, Damian, 175
Lilly, Kristine, 45, 154
Lincecum, Tim, 218
Liston, Sonny, 24
Lloyd, Carli, 140
Logan, Elle, 97
Logano, Joey, 45
Long, Chris, 177, 212
Long, Chuck, 83
Lopes, Davey, 185
Lopez, Nancy, 144
Lott, Ronnie, 32
Louis, Joe, 112
Love, Kevin, 175
Luck, Andrew, 78–79
Lundqvist, Henrik, 148

M

Machado, Manny, 100
Maddux, Greg, 55, 137
Mahorn, Rick, 115
Majerus, Rick, 205
Malkin, Evgeni, 180
Malone, Karl, 94, 205
Manning, Archie, 94, 125
Manning, Peyton, 72, 79,
   94–95, 133, 194, 196,
   218
Mantle, Mickey, 168
Marciano, Rocky, 106
Marino, Dan, 181–182
Mariota, Marcus, 60, 174, 194
Maris, Roger, 158–159
Martin, Mark, 26
Matthews, Clay, 32, 224
Mauer, Joe, 117
Mayfield, Baker, 170–171
Mays, Willie, 11, 36–37
McCollum, C.J., 175
McCoy, LeSean, 182

McEnroe, John, 150
McHale, Kevin, 122
McMahon, Jim, 206
McNally, Dave, 133
Meagher, Mary T., 90
Meyer, Urban, 162, 206
Mickelson, Phil, 22
Mikan, George, 66
Miller, Bode, 138
Miller, Reggie, 78, 229
Miller, Shannon, 168
Miller, Von, 40
Mills, Billy, 191
Molina, Bengie, José, and
   Yadier, 127
Molitor, Paul, 122
Montana, Joe, 74, 181
Moore, Maya, 118
Morris, Jordan, 216
Moss, Randy, 122, 221
Murray, Ty, 22
Musburger, Brent, 68, 133
Mutombo, Dikembe, 38, 234

N

Naismith, James, 84, 86, 103
Namath, Joe, 147, 181
Nelson, Jordy, 86
Newsome, Ozzie, 11
Newton, Cam, 11, 40, 49, 156
Nicklaus, Jack, 161, 165, 188
Nowitzki, Dirk, 200

O

Oher, Michael, 197
Ohno, Apolo Anton, 218
Oladipo, Victor, 78, 99
Olajuwon, Hakeem, 154, 201
Olsen, Merlin, 206
Osborne, Tom, 134
Osweiler, Brock, 133
Ovechkin, Alex, 5, 232, 235
Owens, Jesse, 163

P

Paige, Satchel, 15
Palmer, Arnold, 182

PHOTO CREDITS

FRONT COVER Clockwise from top left: Chris Schwegler/NBAE/Getty Images (Westbrook); Juam Ocampo/NBAE/Getty Images (Moore); Mark Buckner/NCAA Photos/Getty Images (wrestlers); Scott Rovak/St. Louis Cardinals/Getty Images (Molina); Layne Murdoch/NBAE/Getty Images (James); John Russell/NHLI/Getty Images (Subban); Daniel Kucin, Jr./Icon Sportswire/Getty Images (lacrosse); Christian Petersen/Getty Images (Raisman); Sam Greenwood/Getty Images (Thompson); David Rosenblum/Icon Sportswire/Getty Images (bulldog); Rob Tringali/SportsChrome/Getty Images (Brees); Tim Warner/Getty Images (Texas)
TITLE PAGE Mike Stobe/Getty Images (Porzingis); Dave Sandford/NHLI/Getty Images (Crosby); Tim Warner/Getty Images (Texas); Cameron Spencer/Getty Images (Teter); Julian Finney/Getty Images (Williams)
CONTENTS Mascots: Mike Zarill/Getty Images (Alabama, Auburn); Jamie Squire/Getty Images (San Diego Chargers); Thearon W. Henderson/Getty Images (Stanford); Brett Carlsen/Getty Images (Syracuse); Jim McIsaac/Getty Images (Mr. Met); Trophies: David E. Klutho (Super Bowl, World Series, Stanley Cup); Andrew D. Bernstein/NBAE/Getty Images (NBA); Jordan Johnson/NBAE/Getty Images (WNBA); Victor Decolongon/Getty Images (MLS); Mikel Galicia/Icon Sportswire/Getty Images (NCAA); David Rosenblum/Icon Sportswire/Getty Images (College Football National Championship); David E. Klutho (Ovechkin)
ALABAMA Jim Gund/Getty Images (Barons); Wesley Hitt/Getty Images (Saban); John Korduner/Icon Sportswire/Getty Images (Alabama); Mike Zarrilli/Getty Images (Auburn); Sarah Crabill/NASCAR/Getty Images (Talladega); Bettmann Archive/Getty Images (Aaron, Mays); Mitchell Layton/Getty Images (Newsome); Noah Graham/NBAE/Getty Images (Barkley); Kevin C. Cox/Getty Images (Smith); Mike Zarilli/Getty Images (Al the Elephant, Aubie); Alabama/Collegiate Images/Getty Images (Horry); Jerry Lodriguss/The LIFE Images Collection/Getty Images (Jackson); Kevin C. Cox/Getty Images (Greatest Moment); George Silk/The LIFE Images Collection/Getty Images (Paige); Doug Benc/Getty Images (LSU)
ALASKA Paul A. Souders/Corbis/Getty Images (Butcher); Eric Engman/Fairbanks Daily News-Miner/AP (Big Event); Steve Powell/Getty Images (Greatest Moment); Mike Ehrmann/Getty Images (Chalmers); Glenn James/NBAE/Getty Images (Boozer); Brian Bahr/Getty Images (Schlereth); Richard Wolowicz/Getty Images (Gomez)
ARIZONA Courtesy of Larry Fitzgerald (Fitzgerald in Egypt); Focus on Sport/Getty Images (Majerle); Christian Petersen/Getty Images (Fitzgerald action); Jeff Vinnick/Getty Images (Gretzky); Peter Aiken/Getty Images (Wildcats); Justin Tafoya/Getty Images (Booker); Harry How/Getty Images (Goldschmidt); Christian Petersen/Getty Images (Johnson); Barry Gossage/NBAE/Getty Images (Taurasi); Arizona State Collegiate Images/Getty Images (Pedroia); Brian Bahr/Getty Images (Greatest Moment); Barry Gossage/NBAE/Getty Images (Gorilla); Kevin Abele/Icon Sportswire/Getty Images (Sparky); Bryan Terry/NCAA Photos/Getty Images (Finch); Mike Powell/Getty Images (Tillman); Steve Grayson/PGA/Getty Images (Mickelson); Ethan Miller/Getty Images (Murray); Patrick Smith/Getty Images (Suggs); Bettmann Archive/Getty Images (Palmer); Kevin Abele/Icon Sportswire/Getty Images (Big Event); Barry Gossage/NBAE/Getty Images (Suns); Wally Skalij/Los Angeles Times/Getty Images (Dodgers)
ARKANSAS Mike Jones/Four Seam Images/AP (Travelers); Collegiate Images/Getty Images (Pippen with Arkansas); Focus on Sport/Getty Images (Pippen with Bulls); Bettmann Archive/Getty Images (Dean); Brian Bahr/Getty Images (Arkansas); Courtesy of the Arkansas Department of Parks & Tourism (Big Event); Focus on Sport/Getty Images (Bryant); Jason Wise/MLB Photos/Getty Images (Lee); Warren Little/Getty Images (Daly); John Harrelson/Getty Images for NASCAR (Martin); Herb Scharfman/Sports Imagery/Getty Images (Greatest Moment); Dilip Vishwanat/Sporting News/Getty Images (The Numbers); Andrew D. Bernstein/NBAE/Getty Images (Johnson); Tom Pennington/Getty Images (Jones)
CALIFORNIA Noah Graham/NBAE/Getty Images (Kings); Julian Finney/Getty Images (Williams); Tim Clayton/Corbis/Getty Images (Kim); Gregory Shamus/Getty Images (Curry); Jamie Squier/Getty Images (Kershaw); Brian Rothmuller/Icon Sportswire/Getty Images (Posey); Bob Levey/Getty Images (Trout); Stephen Dunn/Getty Images (Carr); James Devaney/Getty Images (Johnson); Dan Avila/RePlay Photos/Getty Images (USC); George Gojkovich/Getty Images (Lott, Polamalu); Focus on Sport/Getty Images (Allen); Christian Petersen/Getty Images (Smith); Andrew Weber/Getty Images (Matthews); Robert B. Stanton/WireImage/Getty Images (Big Event); Focus on Sport/Getty Images (Johnson); Jamie Squire/Getty Images (Boltman); Thearon W. Henderson/Getty Images (Tree); Mark Ralston/AFP/Getty Images (Surf Dog); NY Daily News/Getty Images (Greatest Moment, newspaper); Matt Zambonin/Freestyle Photo/Getty Images (Wild Wing, Sharkie); Bettmann Archive/Getty Images (Robinson, DiMaggio); Dick Raphael/NBAE/Getty Images (Russell); MLB Photos/Getty Images (Henderson); Robyn Beck/AFP/Getty Images (Woods); John W. McDonough (Murray); Andrew D. Bernstein/NBAE/Getty Images (Celtics)
COLORADO John Leyba/The Denver Post/Getty Images (Mutombo); Focus on Sport (Elway); Rick Madonik/Toronto Star/Getty Images (Rapids); Justin Edmonds/Getty Images (Coors Field); Doug Pensinger/Getty Images (Miller); Garrett Ellwood/NBAE/Getty Images (Jokic); Thearon W. Henderson/Getty Images (Arenado); Dustin Bradford/Getty Images (Howard); Elsa/Getty Images (Greatest Moment); RJ Sangosti/The Denver Post/Getty Images (Broncos); Keith Simonsen/Getty Images (Colorado); Leon Neal/AFP/Getty Images (Franklin); Hulton Archive/Getty Images (Dempsey); Russell Lansford/Icon Sportswire/Corbis/Getty Images (Ralphie); Dustin Bradford/Getty Images (Thunder); Kent Nishimura/The Denver Post/Getty Images (Big Event); Jed Jacobsohn/Getty Images (Raiders)
CONNECTICUT M. Anthony Nesmith/Icon Sportswire/Getty Images (Suns); Bob Stowell/Getty Images (Greatest Moment); Andy Lyons/Getty Images (Auriemma); David Madison/Getty Images (Lilly); Jeff Zelevansky/Getty Images for NASCAR (Logano); Bettmann Archive/Getty Images (Rodgers); Bill Wippert/NHLI/Getty Images (Drury)
DELAWARE Jadin Miller/Wilmington Blue Rocks (mascots); G. Fiume/Maryland Terrapins/Getty Images (Delle Donne); Delaware/Collegiate Images/Getty Images (Greatest Moment); Jamie Squire/Getty Images (Flacco); Focus on Sport/Getty Images (White); Jean Catuffe/Getty Images (Weir)
FLORIDA Mike Carlson/Getty Images (Lightning); Samuel Lewis/Corbis/Getty Images (Tebow); Alex Menendez/Getty Images (Raymond James Stadium); David Rosenblum/Icon Sportswire/Getty Images (Florida); Focus on Sport/Getty Images (Smith); Christian Petersen/Getty Images (Wambach); Maddie Meyer/Getty Images (Horford); Joe Robbins/Getty Images (Fowler); S&G/PA Images/Getty Images (Caulkins); Nathaniel S. Butler/NBAE/Getty Images (Carter); Tim Warner/Getty Images (Bosa); Todd Kirkland/Icon Sportswire/Getty Images (Freeman); David Berding/Icon Sportswire/Getty Images (Cook); Heidi Gutman/ABC/Getty Images (Sanders); Focus on Sport/Getty Images (Greatest Moment, Irvin); Sam Greenwood/Getty Images (Thompson); Brian Bielmann/AFP/Getty Images (Slater); Mike Ehrmann/Getty Images (Stamkos); Logan Bowles/Getty Images (Ramsey); Fernando Medina/NBAE/Getty Images (Gordon); Issac Baldizon/Getty Images (Haslem); Jared C. Tilton/Getty Images (Big Event); Bill Frakes (Rodriguez); Joe Robbins/Getty Images (Georgia)
GEORGIA Scott Cunningham/NBAE/Getty Images (Schroder); Todd Kirkland/Icon Sportswire/Getty Images (Ryan); Sporting News/Getty Images (Braves); Scott Bruhn/NCAA Photos/Getty Images (Georgia); Rob Tringali/Sportschrome/Getty Images (Georgia Tech); Ethan Miller/Getty Images (Holyfield); Focus on Sport/Getty Images (Walker); Andrew D. Bernstein/NBAE/Getty Images (Wilkins); Kevin C. Cox/Getty Images (Bailey); Fred Vuich (Big Event); Jeffrey Vest/Icon Sportswire/Getty Images (Uga); Chris Rodier/Icon Sportswire/Getty Images (Buzz); Scott Cunningham/NHLI/Getty Images (Thrashers, Jones, Smart); Scott Winters/Icon Sportswire/Getty Images (Gressel); Tim Clayton/Corbis/Getty Images (Inciarte); Tony Triolo (Greatest Moment); Joe Robbins/Getty Images (Florida); Mark Rucker/Transcendental Graphics/Getty Images (Cobb)
HAWAII David Madison/Getty Images (Rowan); Alex Goodlett/Getty Images (Mariota); Sam Greenwood/Getty Images (Wie); Tom Servais/AFP/Getty Images (Hamilton); Lisa Blumenfeld/Getty Images (Victorino); Pierre Tostee/Getty Images (Garcia); Tom Pennington/Getty Images for Ironman (Ironman); Darryl Oumi/Getty Images (Johnson)
IDAHO Stephen Smith/Four Seam Images/AP (Chukars); Simon Bruty (Street); James Flores/NFL/Getty Images (Kramer); Kidwiler Collection/Diamond Images/Getty Images (Killebrew); Jed Jacobsohn (Plummer); Steve Grayson/WireImage/Getty Images (Greatest Moment); Jonathan Ferrey/Getty Images (Wie); Steve Conner/Icon Sportswire/Corbis/Getty Images (Boise State)
ILLINOIS Manny Millan (Parker); Bruce Bennett/Getty Images (Blackhawks); Nathaniel S. Butler/NBAE/Getty Images (Jordan); Brian Drake/NBAE/Getty Images (King & Jordan); Jonathan Daniel/Getty Images (Wrigley Field); Kidwiler Collection/Diamond Images/Getty Images (Bears); Stacy Revere/Getty Images (Bryant); Jonathan Daniel/Getty Images (Howard); Bill Smith/NHLI/Getty Images (Toews); Ezra Shaw/Getty Images (Greatest Moment); Sandra Dukes/Getty Images (Illinois); Rich Barnes/Getty Images (Northwestern); Focus on Sport/Getty Images (Butkus); Simon Bruty/Getty Images (Blair); Tony Duffy/Getty Images (Joyner-Kersee); Bettmann Archive/Getty Images (Grange); Ron Hoskins/NBAE/Getty Images (Benny the Bull); Tom Hauck/Getty Images (Saluki); Robin Alam/Icon Sportswire/Getty Images (Packers); Jamie Squire (hockey)
INDIANA Andy Lyons/Getty Images (Manning); Rich Clarkson/NCAA Photos/Getty Images (Bird); Robert Laberge/Getty Images (Indianapolis Motor Speedway); Rich Clarkson/NCAA Photos/Getty Images (Wooden); Matthew Holst/Getty Images (Indiana); Jon Durr/Getty Images (Schwarber); Andrew D. Bernstein/NBAE/Getty Images (Thomas); Bettmann Archive/Getty Images (Spitz); Focus on Sport/Getty Images (Montana); Shane Bevel/NBAE/Getty Images (Diggins); Thearon W. Henderson/Getty Images (Samardzija); Jonathan Ferrey/Getty Images (Big Event); Joe Robbins/Getty Images (Purdue Pete, Leprechaun); Bettmann Archive/Getty Images (Robertson); Rusty Jarrett/Getty Images (Gordon); Travis Lindquist/Getty Images for NASCAR (Stewart); Jared C. Tilton/Getty Images (Sato); Nathaniel S. Butler/NBAE/Getty Images (Miller); Rob Carr/Getty Images (Luck); Joe Robbins/Getty Images (Oladipo); Mondadori Portfolio/Getty Images (Greatest Moment); Jamie Squire/Getty Images (Manning & Brady)
IOWA Jonathan Daniel/Getty Images (Field of Dreams); University of Iowa/WireImage/Getty Images (Greatest Moment); Focus on Sport/Getty Images (Warner); Carl Skalak (Fry); Brad Krause/Four Seam Images/AP (Iowa Cubs); Mark Buckner/NCAA Photos/Getty Images (Iowa); David K. Purdy/Getty Images (Iowa State); Iowa State/Collegiate Images/Getty Images (Gable); D. Clark Evans/NBAE/Getty Images (Collison); Gjon Mili/The LIFE Picture Collection/Getty Images (Feller); David K. Purdy/Getty Images (The Numbers); Stuart Franklin/Getty Images (Johnson); Tom Pennington/Getty Images (Hoiberg); Matthew Holst/Getty Images (Penn State)
KANSAS Katy Kildee/The Hutchinson News/AP (Pancake Day); Sean M. Haffey/Getty Images (Self); Rich Sugg/Kansas City Star/MCT/Getty Images (Embiid); Jay Drowns/Sporting News/Getty Images (Greatest Moment); Hy Peskin/Getty Images (Kansas); Joe Robbins/Getty Images (Nelson); Rick Stewart/Getty Images (Sanders); Rich Clarkson/The LIFE Images Collection/Getty Images (Smith); Jamie Squire/Getty Images (Missouri Tigers); iStockphoto/Getty Images (horseshoe); Rob Leiter/Getty Images (Sproles); Melissa Majchrzak/NBAE/Getty Images (Wiggins)
KENTUCKY The Stanley Weston Archive/Getty Images (Ali); Andy Lyons/Getty Images (Calipari); TMB/Icon Sportswire/Getty Images (Louisville Bats); Andy Lyons/Getty Images (Kentucky); Larry French/Getty Images (Louisville); Greg Wood/AFP/Getty Images (Meagher); Jim McIsaac/Getty Images (Simms); Bettmann Archive/Getty Images (Reese); Robert Beck (Waltrips); Rob Carr/Getty Images (Big Event); Ian Johnson/Icon Sportswire/Getty Images (Duke)
LOUISIANA Focus on Sport/Getty Images (Robinson); Rob Tringali/Sportschrome/Getty Images (Brees); Jonathan Bachman/Getty Images (Davis); Layne Murdoch/NBAE/Getty Images (Pelicans); Steve Grayson/WireImage/Getty Images (Forte); David Sherman/NBAE/Getty Images (Augustus); Frederick Breedon/Getty Images (Beckham Jr.); Jason LaVeris/FilmMagic/Getty Images (Bradshaw); Stephen Dunn/Getty Images (Robinson); Chris Graythen/Getty Images (Greatest Moment); Kevin C. Cox/Getty Images (Alabama)
MAINE John Ewing/Portland Press/Getty Images (Sea Dogs); Tony Duffy/Getty Images (Benoit Samuelson); Dave Sandford/NHLI/Getty Images (Kariya); Richard Heathcote/Getty Images (Logan); Chuck Solomon (Big Event); Antonio Scorza/AFP/Getty Images (Crocker); Mitchell Leff/Getty Images (Brown); Rich Schultz/Getty Images (Yankees)
MARYLAND Rob Carr/Getty Images (Orioles); Harry How/Getty Images (Phelps); Jamie Schwaberow/NCAA Photos/Getty Images (Harper); Robert Riger/Getty Images (Greatest Moment); Elliott Brown/Icon Sportswire/Getty Images (lacrosse); Nick Cammett/Diamond Images/Getty Images (Suggs); Justin Berl/Getty Images (Machado); Rob Carr/Getty Images (Jones); Julie Thurston Photography/Moment Editorial/Getty Images (Big Event); Joe Robbins/Getty Images (Steelers); Focus on Sport/Getty Images (Ripken); Louis Van Oeyen/Western Reserve Historical Society/Getty Images (Ruth); Michael Bezjian/WireImage/Getty Images (Pastrana); David Madison/Getty Images (Dawes)
MASSACHUSETTS Steve Babineau/NHLI/Getty Images (Bruins); Michael Ivins/Boston Red Sox/Getty Images (Brady); Joe Robbins/Getty Images (Fenway); Adam Glanzman/Getty Images (Green Monster); Michael Regan/Getty Images (Raisman); The Stanley Weston Archive/Getty Images (Marciano); Doug Pensinger/Getty Images (Flutie); Craig F. Walker/The Boston Globe/Getty Images (Big Event); Focus on Sport/Getty Images (Celtics); Mike Ehrmann/Getty Images (Greatest Moment); Omar Rawlings/Getty Images (Betts); Layne Murdoch/NBAE/Getty Images (Irving); Maddie Meyer/Getty Images (Bergeron, Gronkowski); Mike Ehrmann/Getty Images (Belichick); Bettmann Archive/Getty images (Yankees)
MICHIGAN John Iacono (Fidrych); Rich Clarkson/NCAA Photos/Getty Images (Johnson); Mark Cunningham/MLB Photos/Getty Images (Comerica Park); Chris Schwegler/NBAE/Getty Images (Pistons); Duane Burleson/Getty Images (Brady, Harbaugh); Corbis/Getty Images (Ford); Ron Vesely/MLB Photos/Getty Images (Larkin); Bettmann Archive/Getty Images (Louis); Maddie Meyer/Getty Images (Izzo); Doug Pensinger/Getty Images (Jeter); Paul Warner/Getty Images (Bing); G.N. Lowrance/NFL Photo Library/Getty Images (Bettis); Rey Del Rio/Getty Images (Big Event); Harry How/Getty Images (Sparty); Dave Reginek/NHLI/Getty Images (Octopus); Bruce Bennett/Getty Images (Howe); Duane Burleson/Getty Images (Cabrera); Dave Reginek/NHLI/Getty Images (Larkin); Joe Robbins/Getty Images (Stafford); Andrew D. Bernstein/Getty Images (Greatest Moment); Gregory Shamus/Getty Images (Ohio State)
MINNESOTA Bruce Bennett Studios/Getty Images (North Stars); Nick Wosika/Icon Sportswire/Getty Images (Mauer with Twins); Tom Dahlin (Mauer in high school); Saurabh Raj Sharan/Moment Editorial/Getty Images (sailboat); Jordan Johnson/NBAE/Getty Images (Towns); Garrett Ellwood/NBAE/Getty Images (Moore); Andy Lewis/Icon Sportswire/Getty Images (Thielen); Nick Wosika/Icon Sportswire/Getty Images (Parise); Elsa/Getty Images (Big Event); Jordan Johnson/NBAE/Getty Images (Brunson);